Decline and Fall of Napoleon's Empire

THE NAPOLEONIC LIBRARY

Other books in the series include:

1815: THE RETURN OF NAPOLEON
Paul Britten Austin

ON THE FIELDS OF GLORY
The Battlefields of the 1815 Campaign
Andrew Uffindell and Michael Corum

LIFE IN NAPOLEON'S ARMY
The Memoirs of Captain Elzéar Blaze
Introduction by Philip Haythornthwaite

THE MEMOIRS OF BARON VON MÜFFLING
A Prussian Officer in the Napoleonic Wars
Baron von Müffling

WATERLOO LECTURES
A Study of the Campaign of 1815
Colonel Charles Chesney

WATERLOO LETTERS
A Collection of Accounts From Survivors of the
Campaign of 1815
Edited by Major-General H. T. Siborne

www.frontline-books.com/napoleoniclibrary

DECLINE AND FALL OF NAPOLEON'S EMPIRE

HOW THE EMPEROR SELF-DESTRUCTED

Digby Smith

Frontline Books

Decline and Fall of Napoleon's Empire

A Greenhill Book

First published in 2005 by Greenhill Books, Lionel Leventhal Limited
www.greenhillbooks.com

This edition published in 2015 by

Frontline Books
an imprint of Pen & Sword Books Ltd,
47 Church Street, Barnsley, S. Yorkshire, S70 2AS
For more information on our books, please visit
www.frontline-books.com, email info@frontline-books.com
or write to us at the above address.

ISBN: 978-1-84832-818-1

CIP data records for this title are available from the British Library

Printed and bound by CPI Group (UK) Ltd, Croydon, CR0 4YY

～ Contents ～

Appendices

Bibliography

~ Illustrations ~

~ Map ~

～Introduction～

I HAVE BEEN WRITING BOOKS on the Napoleonic era for over thirty years. Back then, most published literature on the topic centred on the French and British armies, the 'Glory Years' from 1805 to 1809, Waterloo and – of course – Napoleon himself. Thanks to a bold editing decision by Martin Windrow, I was able to launch a series of booklets, under the pen name of Otto von Pivka, on the various German armies – and others – which also played their parts in those dramatic years. The market responded well to this innovation, and has now blossomed to offer a truly broad pallet of information on all the players on the Napoleonic stage.

Until recently I had deliberately avoided writing anything about Napoleon himself. Then, in 1996, I was introduced to the Internet and to the goldmines of the Napoleon Series and the New Napoleon Series fora, where it is possible to have almost any question on any Napoleonic topic answered in great detail.

Over the last three years, it became clear to me that – almost by accident – I had acquired a considerable wealth of knowledge on certain aspects of the Emperor and his environment. What I had learned reinforced my initial opinion of the man: an undoubtedly incredibly competent character, bordering on the genius in many fields, head and shoulders above any other figure of his own era or any other.

However, this undeniably great man was but human; despite possessing massive strengths and virtues in the fields of military command, strategy, domestic and international politics and civil administration, he was almost incompetent in other fields, such as interpersonal relations and diplomacy. A natural bully, he was fully capable of applying pressure to his subordinates to achieve his own ends. Once Emperor of the French in late 1804, his ego flared into incandescent brilliance and dominated mainland Europe. He re-established a court in France which challenged any other in pomp, etiquette and ritual; he became the centre of a solar system, a system which existed purely to serve his own ends. His brothers were placed on neighbouring thrones, and were left in no doubt at all that their first duty was to reinforce his grip on power, both within France and on all the vassal states that he had created from the debris of the Holy Roman Empire.

In 1810, he finally realised that to cement his grip on the throne, he needed a legitimate heir. With little ado, the barren Josephine was sent packing and a suitably qualified replacement 'womb' was soon discovered in Vienna. The plan worked and the King of Rome was born on 20 March 1811; the imperial future seemed assured. But, following the Glory Years, Napoleon's unchallenged power on continental Europe led to ever more repressive economical policies, aimed at benefiting France's economy at the expense of those of his allies, including Russia. His inexorable march towards the annexation of coastal European territories in an effort to stop the rampant smuggling of British goods, and the economic blight which he deliberately inflicted on the vassal states, used up all of the good will that his efforts in civil emancipation had initially given him.

The gargantuan error of his invasion of Russia in June 1812, his vacillation throughout that campaign and his inability to acknowledge his errors, all contributed to the massive extent of the destruction of his Grande Armée. Napoleon's unwillingness to compromise at the repeated allied diplomatic offerings of 1813 and 1814 saw him painting himself into a corner with increasing rapidity. Though the campaign of 1814 saw flashes of his old brilliance as a field commander, his scatterbrained lunge off to the east of Paris in March of that year handed Paris to the allies, and his first abdication followed.

Elba was never going to be big enough to hold that massive ego, and Louis the Unavoidable merely hastened events by failing to pay Napoleon's agreed pension. When 'the violets bloomed again' in 1815, Napoleon was unleashed on the world once more, conjuring armies out of nothing and marching to smash the allied threat on his northern border. Then followed Waterloo, his second abdication and his final exile to St Helena, where he died in 1821, frustrated and impotent, rewriting the recent history of Europe to suit his own ends.

I am frequently accused of insufficient reverence for the Great Man; I plead guilty – gleefully! Irreverence does not necessarily mean blind bias and a refusal to recognise his great deeds in many fields. It does, however, mean that I have looked beyond the glorious chapters of his life and examined many other aspects of the man and his career.

I hope that readers will learn something new about Napoleon, something more than is offered by the usual panegyrics.

As mentioned above, I have made much use of the Internet for my researches, the most profitable discussion fora that I have used being the Napoleon Series, administered by Max Sewell, and the Napoleon Series New Forum, administered by Bob Burnham. Both are repositories of much detailed, reliable information, generously placed at my disposal when requested. Participation in the lively debates on both sites has helped rub the rough edges from many of my initially crude concepts and has led to much new knowledge (for me).

Among those who were of greatest assistance, I would like to thank Tony Broughton, Dominique Contant, Philip Haythornthwaite, Peter Hofschroer, David Hollins, Tom Holmberg, Susan Howard, Kevin Kiley, Katherine Lucini, Ron McGuigan, Marc Moermann, Robert Mosher, Howie Muir, Robert Ouvrard, Mark Urban and Hans-Karl Weiss.

DIGBY SMITH

～ Chronology ～

1769   *15 August:* Napoleon is born.

1778   *15 December:* he leaves Corsica to be educated in France at Brienne. This was a scholarship, based on the proof that he had four quarterings in his family's coat of arms – they were minor Italian nobility.

1785   Napoleon is commissioned into the Artillery Regiment de la Fère. His father dies of stomach cancer.

1789   The French Revolution breaks out. The Corsican patriot leader Pascal Paoli returns to the island with British help, to wrest rule of his homeland from France. Hearing of this, Napoleon also goes to Corsica and offers to fight at Paoli's side; his offer is rejected.

1792   Napoleon is elected lieutenant-colonel of the Ajaccio National Guard. He witnesses the Paris mob storming the Tuileries and the massacre of the Swiss Guard.

1793   *April:* Napoleon and his whole family are expelled from Corsica by Paoli to 'perpetual execration and infamy'.
       June: Napoleon becomes politically active as a Jacobin. He writes a political pamphlet, *Le Souper de Beaucaire*, extolling the virtues of the Revolutionary government, the Committee of Public Safety. By this time he is in close contact with Augustin Robespierre, younger brother of Maximilien, who virtually runs the government.
       18 December: by clever use of his artillery, Napoleon forces the allies to evacuate the French naval base at Toulon, which had been handed over to them by the citizens in September. Napoleon rises in rank and becomes closer to the influential politicians in Paris.

1794   *27 July:* Maximilien Robespierre is toppled from power; Napoleon, now a brigadier general, is arrested in the subsequent period of disorder as being part of his gang.

1795   *5 October:* Napoleon fires the 'whiff of grapeshot' which saves the government (the Directory) from a pro-royalist mob; over two hundred of the mob are killed.

1796   *7 March:* Napoleon marries Josephine; two days later he leaves Paris to take command of the Army of Italy.

1798   Napoleon mounts the expedition to invade Egypt, using many of the units of his old Army of Italy.

11 June: he seizes Malta.

2 July: he storms Alexandria.

21 July: he wins the battle of the Pyramids.

1 August: his expedition is severely compromised by Rear Admiral Nelson's crushing victory over the French fleet of Vice Admiral Brueys in Aboukir Bay. Cut off from France, Napoleon decides to invade Syria.

1799   *20 February:* he takes El Arish.

7 March: he forces the surrender of Jaffa. Over the next few days, at Napoleon's express orders, some 2,600 prisoners of war are executed. Four days later he makes his famous visit to the French hospital, filled with those sick with the plague.

17 March–21 May: the invasion of Syria continues; Napoleon attempts to take Acre, but is thwarted by the Turkish garrison supported by Royal Navy forces under Commodore Sir Sydney Smith.

20 May: falling back into Egypt, he passes through Jaffa, where there are many very sick French soldiers. Napoleon wants them killed by overdoses of opium, but the medical officer, Desgenettes, refuses.

25 July: Napoleon assaults and takes the fort at Aboukir from the Mamelukes.

11 August: hearing news of French reverses in Europe, Napoleon returns to Cairo, and orders Admiral Ganteaume to keep two frigates ready to set sail for France at short notice.

17 August: the admiral reports to Napoleon that the Royal Naval blockading squadron has departed and that the coast is clear. At midnight that night, Napoleon and his small party leave Cairo and hurry to Alexandria.

22 August: they embark by night and set sail for France. From Alexandria Napoleon writes to his successor to command in Egypt, General Kléber, informing him of his good fortune.

16 October: Napoleon arrives in Paris to find the nation in crisis: the Directory is utterly discredited and political turmoil prevails, in which Jacobin and royalist factions are active everywhere. Concealing the true

state of affairs in Egypt and trumpeting his victory at Aboukir, Napoleon is very popular with the Parisians. Lucien Bonaparte, one of Napoleon's younger brothers, is now President of the Council of Five Hundred. Together with the Directors Sieyès and Roger Ducos, he engineers a plot to have Napoleon proclaimed the new strongman in France.

9 November: the senators of the Council of Ancients declare Napoleon commander of the troops in the capital, and the government is moved from the centre of Paris to the suburb of Saint-Cloud.

10 November: escorted by grenadiers, Napoleon storms into the sitting of the senators, informing them that he is taking command. He is thrown out and goes to the Council of Five Hundred, where the scene is repeated. Sieyès and Lucien convince Napoleon to send in his grenadiers to clear the chamber, which he does. The conspirators fill the power vacuum thus created. In short order, Napoleon promotes himself to First Consul and pushes Sieyès and Ducos into the background.

1800   Napoleon's peace overtures to Austria are rejected; he thus pre-empts their offensive in northern Italy, and orders General Moreau to act against their Second Army in southern Germany.

10 May: General Lannes crosses the Great St Bernard pass; Napoleon follows.

14 June: the battle of Marengo; the Austrian general, Baron Melas, advances out of Alessandria fortress to attack the French; having detached too many of his troops to flanking duties, Napoleon finds his army in full retreat by mid-afternoon. General Desaix arrives in the nick of time with his division and restores the combat. A devastating charge by Kellermann's cavalry catches the Austrians by surprise and reverses the situation in an instant. Desaix is killed in the moment of victory. The Austrian position in Italy collapses; France gains Lombardy, the port-city of Genoa and the fortress of Ancona.

3 December: General Jean-Victor Moreau inflicts a heavy defeat on the Austrians at the battle of Hohenlinden.

1801   *9 February:* Austria signs peace with France at the Treaty of Luneville. Relative peace reigns in Europe until 1805.

1802   *25 May:* by a vote of 3.5 million to eight thousand, Napoleon is elected Consul for life by the French electorate.

1 August: the Senate confirms the vote and Napoleon's election.

1803   After several attempts on his life, some financed by Britain, Napoleon decides to eliminate one of his most active opponents, Louis-Antoine the émigré Duke of Enghien, then residing in neutral territory in Baden. Napoleon sends a force of soldiers to kidnap him and bring him to the fortress of Vincennes near Paris.

21 March: after a kangaroo court at Vincennes, Louis-Antoine is shot.

Middle of the year onwards: Napoleon prepares to invade Britain and concentrates the Grande Armée of over one hundred thousand men in camps at Boulogne and along the Channel coast. The plan calls for the French fleet under Admiral Villeneuve to lure the Royal Navy away from the English Channel long enough for the flotilla of French landing craft to cross unopposed.

1804 *18 May:* Napoleon is elected Emperor of the French Republic by the Senate.

2 December: he is crowned in the cathedral of Notre-Dame.

1805 *Early September:* Villeneuve having failed to carry out Napoleon's plans, the invasion of Britain is abandoned; Napoleon marches his Grande Armée east to southern Germany, where an Austrian army under General Mack has invaded Bavaria. Moving with great speed, and cloaked in secrecy, Napoleon surrounds the bulk of Mack's force in the city of Ulm.

15 October: Mack capitulates with twenty-four thousand men.

21 October: Admiral Horatio Nelson defeats the Franco-Spanish fleet off Cape Trafalgar. Although it costs him his life, Nelson's victory guarantees Britain's naval supremacy for the next century. The danger of a French invasion is gone.

2 December: Napoleon defeats a combined Austro-Russian army at Austerlitz in the 'Battle of the Three Emperors', bringing to an end the old Holy Roman Empire of German Nations of which Kaiser Franz of Austria had been emperor.

1806 *12 July:* the Treaty of Paris is signed and the Confederacy of the Rhine created, replacing the Holy Roman Empire of German Nations.

14 October: the Prussian king, Friedrich Wilhelm III, decides to challenge the might of France, with only Saxony at his side. Moving with customary speed and secrecy, Napoleon rushes upon the divided allies, who are scattered at the twin French victories of Jena and Auerstädt. Although defeated, a Prussian corps remains in East Prussia and resistance continues.

21 November: from his enemy's capital, Napoleon issues his Berlin Decree, declaring a trade war (the Continental System) on Britain's export of colonial produce and cheap, mass-produced wares into Europe. Napoleon now places his siblings on the thrones of Naples, Holland, Westphalia and Cleve-Berg.

1807 *14 June:* the war against Prussia and Russia ends after the French victory at Friedland.

7 July: in the subsequent Treaty of Tilsit, Tsar Alexander I agrees to extend the Continental System to Russia.

23 November and 17 December: Napoleon issues the Milan Decrees, extending his trade blockade to neutral nations.

1808 *9 May:* Napoleon kidnaps the Spanish royal family, invades Spain and puts his elder brother, Joseph, on the Spanish throne. His brother-in-law, Joachim Murat, is promoted from Grand Duke of Cleve-Berg to the now vacant throne of the Kingdom of Naples. Much to Napoleon's surprise, the Spanish people rise in revolt against the French and their new king.

1809 *21–2 May:* Napoleon crushes Austria at the battle of Aspern-Essling.

5–6 July: Austria is again defeated at Wagram.

December: realising the need for an heir to legitimise his dynasty on the throne of France, and knowing that Josephine is barren, Napoleon divorces her in December.

1810 *11 March:* Napoleon marries the Austrian archduchess, Marie-Louise, Louis-Alexandre Berthier acting as his proxy in Vienna.

1811 *20 March:* the King of Rome, Napoleon's son, is born.

1812 *25 June:* Napoleon invades Russia with over half a million men.

17–18 August: the battle of Smolensk.

19 August: the battle of Valutina Gora; the French and their allies push on eastwards after the Russians, towards Moscow.

7 September: the battle of Borodino; the Russians withdraw again towards Moscow, just over a hundred kilometres to the east. They then abandon the city to the invaders.

14 September: Napoleon enters Moscow.

19 October: after waiting in vain for overtures of peace from Tsar Alexander, Napoleon leaves Moscow.

28 November: Napoleon forces the crossing of the Beresina river.

5 December: Napoleon abandons his army and returns to Paris. His Russian adventure has cost the lives of over half a million of his own soldiers; Russian losses are probably of the same order.

1813 With a new army of conscripts, Napoleon enters Saxony to confront the Russo-Prussians.

2 May: he wins the battle of Lützen, but is unable to exploit it due to his lack of cavalry.

20–1 May: he wins the battle of Bautzen (Würschen), but is again unable to exploit it. He agrees to an armistice, which lasts until 22 August. Austria enters the war against France.

26–7 August: Napoleon wins the battle of Dresden, but subsequent allied victories cancel out all his advantages.

16–19 October: the massive 'Battle of the Nations', the bloodiest action of the Napoleonic wars, takes place at Leipzig; Napoleon is thoroughly defeated; he loses his grip on Germany and is forced to withdraw into France. His German allies abandon him.

1814　*Spring:* fighting for his very survival, Napoleon conducts the Nine Days campaign in Champagne, which shows him – at times – at his strategic and tactical best. On the diplomatic front he is less intelligent and throws away repeated chances to negotiate an honourable end to the war.

30 March: Paris falls to the allies.

4 April: his assembled marshals at Fontainebleau force the Emperor to abdicate.

11 April: he signs the document of abdication and attempts suicide the next day.

28 April: Napoleon leaves Fréjus aboard the British frigate HMS *Undaunted,* to sail to exile on the island of Elba.

1815　*Late February:* Napoleon leaves Elba to risk all in a final attempt to reclaim power over France.

1 March: he lands near Antibes, in the Golfe Juan, accompanied by about a thousand men. Avoiding royalist areas, he makes his way through the hills towards Paris, gathering support as he goes; Louis XVIII leaves Paris for Ghent.

19 March: Napoleon enters Fontainebleau again and begins to reorganise the government and the army, preparing to fend off another allied invasion. The allies abandon the Congress of Vienna in order to mobilise their forces against him. The greatest threat to Napoleon is posed by the Anglo-Dutch-German-Prussian troops on his northern borders; he resolves to strike at them first.

16 June: Napoleon strikes the Prussians under Blücher at Ligny and defeats them; on the same day, Ney attacks the Anglo-Dutch-Germans at Quatre-Bras, but is unable to break through. The allies fall back and regroup; Napoleon follows the international force under Wellington towards Brussels, sending Marshal Grouchy to keep the Prussians away to the east and apart from Wellington's army.

18 June: Wellington wins the battle of Waterloo, with crucial help from the Prussians, who had shaken Grouchy off. Napoleon's support in France evaporates.

22 June: Napoleon abdicates for the second time, throwing himself upon the mercy of the Prince Regent of Great Britain.

15 July: accompanied by a small party, Napoleon boards HMS *Bellerophon*, but his hopes of comfortable exile in England are dashed. He is sent to the remote island of St Helena on HMS *Northumberland*.

15 October: Napoleon lands at St Helena.

1821   *5 May:* Napoleon dies. His death certificate gives the cause of death as cancer of the stomach, but conspiracy theorists at once theorise that he was poisoned – but by whom?

1840   Napoleon is disinterred, to be returned to his final resting place in Les Invalides in Paris. Again, controversy flares, this time regarding the identity of the corpse in the coffin. The issue remains unresolved to this day.

I

~ The Steps to the Throne ~

*I*N 1802 (YEAR X) NAPOLEON was elected Consul for life, with the right to nominate his own successor, apparently by a massive majority of over three million ayes to a few thousand nayes. But was the decision so clear-cut? At that point about five million French citizens were entitled to vote. In actual fact, it would appear that Napoleon's younger brother, Lucien Bonaparte (then head of the Ministry of the Interior which ran the election) fudged the figures. There were only 1.5 million ayes; Lucien's willing minions added half a million for the men of the army and navy and a further nine hundred thousand for good measure. On top of this, the number of abstentions (sure indicators of electoral apathy) was also high. As Jean Tulard said: 'There was more antipathy for the fallen government than sympathy for the new one.'

Perhaps Napoleon's first major error was committed on 2 December 1804, when he crowned himself 'Emperor of the French Republic'. Prior to this event, he had declared:

> The name of king is outworn. It carries with it a trail of obsolete ideas and would make me nothing more than the heir to dead men's glories. I do not wish to be dependent upon any predecessor. The title of emperor is greater than that of king. Its significance is not wholly explicable, and therefore it stimulates the imagination.

Again, as in 1802, the five million voters were asked for their opinion as to whether the fate of France should be placed in the hands of Napoleon, this time as hereditary emperor: 3,572,329 said yes; 2,569 said no. We assume that some 1.4 million abstained, and thus roughly this number of people were not positively in favour of giving Napoleon the throne. Carnot was not alone in his opposition to Napoleon becoming emperor.

On 2 December 1805 Napoleon had provoked, fought – and very convincingly won – the 'Battle of the Three Emperors' at Austerlitz. At one stroke, thanks to the magnificent performances of the commanders, men and the systems of the Grande Armée, his most powerful opponents in mainland continental Europe – Austria and Russia – were humbled before him. Their armies wrecked, they were anxious to be allowed to sign disadvantageous peace treaties with him which would permit them to continue to exist without losing too much face, territory and money, and to retain power bases for possible future action.

The ailing edifice of the Holy Roman Empire of German Nations was given its final deadly blow with this victory. Kaiser Franz of Austria had been elected Emperor Franz II of this ramshackle house of cards in 1792; in early 1806 he renounced this title and became Kaiser Franz I of Austria, leaving the now leaderless sheep of the defunct empire to mill aimlessly about in an area roughly occupied by that of modern Germany, with the Kingdom of Prussia to the north-east. These sheep came in several different breeds: some were electorates, some duchies, some counties and other minor principalities, some independent imperial city states. The map of the Holy Roman Empire's German nations resembled nothing so much as a patchwork quilt that had been stitched together by several witless geriatrics, with many states owning tiny parcels of territories acquired by marriage over the centuries, scattered over the length and breadth of the place, all divided by foreign soil.

The member states were all absolute monarchies, with more or less benignly inclined rulers, firmly embedded in the feudalistic age. Many strove to emulate the Prussian example, particularly in the military sphere. Customs barriers between all these mini-states inhibited trade and drove up consumer prices. Many of the tiny entities were on or below the verge of national viability. Literacy was very limited and the press frequently subject to censorship – although this latter feature had also become an established practice in Napoleon's supposedly enlightened and exemplary republic. Early in the Revolutionary period, there had been flourishing republican political movements in many of the western German states, but these had withered on the vine as the excesses of the Terror flared out of control in 1793 and 1794.

Despite this, the 'orphaned' states of the Holy Roman Empire presented Napoleon and his increasingly grandiose political ambitions with a spectrum of possibilities. He was Emperor of the French. He had crushed her enemies and destroyed their institutions. Why not salvage all that was left of these old liabilities and convert them, at one masterful stroke, into assets for himself – and for France? There was no effective, coherent opposition to his plans:

Austria was too preoccupied with trying to live on reduced means to bother; Russia was in disarray; Prussia was dithering, and England, although very concerned to recover the Electorate of Hanover (the origin of her royal house) had no field army that could achieve the slightest successes against the French in mainland Europe.

On 12 July 1806, sixteen princes in southern Germany joined with France to form the Confederation of the Rhine by the terms of the Treaty of Paris; they would later be joined by others from the north of Germany. Napoleon's fertile mind had been working frantically towards this conclusion for months, analysing the political entities which lay at his feet, moulding and shaping them like plasticine into new forms which would more ideally suit his aims: a 'United States of Europe', with one common system of weights and measures, one common legal code (the Code Civile or Code Napoléon), one common currency, one common customs organisation, one common military system, all formed to serve the interests of France. Two hundred years later, Europe is still in the controversial birth throes of this potential superstate.

Those old German (and Bourbon) rulers that had crossed Napoleon's path, or did not fit his plans, were simply dispossessed and exiled. Their realms were then shuffled with other territories to form the new kingdoms, grand duchies and principalities, upon whose thrones Napoleon would place grateful, and hopefully reliable, new sovereigns, pliable to his imperial orders and whims at the expense of their own new realms.

Feudal rights were to be abolished in all these new states – a genuine step forward – and a liberal sprinkling of French secret agents was introduced to observe everything that went on in this *cordon sanitaire* and to report events back to Joseph Fouché (Napoleon's Chief of Secret Police) on a frequent and regular basis. This included close monitoring of the local press and the closing-down of those newspapers and periodicals which did not toe his party line. Being the editor of a newspaper in France and the Confederation of the Rhine from now until 1814 was to be a high-risk career.

From 2 December 1804 Napoleon was an emperor. But he was the emperor of a republic, with none of the usual tiers of aristocracy below him; in their place he had only republicans, some of them regicides. He recognised that any society needs a system of rewards and baubles with which to motivate and steer the aspirations of the upper classes. In a traditional absolute monarchy, such as almost all other European states of this time, the hereditary aristocracy automatically headed the class race. But France had bloodily rooted out her *aristos*. There was a vacuum in the state structure. In post-revolutionary Russia, Heroes of the Soviet Union were invented to fill the vacuum; Napoleon was much less radical than Lenin.

In late 1806, to reward those who had served him outstandingly, he recreated a titled aristocracy for France. This system he extended to all those vassal states where his writ ran. An entire panoply of kings, princes, dukes, counts and barons, a sort of crowned *cosa nostra*, not perhaps so different from the traditional aristocracies, sprang up. And with it returned all the tortuous ritual and etiquette of the medieval courts as practised in those of the absolute monarchs whom he – and France – had despised. With the fervour of the convert, he embraced it all.

Some of these new *aristos* were created in reward for services rendered on the battlefield, some for diplomatic or commercial skills in his service. In most cases the system was a genuine meritocracy and the titles were for the lifespan of the recipient only. They often carried considerable financial bonuses and pensions, often drawn from states outside France, such as Westphalia.

The marshals were the leaders who had fought his victorious battles and campaigns: it was only right that they should benefit accordingly. The bestowed wealth and titles of some of them are shown below. What they looted from the lands they conquered, in cash and in kind, is over and above these sums. Many of them bought expensive houses in Paris:

	Endowment (francs)
Augereau, Duke of Castiglione	196,764
Bernadotte, Prince of Ponte Corvo	291,631
Berthier, Prince of Neuchâtel	1,114,945
Bertrand, Count	226,230
Bessières, Duke of Istria	262,769
Davout, Duke of Auerstädt, Prince of Eckmühl	980,484
Duroc, Duke of Frioul	370,882
Lannes, Duke of Montebello	327,820
Marmont, Duke of Ragusa	120,882
Masséna, Duke of Rivoli, Prince of Essling	933,375
Ney, Duke of Elchingen, Prince of the Moskowa	728,973

Among those to benefit from this significant political move were all of Napoleon's relatives. Nepotism occurred – and occurs – in most societies; with his Corsican upbringing, Napoleon was just as liable to come under family pressure to share the spoils of his imperial crown as any other successful *parvenu*. But precisely this nepotism was to be a major factor in his downfall.

Although he was only too well aware of the personal and professional limitations of each of his relatives – now salivating expectantly in his shadow – and of their lack of suitable training for the hugely complex tasks of ruling states, he needed them to be sitting obediently on the thrones of those states which *had* to be allied to France. Napoleon needed not only the *cordon sanitaire* of the Confederation of the Rhine, whose states could well be ruled by Germans loyal to him, but also his relatives as allies up among the crowned heads of Europe. As far as his royal siblings were concerned, quality mattered little – their role was simply to extend the reach of his influence. Napoleon was supremely, and cynically, confident of being able to micro-manage each of his puppet kings into doing his will, by constant use of the string-pulling of which his *Correspondance* has left us so many revealing examples.

On being presented with – sometimes cajoled into accepting – a throne, each sibling would be given a motivational harangue, in which Napoleon clearly stressed that the lucky monarch's first duty was to rule his state totally in the interests of Napoleon and as he directed. Each new monarch would be offered a French team of trusty 'management consultants', experts in civil, financial, legal and military affairs, who would accompany them to their new realms. The role of these consultants was twofold: to set up copycat French systems in the satellite state, and to spy on the monarch, sending frequent and regular information on how and what he was doing back to Napoleon.

Napoleon sent other spies covertly into these allied states to probe and snoop on various matters as he saw fit. The information sent back to him generated veritable floods of letters, orders, complaints, instructions and threats to each of his unfortunate relatives, who, it seems, could do nothing right.

Of course, in this cornucopia of nepotistic greed no kingdom or principality that he so distributed was absolutely equal in all respects to any other. Some were larger, richer, warmer, more or less beautiful than others. Thus, instead of creating a happy and contented bunch of new monarchs, eager and willing to serve him, Napoleon merely increased the backbiting and envy among most of his family circle.

His brother, Lucien, was the outstanding exception of the family. By now he had managed to make himself so rich that he had no need of help from Napoleon; his greed was satisfied. Lucien refused to accept a crown in return for abandoning his mistress to marry into a dynasty of which his brother approved, and in 1810 he left Europe, intending to settle in America. His ship was taken by the Royal Navy and he settled in England for some years. He was to experience Napoleon's displeasure.

Joseph, Napoleon's elder brother, was also unwilling to mount a throne, but allowed himself to be talked into becoming King of Naples and then of Spain,

LUCIEN BONAPARTE

where he acted as the Emperor's utterly miserable whipping boy for years.

The rest of the pack hastened to grab the proffered thrones – and endured years of misery as, with merciless frequency, the missiles of Napoleon's *Correspondance* bombarded them with cutting criticism.

Napoleon's brother Louis accepted the throne of the Kingdom of Holland and threw himself into his new role with great gusto, trying to become more Dutch than the Dutch themselves. This brought him into immediate conflict with his imperial brother, who shortly made it very clear that Louis's duties were to Napoleon first, France second and Holland only third.

In this series of appointments we see very clearly demonstrated one of the major causes of the Emperor's ultimate downfall: his willingness to prop himself up knowingly with broken reeds. Because of Napoleon's total inability to delegate authority, these flimsy characters required his constant attention, monitoring and intervention. These endless, repetitive rituals of familial espionage and chastisement must have robbed Napoleon of a large amount of his valuable time and energy.

When Napoleon became Consul, he declared that 'the revolution is over'. Ending a period of turmoil was perhaps necessary; reintroducing the pomp and circumstance of the hated *aristos*, many of whom had been murdered in the years up to 1795, was a monumental error, truly stamping on the graves of all the patriots who had fought and died to overthrow the Bourbon dynasty.

This error was compounded by the fact that, only a few weeks before, he had ridiculed his brother, Louis, for instituting his own system of orders of chivalry in Holland. These were the Orde van de Unie and the Koninklijke Orde van Verdienste. Poor Louis probably thought that by aping the creation of the Legion of Honour he was finally doing something of which his imperial brother might approve.

Napoleon abolished these Dutch orders on 18 October 1811.

The Totalitarian Dictator

Napoleon's interest in what went on in his empire knew no bounds; he sniffed around the darkest and most remote corners of the state, squandering his energies and time; he even went so far as to meddle in the content of church services. In this respect, he was totalitarian.

As under the Constitution only the Emperor was empowered to introduce new legislation, and as there was no opposition, he was a dictator. Below are some examples of the trivial matters which he allowed to distract him:

To M. Bigot de Préameneu, Minister of Public Worship.*

> *Paris, 3 March 1809.*
> Let me know why the Archbishop of Aix has ordered a Novena because of the illness of Queen Louisa,† and why the clergy ask the people's prayers for any person, without leave from the government.

And again:

To Count Fouché, Minister of Police.‡

> *Rambouillet, 14 March 1809.*
> ... Arrest the Vicar of Noyon, who has ventured to make improper allusions to the conscription in one of his sermons. You will have him brought to Paris, and examined by one of the Councillors of State. You will make a report of the enquiry to me.

The press enjoyed Napoleon's special scrutiny; in his eyes it should exist purely as an instrument of his propaganda, yet another of his tools for leading the nation (and later the whole of Europe) along the path he had chosen for it. By means of articles which he wrote, and which appeared anonymously in *Le Moniteur*, he fed the 'right' responses to the public's concerns on lack of political freedoms.

By 1811, he had not only forbidden all newspapers not to print articles on a whole range of topical (political and military) themes and installed a resident censor within each editorial office, but he had reduced the number of newspapers to four in Paris and one in each Department. He personally maintained an eagle eye on every activity of these survivors. His powers extended well beyond the borders of France, as may be seen here:

To General Clarke, Count of Huneburg, Minister of War.§

> *Paris, 27 March 1809.*
> There is a Courier d'Espagne, published in French, by a set of intriguers, which appears at Madrid, and which cannot fail to do great harm. Write to Marshal Jourdan that there is to be no French newspaper in Spain, and that this one is to be suppressed. I do not intend to allow any French

---

* *Correspondance* CLXIV.

† Ex-queen of Spain, then in Provence.

‡ *Correspondance* CLXVI.

§ *Correspondance* CLXX.

newspaper wherever my troops are, except such as are published by my order. Besides, do not the French receive Gazettes from France? And as for the Spaniards, they must be spoken to in their own language. Your letter on this subject must be a positive order.

Not only sermons and newspapers fell under Napoleon's censorship; books and plays were also included:

To Count Fouché, Minister of Police.[*]

> *Paris, 3 April 1809.*
> There is a work on Suwaroff, many of the notes to which are very objectionable. This book is said to have been written by an Abbé. You must put the seals on that Abbé's papers, you must have all the notes cancelled, and you must even stop the publication of the work, which is anti-national.

His meddling in affairs of the Church, the press and the theatre must have absorbed hours of his valuable time every day.

∽ Repression ∾

Whenever any sections of the population of his empire showed signs of trying to throw off his yoke – either inside or outside France – Napoleon was swiftly informed, either by the commanders in the affected regions or by his ubiquitous spies, who infested his realm like lice. His reactions were universally fierce and aggressive.

In the 1809 campaign, the Tyroleans, whose province had been ceded by Austria to Bavaria after the 1805 war, rose in revolt against the Bavarians and their French allies. They were an embarrassing thorn in Napoleon's side for months; his repressive measures were extremely severe:

To Marshal Lefebvre, Duke of Danzig, Commanding the 7th Corps of the Army in Germany.[†]

> *Schönbrunn, 30 July 1809.*
> I have this moment received your letter, dated 5 a.m., of the 28th. I see the Communes of Tauffers[‡] have submitted. I am sorry that

---

[*] *Correspondance CLXXIII.*

[†] *Correspondance CXCIX.*

[‡] In the original draft the word is Lowfers.

you have not punished them. My intention is that on receiving this present letter, you shall demand 150 hostages, taken from all the Tyrolese Cantons; that you shall cause at least six large villages, all through the Tyrol, and the ringleaders' houses to be sacked and burned, and that you shall let it be known that I will put the whole country to fire and sword, if all the muskets – eighteen thousand at the very least – are not given up to me, with as many brace of pistols, which I know to be in existence. You will have the 150 hostages taken, under good and safe escort, to the Citadel of Strasbourg. When I made my armistice, I did it principally to reduce the Tyrol.

After what has happened at Tauffers, I fear you may allow yourself to be fooled by that rabble, which will be worse than ever, the moment your back is turned. Frenchmen and Bavarians have been massacred in the Tyrol. Vengeance must be taken and severe examples made there. As for the Austrians, I have already made my intentions known to you. They must be aware of the armistice. They are a most egregiously false set. They are in far too close relations with the Austrian headquarters. No parleying! If they do not evacuate the country promptly, have them arrested. They are mere ruffians; they gave authority for the massacres. Give orders, then, that 150 hostages are to be made over to you; that all the worst characters are to be given up, and all the guns, at all events until the number reaches eighteen thousand. Make a law that any house in which a gun is found shall be razed to the ground, and that every Tyrolese found with a musket shall be put to death. Mercy and clemency are out of season with these ruffians. You have the power in your hands. Strike terror! And act so that a part of your troops may be withdrawn from the Tyrol, without any fear of its breaking out afresh. Six large villages must be sacked and burned, so that not a vestige of them remains, and that they may be a monument of the vengeance wreaked on the mountaineers. My orderly officer, L'Espinay, has taken you my orders. I long to hear that you have not allowed yourself to be caught, and that you have not rendered my armistice useless; for the chief benefit I desired to draw from it was to take advantage of the six weeks it gave me, to reduce the Tyrol. Send columns to Brixen.

For all this, the Tyroleans were not finally crushed until November of that year.

Trouble had also broken out in other Austrian provinces, although not on the same scale as in the Tyrol:

TO THE PRINCE OF NEUCHÂTEL, MAJOR GENERAL OF THE ARMY IN GERMANY.[*]

Schönbrunn, 5 August 1809.

Write to General Beaumont that I conclude him to have entered the Vorarlberg; that he is not to busy himself with issuing absurd proclamations, but to take measures for insuring tranquillity; that the most urgent of these is complete disarmament – not only as regards guns, pistols and swords, but also as regards gunpowder and war material. That country must give up at least twelve thousand weapons. Two hundred hostages, also, must be taken, and sent to a French citadel, and ten or twelve houses, belonging to the ringleaders, must be burned and sacked by the troops, and all the property of these ringleaders must be sequestered, and declared confiscated.

The Emperor had to have his ears and eyes everywhere; if he relaxed for a second, something was sure to go wrong. In 1809 his much-maligned naval squadron in the Scheldt was the recipient of a further burst of wrath:

TO COUNT FOUCHÉ, MINISTER OF POLICE.[†]

Schönbrunn, 9 August 1809.

. . . If my idiots of sailors have had the sense to run into Antwerp, my squadron is safe. The English expedition will come to nothing. They will all perish from inaction and fever.

His forecast of the fate of the British Walcheren expedition was spot on.

It is incredible to see how much of his precious time Napoleon diverted to trivial peripheral matters, which surely ought to have been delegated to a competent subordinate. His immense sense of his own importance emerges clearly in this letter:

TO COUNT FOUCHÉ, MINISTER OF POLICE.[‡]

Schönbrunn, 10 August 1809.

I send you the Bishop of Namur's Charge, which seems to me written with an evil intention. Find out who drew it up.

I see by your report of the 3rd that the Commissary-General of Police at Lyons discloses the fact that, on being informed that the order

---

* *Correspondance* CCIII.

† *Correspondance* CCVI.

‡ *Correspondance* CCVII.

for the Te Deum* on the 30th was not, according to the usual custom, to be preceded by my letter, he pointed out the omission. If this be so, you will have a conversation with Cardinal Fesch, and you will make him understand that unless he instantly withdraws the order he has given, and causes my letter to be reincorporated with his mandate, I shall consider him my enemy, and the enemy of the state.

Make him understand that there is nothing contrary to religion in my letter; that I do not permit anyone, and him least of all, to fail in respect to the authority with which I am invested. Settle this matter with him, if you can, and let my letter appear in his mandate. You will send for M. Emery, who is the Cardinal's councillor, and you will speak to him in this sense: 'Either my letter is contrary to religion or it is not; and has any bishop the right to change the sense I have given it?' I am as much a theologian as they are, and even more. I shall not go out of my province, but I will allow nobody else to go out of theirs.

At Bussaco on 27 September 1810 the overconfident André Masséna, advancing to invade Portugal, suffered a major defeat at the hands of Wellington's well-concealed Anglo-Portuguese army. News of this leaked into France from foreign newspapers; Napoleon at once set the record straight in his usual fashion. His comments about the good supply situation of French and allied troops in Spain, and their total control of the security there, are quite revealing; even at this time, in many areas the invaders were hanging on with great difficulty. His reference to the perfect harmony reigning among the various French commanders in Spain, following Napoleon's measures of the previous February, is a joke. He admits to having over 230,000 men in the peninsula; the true figure was probably slightly higher.

To the Count of Montalivet, Minister of the Interior.[†]

Fontainebleau, 13 October 1810.

False reports are too easily put about by evil-disposed and idle persons, under the influence of England, and even by means of echoes from foreign newspapers. There are certain objections to contradictions in our own newspapers, and besides, such a course is not always sufficiently dignified. I beg you will send the Prefects a weekly circular, to make them aware of the real truth as to current reports, and thus direct their opinions and language. You will order them to keep your dispatches to themselves, and to make use of

---

* For the victory of Wagram.

† *Correspondance* CCXCVII.

them in every way which may influence the public opinion of their Department.

I should wish the objects of your circular to be – first, to make known our system against England; that it is not want of money which dictates these measures to the government, but the desire to harm England, and that the advantage of this system has been proved by experience. Second, to make known the prosperous condition of French finances. This year's revenue amounts to over eight hundred million, as is proved by the accounts of the Ministers of Finance, and of the Public Exchequer, which will shortly be published. This proves the absurdity of the reports spread in certain Departments, as to the creation of a paper currency, of mortgages, of new taxes, and even of contributions to be levied on the Funds – the authors of which would fain apply the disastrous measures taken in Austria, Russia, Prussia and England, to France.

The third point of the circular should refer to the affairs of Spain. The French armies there are in the best possible condition and abundantly supplied. The Army of Andalusia, which occupies Seville, Granada, etc., has more than ninety thousand men fit for active service, under the orders of Marshals the Dukes of Belluno and Treviso, Count Sebastiani and the Duke of Dalmatia; the Army of Portugal, under the orders of the Prince of Essling, the Dukes of Elchingen and Abrantes, and Count Reynier, has more than seventy thousand men under arms. It has seized Ciudad Rodrigo and Almeida, and was face-to-face, on the 24th, with the English army, which it had forced to retire for ten marches, and which seemed to be falling back on its vessels. A battle was imminent, and the English were reinforcing their army, which amounted, possibly, to some thirty-six thousand men.

You will say that the reports circulated against the Duke of Abrantes are calumnious and false, that the general in question is winning the greatest distinction, and that the most perfect harmony reigns among the various generals; that Aragon, which was the most disturbed of all the Spanish provinces, is now the most submissive; that General Suchet, who has a fine army, numbering forty thousand men, is besieging Tortosa and threatening Valencia; that the Duke of Tarento having moved towards Tarragona, a few armed bands have taken advantage of his absence to gather about his rear and violate certain parts of the Pyrenean frontier, that other strong bodies of French troops occupy Navarre, the Asturias, Biscay and the other provinces; that a few smugglers, and the remnants of the Spanish army, have formed themselves into bands, which seize travellers –

hardly to be wondered at in such a large country as Spain – but that, on the whole, things are going very well indeed.

If the chief functionaries of the Departments are thus warned, every week, against false rumours which are rife, their tone will be steady, and this will react on Paris itself. You will submit these letters to me at a business sitting.

Napoleon's obsession that he must dominate and control all aspects of life in the ever-increasing realm over which he ruled is again demonstrated by these orders against the press:

TO GENERAL SAVARY, DUKE OF ROVIGO, MINISTER OF POLICE.[*]

Fontainebleau, 20 October 1810.

In the *Gazette de France* I see an article about a Minister of the Spanish Junta to the United States, in which Ferdinand VII is referred to. Who gave the *Gazette de France* authority to insert so mischievous an article? Inform the *Gazette de France* that the first time such an article is copied, the paper will be suppressed.

TO GENERAL SAVARY, DUKE OF ROVIGO, MINISTER OF POLICE.[†]

Fontainebleau, 25 October 1810.

I see by your police report that the blocks of a will of Louis XVI which was being printed for a certain Bonneville, a dealer in engravings, have been seized in the house of one Farge (No. 2, Cloître Saint-Benoît). Have these two persons arrested. Write to the Director of the Censure Department to have their charter revoked, and that they are never to be allowed either to print books, or sell engravings, again; then you will have them shut up in a state prison, until the millennium. When the Censorship was instituted, provision was made for depriving any handful of wretches who might attempt to disturb the public peace, of all right either to print or sell books. Send me a statement of the booksellers and printers who are known to be evilly inclined, and cannot be depended upon, so that I may revoke their licence. Follow this up vigorously; it is time to make an end of it. There can be no greater crime than that committed by these people.

Even as his empire crumbled in the wake of his Russian disaster, Napoleon struggled frantically to maintain the façade that he had created.

Early in 1813 a small force of Cossacks under Colonel Tettenborn approached the great old Hanseatic city state of Hamburg on the lower Elbe. Hamburg had been swallowed up by Napoleon in 1810 as part of his obsessive drive to enforce his hated Continental System and to eliminate the smuggling into 'Fortress Europe' of British goods. The area became the 32nd (French) Military Division, and all aspects of political and commercial life were at once forced into the homogeneous Napoleonic template. General Carra Saint-Cyr was in command of the 1st Division in the city, the commercial life of which had been ruined by that same System. Hearing of the advance of Tettenborn's hostile force, Saint-Cyr lost his head and fled with his troops to Bremen on 12 March, thus tearing a great gap in the Emperor's coastal defence network.

Tettenborn was invited into the city by the jubilant citizens, but refused to enter unless they abandoned all the French-style political institutions and customs that had been imposed in 1810. They readily agreed and the great port fell into allied hands without a shot being fired.

Napoleon was enraged:

To the Prince de Neuchâtel, Major General of the Grande Armée.[*]

Waldheim, 7 May 1813.

Send an officer to Bremen, to inform the Prince of Eckmühl of the events which have just occurred, that we shall probably be at Dresden tomorrow, and that the Prince of the Moskowa is about to cross the Elbe and march on Berlin. It is indispensable that the Prince of Eckmühl should move on Hamburg, seize that town, and forthwith send General Vandamme into Mecklenburg. This is the course he must take.

He will at once arrest all subjects of the town of Hamburg who have taken service under the title of 'Senators of Hamburg'. He will bring them before a court martial; he will have the five worst culprits shot, and he will send the rest, under strong escort, to France, where they will be detained in a state prison. He will have their property sequestered, and declare it confiscated. The Crown will take possession of all houses, landed property, etc.

He will have the whole town disarmed. He will have the officers of the Hanseatic Legion shot, and he will send all persons who have enlisted in that corps to France, to the galleys.

As soon as my troops have reached Schwerin, he will endeavour, without saying a word, to lay hands on the prince and

---

[*] *Correspondance* CDXXXIX.

his family, and will send them to France, to a state prison. These dukes have been traitors to the Confederation. Their ministers will be treated in the same way.

He will not permit any hostile act against the Swedes, so long as they remain in Pomerania, and undertake to remain quiet.

He will draw up a proscription list of five hundred of the richest and most ill-behaved persons belonging to the 32nd Military Division; he will have them arrested, and will have their property sequestered; it will be taken over by the Crown. This measure is particularly necessary in Oldenburg. He will mulct the towns of Hamburg and Lübeck, in a sum of fifty million. He will take steps to have this contribution assessed in a manner as to ensure its prompt payment.

He will have the whole country disarmed, and will have all gendarmes, gunners, coastguardsmen, and officers, soldiers, or officials, who have behaved as traitors, arrested. Their goods must be confiscated. Let him especially remember those Hamburg families which have behaved ill, and those whose intentions are evil. The landed proprietors must be turned out, or we shall never be sure of the country.

He must have the fortress of Hamburg armed; he must have drawbridges made to the gates, place guns on the ramparts, raise the parapets, and make a citadel on the Hamburg side, in which four or five thousand men may be out of reach of the populace. He will also have Lüneburg armed, so that it may be secured against sudden attack, and he will reorganise Cuxhaven.

All these measures are indispensable, and the government must not be allowed to modify any one of them. The Prince of Eckmühl must declare these my express orders, and must act, in due time and place, with the necessary caution. All known ringleaders of rebellion are to be shot, or sent to the galleys.

As to Mecklenburg, my general view is that the princes of that country have forfeited the Emperor's protection; but you must not allow this to become apparent, and I shall probably have time to give orders. As the Prince of Eckmühl may not be aware of these arrangements, he may, in the first instance, promise anything he is asked, under the sole reservation of the Emperor's approval being obtained. When that approbation is obtained, everything will be in order.

You will observe this letter is in cipher.

Hamburg being in a state of siege, the Prince of Eckmühl will appoint a strong commanding officer to keep order. He will send General Vandamme forward, with his headquarters, but he will spare the general, for such warriors are growing rare. Write to General Vandamme that I am well pleased with his conduct at

Bremen, and that I intend to give him a good command; that, meanwhile, he must second the Prince of Eckmühl by every means in his power; that I shall be obliged to him for doing so, and shall take due account of what he does in this respect.

The city of Hamburg was retaken by Marshal Davout on 30 May and awful retribution was exacted upon it. The 'Iron Marshal' became known to the citizens as 'Davout the Terrible', a reference to Tsar Ivan of Russian history. Bad as his rule of the city for the rest of the war was, it would seem that he did not apply all the repressive measures that Napoleon ordered.

General Carra Saint-Cyr was removed from his post, but on 30 March was back in command of a division under Dominique-Joseph Vandamme. He became a count in the first restoration and died in 1834.

The Emperor kept a close and baleful eye on Hamburg:

To Marshal Davout, Prince of Eckmühl, Commanding the Grande Armée.*

Bunzlau, 7 June 1813.

I need not tell you that you are to disarm the inhabitants (of Hamburg), to seize all muskets, swords, guns and powder, to make domiciliary visits wherever necessary, and to utilise everything for the defence of the town. Nor need I tell you that you are to press all the sailors, up to three or four thousand, and send them to France; that you are to press all bad characters and send them to France also, to be enrolled in the 127e, 128e and 129e Regiments. You will thus clear the town of five or six thousand men, and the hand of justice will be heavy on the rabble, which, it appears, could hardly have behaved worse. As regards other arrangements, I refer you to the Major General's letter, dated 7 May.

The financial effects of his handling of this great port-city raised concerns even in the commercial world of Paris. Napoleon's Minister of Police, Savary, reported nervously to his master that unease was growing. He was swiftly put back on track:

To General Savary, Duke of Rovigo, Minister of Police.*

Dresden, 18 June 1813.

I have your letter.
It is my intention that Hamburg shall be treated with great severity.

---

* *Correspondance* CDXLIII.
† *Correspondance* CCCXLVI.

The various decrees you have received will give you proof of this. I desire all proprietors, and all guilty persons, may be driven out, so that all property in the Military Division may change hands. The Prince of Eckmühl is therefore only carrying out my orders, and you, instead of thwarting him, must help him by every means in your power. The cackling of the Paris bankers matters very little to me. I am having Hamburg fortified. I am having a naval arsenal established there. Within a few months it will be one of my strongest fortresses. I intend to keep a standing force of fifteen thousand men there.

As for M. A?, I do not know him. But I am inclined to think him not overscrupulously honest, seeing he sends sums of sixty thousand francs to his wife in Paris, for her to buy property in Normandy. As regards his influence on military matters, the fault lies with the generals, who should not listen to a man who knows nothing about war, much less consult him.

Generally speaking, the police does not do a good service; it accepts all false rumours that come from London, and dins them into the general's ears. The Antwerp Commissary never does anything else. All these police reports mean nothing, and, luckily, do no harm when they are sent to me, but generals who have no habit of command and no readiness of mind take them for official documents. They mind what they are told and act accordingly, to clear their responsibility. Forbid the Commissaries of Hamburg and Antwerp, as well as the Commissary at Amsterdam, to give this sort of information to the military authorities. They are all three duped by the English, who purposely spread reports of steps they have no real intention of taking.

The depth and breadth of Napoleon's knowledge of all that was going on within his empire is demonstrated by the reference to 'M. A?' and his financial dabblings.

Napoleon's astounding ability to absorb and assess the import of countless reports, on a whole spectrum of topics on a daily basis – even when involved in a war for survival in Saxony as he was – is mind-boggling. Despite all the crises with which he was faced, Napoleon could still find time to keep his finger on popular matters by reading the local German press:

To the Prince of Neuchâtel, Major General of the Grande
Armée.*

Dresden, 18 June 1813.

Here is a very extraordinary article out of the *Journal de Leipsic*.
Send it to the officer in command that he may get an explanation of
it. Let him have the gazetteer arrested on the spot, brought before a
court martial, and shot, if there is the smallest evidence of evil
intent.

Evidence that Napoleon permitted corruption to flourish under his rule is
found in this letter, firing a warning to Louis-Antoine Fauvelet de Bourrienne,
a school friend of the Emperor who had risen to high rank on his coat-tails.
Bourrienne, a lawyer and diplomat, had accompanied Napoleon to Egypt as his
secretary and had assisted in the coup of Brumaire. Later he lost his post when
his shady financial dealings became too blatant. From 1805 to 1810 – back in
favour despite his track record – he was French envoy to Hamburg and made a
fortune in bribes by facilitating evasions of the Continental System. He later co-
operated in the writing of the so-called 'Memoirs of Napoleon Bonaparte',
published in 1829 and widely regarded as being somewhat unreliable.

To General Savary, Duke of Rovigo, Minister of Police.†

Dresden, 30 June 1813.

You will inform M. Bourrienne that he is to break off all correspondence, on any pretence whatsoever, with Hamburg; for the first time
he writes about, or concerns himself, directly or indirectly, with
Hamburg affairs, I will have him arrested, and I will make him
disgorge everything he has stolen from that city.

---

* *Correspondance* CDXLVIII.

† *Correspondance* CDLI

2

~ Military Blunders ~

~ 1800: Marengo ~

*M*ANY READERS WILL BE surprised that Napoleon, the greatest general that ever lived, should have begun to exhibit feet of military clay so early in his meteoric career, when only thirty-one years of age. It is, however, at Marengo that we see for the first time the sort of miscalculation that was to lose him that battle on 14 June 1800 to the Austrian General der Cavallerie Baron Michael Friedrich Benedikt Melas, then aged seventy.

Lose that battle? Oh yes! In direct contravention of his own oft-trumpeted maxim of 'march divided, fight concentrated', the future Emperor of the French had so underestimated his enemy that he had made considerable detachments from his army, including the nine thousand men of General Desaix's corps of the divisions of Boudet and Monnier. The reason for detaching these valuable troops from his total of twenty-eight thousand was that he had convinced himself that Melas, in Alessandria, was aiming to avoid a battle, to execute a flank march south to the port-city of Genoa, which had fallen into Austrian hands on 4 June, and to evacuate his army from the trap it was in by sea on British ships.

Napoleon had crossed the Alps (though not quite 'like a thunderbolt' as he later wrote), taken the Austrian artillery depot at Milan on 2 June after a string of brilliant tactical victories, and placed himself across Melas's lines of communication to the east. He was convinced that Melas had started to evacuate his army from the city of Alessandria, so he sent patrols – and eventually Desaix – south to Novi to intercept this move. He also sent Lapoype's division (some 3,500 men) off to the north to block any possible Austrian retreat in that direction. However, Melas had about twenty-nine thousand men in Alessandria on 14 June, and fully intended to fight.

Despite there being only one bridge across which the Austrian army could defile in order to attack the French, the situation at about ten o'clock was so bad for Napoleon that he sent a courier after Desaix and Lapoype with the infamous 'For God's sake come back!' messages.

From ten o'clock until three in the afternoon, the French army was pushed back, eventually beginning to disintegrate under Napoleon's hand. So sure was Melas that the battle was won, that he handed over command to Feldmarschalleutnant Konrad Kaim and returned to Alessandria to write his victorious report.

Happily for Napoleon, the river Scrivia, which barred Desaix's way south,

Napoleon ascending the Alps

was swollen and too high for him to cross; Napoleon's panic-stricken 'For God's sake come back!' message was delivered in time. It was shortly after three o'clock when Desaix returned to the field, his division hurrying along behind.

'Well,' asked Napoleon of his saviour anxiously, 'what do you think?'

'This battle is surely lost!' replied Desaix. 'But there is time to win another!'

There followed the ambush of the Austrian column by the 9e Légère,

Louis Desaix

Kellermann's legendary cavalry charge and the collapse of the Austrian grenadiers, which sealed the day in favour of the French.

This stunning victory ended the war in northern Italy, and lent so much political weight to the victor that he was able to return to Paris and secure his position as leader of a grateful nation. Conveniently for Napoleon, the faithful Desaix was killed in action at the moment of victory; the First Consul was able to bask alone in the glory of Marengo.

Napoleon's underestimation of the enemy was to recur in 1809 at Aspern-Essling, in 1812 in his invasion of Russia, in 1813 at Leipzig, in 1814 after his brilliant Nine Days Campaign, in 1815 at Ligny and, most tellingly, at Waterloo.

Napoleon was no fool in his ability to assess his fellow men – and women; he knew about human weaknesses and sought to insulate himself against them by setting up comprehensive intelligence-gathering networks across Europe, in allied as well as hostile and neutral countries. By 1809 Bavaria was one of his most reliable allies, but this did not stop him sending his spies into her territory for his own purposes. The total budget for such intelligence work is not clear, but it seems that many large sums were involved:

Napoleon at Aspern-Essling

To the Count of Champagny, Minister for Foreign Affairs.[*]

Paris, 23 February 1809.

Let M. Otto know that I will allow him a sum of ten thousand francs a month, for espionage; that I desire he will organise a spy system at Munich, headed by reliable and intelligent men; and that, to avoid giving umbrage, he will give the king full knowledge of it. The duty of these spies will be to watch all Austrian movements in Styria and Carinthia, and the roads to Vienna and Prague. It would be well that this spy system should consist, at all events as far as the chiefs are concerned, of men who could be attached to the Military Staff, in case of necessity. You will remit the ten thousand francs a month to M. Otto, according as he spends the money. He must set up this spy system on a large scale, so as to be thoroughly informed as to the Austrian movements. You will place five thousand francs a month at the disposal of M. Bourgoing, for the same purpose, so as to have information of what happens at Warsaw, and on the distant frontiers of Austria and Bohemia. Let MM. Bourgoing and Serra understand that they must arrange this spy system so as to have men who will keep them thoroughly informed of what is done in Bohemia and Warsaw. Their reports will be sent in direct to you.

～ 1805: Napoleon and Naval Affairs ～

Napoleon was usually an exceptionally gifted strategist and commander. He weighed the intelligence, planned, calculated and gave the orders needed to achieve his defined objectives. His troops marched, the enemy fell into his traps and the wars were won; it was so simple – on land.

At sea, things were slightly different. The intelligence, planning, calculations and issuing of orders went ahead as before; then the tides and the weather stepped in, problems almost never experienced on land.

The ships of the fleet could only enter or leave most European ports (apart from the Mediterranean and Adriatic) at certain periods of the day and night, at high tide. Tidal activity was governed not by Alexandre Berthier or even by the Emperor himself, but by the waxing and waning of the moon. Time and tide wait for no man.

Seamanship was – and is – a highly skilled craft, requiring constant practice by officers and crew if a ship was to be efficiently handled. Due to the ravages of the French Revolution, about two-thirds of the officers had left the

---

[*] *Correspondance* CLXII.

French navy by 1795. Due to the lure of better pay in the merchant marine, trained, competent replacements were not forthcoming. The quality of the remaining naval officers was not of the best, and a general spirit of defeatism pervaded the corps.

Prior to the Revolution there was a highly trained corps of naval gunners; this was considered as being elitist by the Committee of Public Safety and was disbanded. The new regime also hated the old officer caste (naval as well as military): orders were now a basis for debate among the hands. This meant that in bad weather, when the very survival of a ship might depend on all hands climbing aloft to reduce the spread of canvas, many of them might refuse to go. As flogging had been abolished, officers often had their work cut out just to keep the vessel afloat, let alone fight the Royal Navy.

At this point in history, all ships moved either by oars (galleys) or by wind power. European navies consisted mostly of square-rigged ships. Galleys were extremely rare in high-seas fleets, but the Baltic navies had their share.

Utter dependence on wind power for motion places immense limitations on naval operations. For example, a sea voyage from A to B which takes two days in May might take ten times as long in February or in June. Global wind-and-weather patterns such as the trade winds, the Roaring Forties and the doldrums were factors which every proficient sailor had to take into consideration when planning any operation. Apart from these regular global weather patterns, there were always liable to be random exceptions, which could easily disrupt the best-laid of schemes. A strong onshore wind might imprison a ship in harbour for days; a storm might – and often did – threaten the very survival of a ship or of an entire fleet. The speed and direction of a square-rigged sailing vessel depended on the settings of the various sails, of which there could easily be a score or more on a fully-rigged ship of the line.

These factors disrupted naval operations on a very regular basis and were part of every sailor's life. There was yet another factor, which Napoleon did not have to cope with in land campaigns – navigation. There were no roads or distinctive physical features on the high seas. Once out of sight of land, the position of any ship of this era had to be determined by a complex procedure involving charts, sextants, compasses, and clear daylight so that the height of the sun could be used as the crucial basis of the calculation. Any errors made in this calculation could easily be fatal. To attain the desired speed and direction of a ship involved much dangerous, complex, physical work by the crew members, high up in the yardarms and rigging, often in storm conditions. Man's influence on his environment at sea in this age was so slight that it was common for a ship or ships to be driven to destruction on coasts despite all the best efforts of the officers and crews.

Storms often ripped sails away, broke masts and yardarms, swamped vessels or smashed them together. The Royal Navy – undoubtedly the greatest and best-manned in the world at this point – lost many ships purely to bad weather conditions. If this were true of the best navy, at sea throughout the year and all around the world, consider the challenges faced by a navy unable to achieve that essential sailing experience, with its ships in less-than-optimal condition, its officers and crews at a low state of training, and the naval arsenals in the ports similarly neglected. Such was the unhappy condition of the French navy from 1792 to 1815.

All these factors combined to make the French navy of the period very much the poor relation of the army. The army was, as it were, Napoleon's chosen instrument: he knew it inside and out, and played it as well as any virtuoso that ever lived; it responded promptly and faithfully to his every whim, right to the end. The navy, however, was a different matter altogether.

His impatient mind could not be bothered to consider its very valid limitations in use. He had no confidence in his admirals. He suspected that they were all half-hearted, hiding behind complexities in order to avoid taking on the enemy. This lack of patience is all the more surprising, as he must have divined why it was that he could not get at Britain, was unable to cross that ditch to Dover that he could see but not touch. He must also have understood that if he was the bully boy of Europe, Britain was the bully boy of the world, solely due to naval power.

In 1815, when he boarded HMS *Bellerophon*, he exclaimed: *Je n'ai point fait assez pour la marine* (I have not done nearly enough for the navy). If only he had devoted a little more time to that problem.

In 1798, bored by inaction in Paris, he laid a scheme before the Directory for the invasion of England and was commissioned to put it into action. By 11 January he was at Dunkirk and full of enthusiasm: 'All goes well. We are working hard at the reorganisation of our navy and the formation of the Army of England.'

On 12 February 1798, he wrote: 'It is said that the Dutch have numbers of fast-sailing flatboats; we must obtain from 150 to 250, with as many gunboats as possible. We must then get these vessels to Dunkirk at once, so as to be able to leave that port a month hence, with fifty thousand men, artillery, supplies, etc.'

But by the 23 February, back in Paris, he reported:

> Whatever we do, we cannot command the sea for several years to come. To effect a landing in England without controlling the sea is the boldest and most difficult military operation ever attempted. It would seem, then, that the expedition to England is not feasible. We

must therefore merely keep up the pretence of it, and concentrate our attention and our resources on the Rhine, or else undertake an expedition to the Levant so as to threaten the trade with India. And if none of these operations is feasible, I can see no other course than to make peace with England.

So here we have, at this early stage in his career, a clear understanding of France's naval limitations and the consequences of not rectifying the situation – to 'make peace with England'. But was Napoleon the type to back down from a challenge?

In May 1798 he was mounting his famous expedition to Egypt. His naval commander was Admiral Brueys; the fleet consisted of fifteen ships of the line, twelve frigates and over two hundred transports. But on 17 May he wrote: 'We have been riding at anchor these last three days ready to start, but a strong wind continues to blow from the wrong quarter.' And on the 27th: 'We have been becalmed these two days, ten leagues from the Straits of Bonifacio.' Next day they were able to continue under full sail when a favourable wind came up. Napoleon, then, was familiar with the vagaries of the weather and the effects that it had on naval operations. The expedition disembarked at Alexandria on 2 July. As the harbour of the city was too shallow to accommodate the ships of the line, they went off to Aboukir Bay, where they were destroyed by Rear Admiral Nelson's fleet in his usual, daring manner, on 1 August.

On the 19th he wrote to the Directory:

> Fate has ordained, in this event as in so many others, that if we are given a great preponderance on the continent, to our rivals is given the dominion of the seas . . . Collect all our ships from Toulon, Malya, Ancona, Corfu, Alexandria, to form a new fleet. Had I been master of the sea, I would have been lord of the Orient.

Napoleon had clearly read the right signs from events; the concentration of a new fleet was the only possible course of action. The Egyptian adventure ran its course; the Peace of Amiens brought a temporary ceasefire to Europe.

In 1802, Napoleon took advantage of the removal of the Royal Navy's iron grip on the Atlantic to send an expedition to the West Indies to reimpose French rule – and slavery – on Santo Domingo; so much for *Liberté, Egalité, Fraternité*. Although the operation succeeded, the cost in trained naval officers and men was high: several thousand, to say nothing of the thousands of army personnel who also died of the dreaded yellow fever. Replacement of these lost men was not easy; it took years to train proficient naval officers.

Great Britain declared war on France again on 16 May 1803 and at once reimposed the tried and trusted naval-blockade system against France. Although the Royal Navy was well up to the coming tasks, the army available within the kingdom was woefully inadequate. The famous Martello towers were not yet there; the building programme would not start until 1808. What coastal defensive works existed were mainly simple earthworks, weakly armed and the responsibility of the local authorities, which had to bear the costs of construction and provide the garrisons.

Although the British army had about ninety thousand men, the bulk of these were abroad in the colonies. Apart from this there were the militia, some one hundred thousand men, but these were of indifferent combat value and distributed across the country with the aim of countering civil disobedience rather than defeating an invasion by the Grande Armée. Had Napoleon been able to cross the Channel and land a credible force in Kent, there would soon have been a crisis in London; the wars might well have taken a very different course than they did.

Napoleon was well informed of conditions in Britain; he read all the newspapers and had reports from his agents. All he had to do was to cross the Channel and walk into London.

On 23 August 1803, at Saint-Cloud, Napoleon wrote:

> England will never get other terms from me than those of Amiens; I will face everything, but I will never consent to her holding anything in the Mediterranean. From Malta, Nelson holds all of Italy blockaded. By the help of God and a good cause, the war, however unfortunate it may be, will never make the French people bow before this proud nation that makes its sport of all that is sacred on earth, and that has, these last twenty years, assumed a predominance and arrogance in Europe that menace the very existence of all nations in their industry and commerce, those mainsprings of national existence.

The future Emperor's grasp of the importance of economics, and of the strategic significance of the island of Malta were clear; so what would he do to address these topics?

He realised that Great Britain's mastery of the seas made the serious defence of any of his colonies impossible for as long as the French navy was still the underdog. At this point it still was, despite his acknowledgement of this defect in 1798; in four years he had not tackled the problem of his inadequate navy.

Realising the vulnerability of his colonies, and chronically short of cash to fund his massive army, he sold Louisiana to the United States for 27.3 million dollars. This achieved three things: his coffers filled up, he had less to defend (thus fewer future outgoings) and Britain's truculent ex-colony received a boost. Not at all a bad deal.

Now to those troublesome islanders themselves. Having cowed mainland Europe, he laid elaborate plans to invade England and stamp out the pests who disturbed his vision of a new world order. A huge complex of camps, roads and harbours was built along the Channel coast, arsenals of military stores and weapons were assembled, flotillas of gunboats and transports were built; the bulk of the Grande Armée became the 'Armée d'Angleterre' and marched into north-western France to perfect their skills at arms. French naval assets were redeployed to these harbours to seize control of the Channel at the given signal. At this point the French navy had about sixty ships of the line available, but many were in bad shape, and the state of training of the crews was poor. In Britain, by contrast, an energetic programme of construction was under way to build forty new seventy-fours. Napoleon was to build only eighty-three ships of the line during his entire reign. If he really understood the importance of sea power, why did he not concentrate more resources and attention on his navy? In the end, perhaps the battle of Trafalgar (to come in 1805) knocked the will to fight Britain at sea out of him.

On 29 September 1803 Napoleon wrote to Admiral Eustache Bruix, his navy commander:

> I am glad to see that your port at Boulogne is beginning to fill up. Le Havre, Cherbourg, Granville, St Malo, have large flotillas ready that may reach you at any moment. They will double your strength. In the meanwhile, I have much satisfaction in hearing of the good spirit of the troops and of the zeal with which they work at their naval tactics.

On 5 November 1803, Napoleon arrived with the invasion force in the great camp at Boulogne: 'I arrived unexpectedly at Boulogne on Friday at one o'clock. I set to inspecting with the liveliest interest the preparations for our great expedition; at midnight I was still at it. I am in barracks in the centre of the camp on the seashore, where the eye can measure the space that separates us from England.'

By the 9th, he had seen more: 'I spent Sunday visiting our new ports at Ambleteuse and Wimereux, and in manoeuvring the troops. I inspected today, in the closest detail, the naval workshops; their condition is as bad as it well could be. I have just converted some barracks into a naval arsenal. I have to look after the smallest details in person.' So the neglect of French naval assets of the last ten years was not to be put right overnight; even Hercules might have felt challenged by the tasks which confronted the Emperor.

However, Napoleon went on to remark: 'Our fleet, which already numbers one hundred men-of-war, remains at anchor in the bay, and the English don't dare to close in to short range. Lord Keith is apparently in command and has several sixty-fours; he has suffered some damage even at long range.'

On the 12th: 'I hope that I shall soon reach the goal that Europe is watching. We have the insults of six centuries to avenge.'

Four days later: 'From the cliffs at Ambleteuse I had sight of the English coast. I could make out houses and movement. The thing is a ditch, and with a pinch of courage it can be jumped.' So near yet so far.

On 7 December in Paris, he was to write: 'The combined fleets will start in March, and reach Boulogne . . . with 130,000 men. With a good wind we need the fleet for only twelve hours.' By this time he had assembled over 2,300 flat-bottomed transports on the coast, each capable of carrying up to four field guns and from sixty to a hundred men.

The year 1804 saw a rash of attempts on Napoleon's life, which distracted his attention from his grand designs on Britain for some months, but on 2 July he was back on track and wrote to Vice Admiral Louis-René Levassor de Latouche-Treville, who commanded the French Mediterranean fleet in Toulon:

> Let me know by return what day you can weigh anchor, weather permitting. Inform me also as to the position of the enemy – where Nelson is. Think over carefully the great enterprise you are about to carry out; and let me know, before I sign your final orders, your own views as to the best way of carrying it out.
>
> We have 1,800 gunboats and cutters carrying ten thousand men and ten thousand horses between Etaples, Boulogne, Wimereux and Ambleteuse. If we are masters of the Channel for six hours, we are masters of the world! If you take Nelson in, he will sail for Sicily, Egypt or Ferrol. It would seem better, therefore, to sail very wide, to appear before Rochefort, which would give you a fleet of sixteen of the line and eleven frigates, and then without delay, without touching, whether by circling around Ireland or by carrying out the first plan, proceed to Boulogne. Our Brest fleet, twenty-three of the line, will have troops on board, and will remain constantly under sail, so that Cornwallis must keep close in to the coast of Brittany to prevent its getting out. But before my ideas are quite settled about these operations, which offer great risks, but of which the success would mean so much, I shall wait for the plan you are to send me.

'Masters of the world!' These were not the ramblings of a madman; his plan was excellent. All he needed was one more slice of his customary luck and he would have been master of the world.

But the planners in the corridors of the Admiralty in London had already played this one through dozens of times and were well aware of his build-up of forces across that 'ditch'; even if he succeeded in mastering the Channel for six hours, they had to be the right six hours, with optimal wind, weather and tidal conditions.

On 21 July 1804 Napoleon was at the inn of Pont-de-Briques: 'The wind freshened tonight, and one of our gunboats dragged its anchor and struck on the rocks about one league from Boulogne; I thought all would be lost, the ship and the crew, but we were able to save them. The sight was a grand one.'

A week later:

> Yesterday I reviewed the whole flotilla. Compared with that of England, our situation is most favourable. The war has no ill effect on France, because of its weighing so heavily on England, and I have here around me three hundred thousand men, three thousand cutters and gunboats, that only await a favourable breeze to carry the imperial eagle to the Tower of London. Time and Fate alone can tell what will become of it all.

Prophetic words. Emil Ludwig, in his racy biography of the Emperor, has a dramatic scene on such a day in which Napoleon orders Admiral Bruix to have part of the flotilla to put to sea; Bruix refuses because of strong onshore winds and there is almost a fight between the two men. It ends with Bruix being sent to Holland and Rear Admiral Magon taking command and obediently putting to sea, with the result that the bodies of some two hundred French sailors were washed up next day. Unfortunately, Six does not confirm this for either admiral. As both had their names inscribed on the Arc de Triomphe and both were highly honoured, it seems that the tale is apocryphal.

Unfortunately for Napoleon's plans for world domination, Admiral Latouche-Treville, a very brave and capable officer, suddenly died in Toulon on 19 August 1804. He was to be sadly missed.

Britain, meanwhile, was very active on the diplomatic front, building another coalition against France. On 3 August the Emperor wrote:

> There are signs of a coalition forming; I shall not give them time to complete it; it is not right that Austria, by such equivocal conduct, should hold three hundred thousand men at attention on the shores of the Channel. The court of Vienna will have to come out of its ambiguous attitude, and if Vienna is so mad as to attempt the

fortune of war again, and listen to the suggestions of London, woe betide the Austrian monarchy!

Then on 6 September 1804, another naval plan was hatched; Napoleon wrote to Vice Admiral Ganteaume:

> If you could carry sixteen thousand men and a thousand horses to Ireland in November, it would be fatal to our enemies. Tell me if you could be ready, and what are the probabilities of success. Have a talk with General O'Connor about the points where we might disembark.
>
> I have no naval commanders. I would like to create a few Rear Admirals, but I would prefer to select the men who showed most promise, regardless of seniority.

Six days later, he wrote to Admiral Denis Decrès, his Minister of Marine and a distinguished officer of the Bourbon navy:

> The navy must be tuned up by making a few examples. It is the only way to get a navy. Every naval expedition we have attempted since I have been at the head of the government has failed, because the admirals see double and have picked up the idea, I don't know where, that you can make war without running risks. I have sent you some reports on St Helena.

There had been several French expeditions to Ireland before; all had failed miserably, even when the ships actually managed to land the troops, as in August 1798. British rule in Ireland was, justifiably, unpopular there, but the wild-geese in France tended to talk up the prospects of popular uprisings for their own ends.

Napoleon would not let go of the idea of an expedition to Ireland. On 27 September he wrote to his Chief of Staff, Alexandre Berthier:

> My Cousin:
> The expedition to Ireland will take place. You must confer with Marshal Augereau on the matter. We have at Brest transports for eighteen thousand men. General Marmont is ready on his side with twenty-five thousand. He will attempt to land in Ireland and will be under the orders of Marshal Augereau. At the same time the Grande Armée will embark at Boulogne, and will make every effort to effect a landing in Kent. The navy holds out hope of being ready on 22 October.

But the invasion of Ireland did not take place; neither did the landing in Kent, which was just as well for Britain, as the weak home defence forces would probably have been rapidly and completely overwhelmed once the naval shield had been pierced.

The year 1804 turned into 1805 and still the Grande Armée passed its time in the Channel camps, drilling and perfecting its manoeuvres that were to make the Glory Years possible. Still Napoleon insisted on watching and waiting for a chance to invade Britain. To command the vital fleet, he selected Vice Admiral Pierre-Charles Villeneuve, now commanding in Toulon. Villeneuve had commanded the *Guillaume Tell* at the battle of the Nile. With two other ships, he had escaped from that disaster and gone to Malta. When Malta was taken by the British he was briefly a prisoner of war. Just why he was selected to fill this crucial post, on which Napoleon's plan for world domination hinged, is unclear. He was chosen over Vice Admiral François-Etienne Rosily. It seems that even at the point of selection, Napoleon had misgivings about the qualities of his chosen commander.

The Emperor's plan called for the Toulon fleet to break out into the Atlantic, lead Nelson's ships on a wild-goose chase to the West Indies, then to double back, pick up the Brest squadron and hold the Channel in order to cover the vital crossing of the army. All in all, it was an excellent plan, which almost worked.

At last, on 30 March, Admiral Villeneuve managed to take his squadron out of Toulon, through the straits of Gibraltar and off across the Atlantic to the West Indies. By this time, Britain's high-handedness had caused Spain to join forces with France and to place their fleet at Napoleon's disposal. The chase across the Atlantic succeeded in losing Nelson, and months later, Villeneuve was back off the French coast. So far, so good.

On 22 July Admiral Calder with fifteen ships of the line clashed with Villeneuve off Cape Finisterre. Villeneuve had twenty of the line and seven frigates. Calder caused two of these to strike their colours in stormy conditions and went off home with his prizes; Villeneuve headed north, for the Spanish harbour of Ferrol. Calder was severely censured for not having destroyed the Franco-Spanish squadron completely.

At the third attempt, on 17 August, Villeneuve managed to get out of Ferrol with his twenty-nine ships of the line, with some intention of carrying out his orders and making north for Brest. He sent the frigate *Didon* to find the Rochefort squadron and to direct it also upon Brest, to join Vice Admiral Honoré Ganteaume's squadron. The frigate was promptly taken by the Royal Navy. But just before he sailed, he had written to Decrès: 'The enemy's forces, more concentrated than ever, leave me little other resource than to go to Cadiz.' Hardly had Villeneuve lost sight of land, than British warships appeared on the horizon. His courage failed him and he turned south for the safety of the Spanish port.

On 20 August, the Emperor heard that the combined French and Spanish fleets (twenty-four ships of the line) had left Ferrol. Two days later, he wrote to Villeneuve: 'I hope you have reached Brest. Start; lose not a minute, and, with my combined fleets, sail up the Channel. England is ours. We are all ready, everything is embarked. Appear here for twenty-four hours, and all is over.'

But Napoleon was now facing the prospect of a war on two fronts; Austria was rattling sabres in the Danube valley, and hence time for an invasion of Britain was running out, as the Grande Armée might have to be sent to crush the mainland threat.

British admirals Calder and Collingwood, with twenty-six ships of the line, had followed Villeneuve and at once blockaded him in Cadiz. They sent word to Nelson, at this point back in England on leave. He set sail on 15 September and assumed command of the British fleet off Cadiz on the 28th.

According to Ségur, when Napoleon heard that Villeneuve was at Ferrol he was livid; he said to Pierre-Antoine Daru, his civil councillor: 'Do you know where that f****r Villeneuve is? He is at Ferrol! . . . He has been beaten, he is hiding in Ferrol . . . What an admiral!'

When his rage had subsided a little, Napoleon wrote to Villeneuve on 13 August:

> Inform Admiral Ganteaume of your departure by special courier. Never will a fleet have faced risks for a more important object, and never will my soldiers and sailors have an opportunity of shedding their blood for a greater and more noble result. We might all of us well die content for the sake of helping the invasion of the Power that has for six centuries oppressed France. Such are the sentiments that should animate you, that should animate all my soldiers. England has not more than four line-of-battle ships in the Downs.

Next day, he wrote to Decrès: 'If with thirty ships my admirals fear to attack twenty-four British, we may as well give up all hope of a navy.'

And in reality, Napoleon had absolutely no confidence in the man to whom he had allotted such a key role in his plans for world domination. That same day he wrote:

I believe that Villeneuve has not enough in him to command a frigate. He has no decision and no moral courage. Two Spanish ships have been in collision, a few men are sick on his own ships, add to that two days of unfavourable winds, an enemy ship reconnoitring, a report that Nelson has joined Calder, and his plans are changed, when, taking these facts one by one, they amount to nothing. He has not the experience of war, nor the instinct for it.

On 23 August Napoleon recorded as follows:

My fleet sailed from Ferrol on the 17th with thirty-four ships of the line; there was no enemy in sight. If my instructions are followed, if it joins the Brest fleet and enters the Channel, there is still time; I am Master of England. If, on the contrary, my admirals hesitate, manoeuvre badly, and do not carry out my plans, all I can do is to await winter and then cross with the flotilla; it is a risky operation.

Such being the state of things, I must attend to the more urgent matter. I can place two hundred thousand men in Germany, and twenty-five thousand in the kingdom of Naples. I march on Vienna, and do not lay down my arms until Naples and Venice are mine, and I have so increased the Electorate of Bavaria that I have nothing further to fear from Austria.

But the disappointment of Villeneuve did not stop Napoleon's brilliant mind for long. He heard the news at Pont-de-Briques late one night. He sent for Daru, who appeared at four o'clock in the morning. 'Sit down there and write,' snapped Napoleon. Immediately, and apparently without meditation, he dictated, unhesitatingly and in his concise and imperious manner, the plan of the 1805 campaign, as far as Vienna. Having made certain that his instructions were well understood, he dismissed Daru with the words:

Leave immediately for Paris, but feign to set out for Ostend. Arrive at your destination alone and at night; and let no one know you are there. Go to the house of General Dejean;[*] closet yourself with him, and prepare, but with him only, the orders for the marches, stores, etc., etc. I do not want a single clerk to know of this; you will sleep in General Daru's study, and no one must know you are there.

On 25 August Napoleon turned his back on England and marched the Grande

---

* General Jean-François-Aimé Dejean was then Minister for War.

Armée off to the Danube. Whatever Villeneuve now did was irrelevant, as the Grande Armée was in eastern Austria. His mission should have been aborted.

By 31 August news that his fleet was in Cadiz reached Napoleon in Vienna. On 4 September he wrote to Decrès: 'Admiral Villeneuve has touched the limit! The thing is unthinkable! Send me a report covering the whole expedition. Villeneuve is a low rascal who must be ignominiously cashiered. Without plans, without courage, he would sacrifice everything to save his skin!'

The battle of Trafalgar on 21 October destroyed the Franco-Spanish fleet. Villeneuve was taken prisoner and returned to Britain. On 17 April 1806 he returned to France and was sent to Rennes. On 22 April he was found dead in his room, with six knife wounds in his heart. It was stated that he committed suicide. His name is inscribed on the Arc de Triomphe.

One must sympathise with Napoleon in this case. He had concentrated on the invasion of Britain for over two years, only to have his chances of world domination ruined by the faint-heartedness of Villeneuve. It is evident that Napoleon had now lost faith in his navy ever being able to achieve anything of note. He thus was forced to accept that he was caged in Europe by the Royal Navy.

The flotilla of transports and gunboats rotted; relatively little new construction was undertaken for the French navy and the sailors were used for coastguard duties. In 1813 there were sixty-four ships of the line in the French navy, forty frigates, eleven corvettes and twenty-seven brigs. But their crews were mostly doing shore duty; they also provided four regiments of infantry which fought, very well, in Saxony.

But by this time, Napoleon had ordered an increase in the naval building programme. Money for military expenditure was short, time was of the essence, but he was determined to revive France's naval power. As he wrote in January 1813:

> I can by no means agree to reducing my naval armaments . . . my intention is to increase those in Toulon, Rochefort, Brest and Cherbourg as much as possible . . .
>
> I have fourteen ships on the stocks in Antwerp. Three of them must be launched in March 1814. On eleven of the others you must make enough progress for them to be launched in March, April and June 1814 and the remaining five in 1815.
>
> At Cherbourg the *Jupiter*, *Centaure* and *Inflexible* must be launched in 1814. With the *Zélandais* and *Duguay-Trouin* already complete, that will give me seven of the line there.
>
> At Brest I wish *Orion* to be launched as soon as possible and *Brabaçon* should be launched at Lorient in 1814 with *Magnifique*,

Algéciras and *Jean Bart* in the following year.

Start building an eighty-four-gun ship at Rochefort. At Toulon *Héros* must be launched soon so that work may begin on a 118-gun ship.

Colosse and *Kremlin* should be launched there next year, as should *Scipion* and *Brillant* at Genoa.

Duquesne and *Montenotte* should be launched immediately at Venice, as should *Amphitrite*. Another should be launched in 1814.

By September 1814 I wish to have twenty-six ships of the line at Toulon, five at Venice, which will give me thirty-one in the Mediterranean, with three Italian and two Neapolitan, thirty-six.

At Rochefort eleven, four of them three-deckers, at Lorient three, at Cherbourg seven, one three-decker; at Brest seven, one three-decker; that would give me twenty-eight of the line, including six three-deckers, on the [Atlantic] ocean coast. Then thirty for the Scheldt and ten at the Texel – a total of 104 ships of the line.

Investing such a large part of his scarce resources in such a major naval resuscitation programme clearly shows Napoleon's determination to rival Britain's command of the seas. But numbers of ships are not enough. They had to be equipped, supplied, crewed by trained men, and commanded by skilled and experienced officers and admirals. In 1813 he was to use his precious corps of naval gunners as infantry, and many would be lost at Leipzig; this increased the problems of crewing his new ships.

Though he could order things to be built, he was unable to conjure experienced men from fresh air. Without the time and opportunity to train these crews at sea, the ships were worthless. As soon as they poked their new noses out of harbour, they would have been reduced to flotsam in short order by the Royal Navy.

This programme clearly shows that the Emperor had fully grasped the importance of naval power. It is less clear how he intended to find the months of free time at sea, training his new navy, or where he would find the skilful admirals to lead the new fleets to victory

It was in 1805 that Napoleon said: 'There is only one time in your life for war. I shall be good at it six years longer, after which I must pull myself up.'

3

～Economic Errors～

'*I*N AFFAIRS OF STATE one must never retreat, never retrace one's steps, never admit an error – that brings disrepute. When one makes a mistake, one must stick to it – that makes it right!'

According to Ségur, this statement was uttered by the Emperor in his presence in the Kremlin in October 1812, shortly before he was forced to abandon Moscow. It reveals a man so used to having his own way in all matters that he need only pretend that things are well, for them to be so. Such a philosophy will work for as long as the player adhering to it is holding all the aces. When this ceases to be the case, life very quickly becomes complicated. It is with this in mind that we must regard Napoleon's economic policies.

By 1799 the Directory was utterly incapable of managing the national economy. Financial policy was in disarray, rampant inflation caused increasing hardship to the less well off and bankruptcies increased. The condition of the poor was even worse than it had been prior to the Revolution. In 1794 the gold franc had been quoted at seventy-five paper francs; by the end of 1795 it was worth two thousand paper francs and by 1798 it was quoted at eighty thousand.

In August 1799 the Directory declared an enforced levy of one hundred million francs on the resources of the rich, which included all those who had risen through the revolutionary miasma to their new positions; they were enraged. In the face of growing public unease, the Directory dismissed all the Jacobin ministers, including Bernadotte, the Minister for War.

Napoleon would have been in complete agreement with President Bill Clinton of the United States when the latter famously said: 'It's the economy, stupid!' Finances were always at the forefront of the Emperor's mind, never more than when he contemplated his inevitable wars with Britain.

The old adage that economic wealth was needed in order to wage war was well understood, both in London and Paris. Britain turned all the considerable advantages which she possessed by virtue of her progress in industrialisation and her monopoly of trade in colonial produce to financing her repeated wars against Napoleon. The repeated collapses of her coalitions against France never discouraged her for a minute.

When considered with the advantages of hindsight, one must say that once Napoleon had embarked upon total economic war with Britain, he really had no alternative but to try to control all of Europe's possible entry points for colonial produce and cheap, mass-produced wares. This relentless struggle to stop the importation of goods that everybody in Europe wanted was unrealistic, indeed doomed to failure from the start. Napoleon had taken up arms against market forces. Like the communists of the Warsaw Pact, he would learn his limitations, even if it took a few years.

His draconian measures alienated more and more people and ruined more and more sections of the continent's commerce. He must surely have quickly recognised that if he forced Europe to abandon her traditional commerce, he would have to provide adequate, mutually lucrative alternatives to his vassal states; he had none.

'In affairs of state one must never retreat, never retrace one's steps, never admit an error . . .'

Many in Napoleon's closest circles must also have realised this, though none dared to tell him openly that he was wasting all his efforts. He rushed blindly and ever more quickly to wars on two fronts, dragging millions to destruction in his wake.

Although the trade war at sea had drastic effects on the seaports and their immediate hinterland, commercial activity deep inland seems to have continued more or less as before – except in the area of cloth production in non-French states. As we shall see in the example of the destruction of the traditional weaving trade in the Grand Duchy of Cleve-Berg in 1808, Napoleon's desire to deform established patterns of trade for his own advantage brought widespread commercial and social upheaval.

The chart of French exports (Appendix A, p. 218) shows the commercial importance of the Confederation of the Rhine to Napoleon. These states were the clear front-runners among the international customers of the French economy. There were two great centres for international trade and commerce in Germany at this time: Frankfurt am Main and Leipzig. In these two rich cities, merchants from all over the continent conducted their wheeling and dealing, which was little affected by the restrictions of the Continental System. In their real worlds, contraband British goods were bought and sold as before the beginning of the trade war.

French silks, perfumes, wines and spirits flowed to the east and British contraband flowed (mainly) from Russia into the French Empire, where it found eager buyers. When, in retaliation for Tsar Alexander's breaking of his Continental System, Napoleon refused to buy Russian timber and cordage for his fleet, the Russians simply sold the goods to German middlemen, who sold them on to the French for a handsome profit of their own.

But Napoleon's 'new economic miracle' solution to the trade war with Britain had great disadvantages, as may be seen in the misfortunes of the Grand Duchy of Cleve-Berg. Until 1806 Berg had been a Bavarian province; on 15 March of that year Napoleon – having raised Bavaria to a kingdom by sticking large pieces of Austria and Prussia to it – took Berg from her and added the province of Cleve to form the new Grand Duchy. This he presented to his brother-in-law, Joachim Murat.

Austria was forced to cede to Bavaria Burgau, Eichstädt, Argen, Lindau, Vorarlberg, Hohenems, Tetnang, the old imperial city of Augsburg, Königsegg-Rothenfels and the Tyrol. This last province would prove to be utterly indigestible and would be returned to Austria in 1814. Prussia contributed Anspach-Bayreuth to Bavaria.

The inhabitants of the new Grand Duchy of Cleve-Berg were politically impotent and apathetic, as were the vast majority of other Europeans; they reacted with little interest to this change of ownership of their land, but many had sympathy with the recent civil achievements of France in certain fields.

In due course, French-style political structures were introduced. From 1 August 1808, Joachim Murat was promoted to be the King of Naples and Napoleon assumed direct rule of Cleve-Berg. The old feudal rights and duties in the grand duchy were abolished by Imperial Decree on 12 December 1808; on 11 January 1809 the Code Civile and equality before the law were introduced.

On the economic front, the old Guild of Textile Craftsmen was abolished, along with all other such specialised trade organisations, by a ruling of 7 February 1810. This act was the logical extension of the abolition of the trade guilds in France, which had been enacted by the king in 1791. The abolition had been justified on the grounds that the guilds had become obstacles to economic progress, full of restrictive practices, forcing the prices of their products to unrealistic heights.

Another rule – unpopular in Cleve-Berg as it was in France itself – was the introduction of conscription, under the terms of Article 38 of the treaty which had established the Confederation of the Rhine. This stipulated that the grand duchy must provide a military contingent of five thousand men.

The historic wealth of the grand duchy came mainly from the weaving and exportation of various cloths. The skills for this trade had come to the region in the seventeenth century with the Huguenots, who – as Protestants – had been mercilessly persecuted in their French homeland and had immigrated to more tolerant Germany. Even today, Krefeld, just north of Berg, is known as the Town of Velvet and Silk. The centre of Cleve-Berg's fabric production was the conurbation now known as Wuppertal on the river Wupper, which drove the mills, as satanic as any in Britain.

The major export market for the fabrics of the grand duchy was France, followed by Spain and America. But, as we know, Napoleon was determined to build up his domestic production of cottons and silks and to sell these products to his neighbours.

Krefeld was 'lucky' enough to have been absorbed into France in 1803, and her industry was to benefit directly from this in the following years. Cleve-Berg was foreign territory: hence her textile industry interested Napoleon only in that it represented unwelcome competition for his French produce in the markets of mainland Europe. It had to go. It was that simple.

The blow fell early. On 30 April 1806 he had decreed a ban on the importation to France of cottons, muslins, calicoes, chintzes and lamp wicks. Still permitted to be imported were items of haberdashery, ribbons and raw cotton, but these were now subject to a tariff of sixty francs per hundredweight. Similar items not made of cotton were tariffed at up to 275 francs per hundredweight. The merchants of Cleve-Berg appealed to Murat to save them from imminent ruin; he shrugged his shoulders. Murat was very conscious of whose interests he should serve. This, it was quickly noted, conflicted somewhat with the motto on the triumphal arch under which he had recently passed on entering his new realm: *Il rendra heureux son peuple* (He will make his people happy).

A deputation of Cleve-Berg's leading drapers journeyed to Paris with plenty of samples of their wares, to lay them before the Emperor. The aim was to demonstrate that their products were easily distinguished from those imported from Britain and that thus they should gain exemption from the tariffs and from the importation ban. Napoleon ignored them.

The next blow for the Cleve-Berg fabric industry came with the Turin Decree of 28 December 1807, which forbade the importation of its cottons into the Kingdom of Italy, while allowing French fabrics free access. Another deputation hurried to Paris on 28 January 1808, to be told that they would be unable to be received by Napoleon as he was busy 'making dukes'.

There was more to come. On 8 October 1810 the Tariff of Trianon was published. This decreed illegal the importation, possession or sale of colonial products from Britain, except by licence to be bought from France, and was retrospective. This gave an army of French customs officials the right to seek out such wares, even in private dwellings; the incentive to do a good job was provided by the promise of one-fifth of the value of the items that they confiscated. Informants were encouraged to betray anyone who had as little as four hundred grams of sugar or tea or even thirty grams of pepper.

So, the advantages of the legal and social reforms in the grand duchy were very soon perceived as vastly outweighed by the ruin of the domestic industry, the burdens of conscription and the draconian stamping-out of the enjoyments of sugars and spices, tea and coffee. That tobacco was grown along the Rhine was a last remaining comfort to some addicts.

Smuggling of the forbidden goods flourished, as did public hatred of Napoleon and his minions. On 27 January 1813, when news of the scope of Napoleon's defeat in Russia became general knowledge, there was a popular rebellion against French rule, which had to be put down with some bloodshed by the 3rd Battalion of the 146e French Infantry Regiment.

Napoleon was enraged. On 8 May 1813 he published the Edict of Nossen, by which 260 French customs officials were dispatched into the grand duchy to hunt down British colonial goods that everyone knew were there. Mass house-to-house searches under the protection of the French army ensued. The goods found were confiscated and sold in the then French city of Cologne. The two towns of Barmen and Elberfeld reckoned their losses at over two million francs.

With Napoleon's star now on the wane, the young men of the grand duchy were no longer willing to answer the call to present themselves for conscription as fresh cannon fodder for his ambitions. They fled into the countryside and hid. The situation became so grave that Napoleon ordered the parents of any absentee conscript to be arrested and held until he surrendered himself to the military. There were so many such unfortunate parents arrested that they had to be confined in the comedy theatre in Elberfeld.

Within seven years, Napoleon's futile economic master plans and ever-growing needs for military manpower had resulted in a state of social misery and economic ruin. The case of Cleve-Berg was a microcosm of what was going on all over those parts of Europe that he controlled. As the size of his realm was ruthlessly expanded, so more and more Europeans slipped from being Napoleon's passive subjects to his embittered opponents.

But it has to be a really ill wind that blows nobody any good, as James Stephen noted in his book *War in Disguise; or, the Frauds of the Neutral Flags*:

> The merchant flag of every belligerent, save England, disappeared
> from the sea. France and Holland absolutely ceased to trade under

their own flags. Spain for a while continued to transport her specie in her own ships, protected by her men-of-war. But this too, she soon gave up and by 1806 the dollars of Mexico and the ingots of Peru were brought to her shores in American bottoms.

It was under our [the American] flag that the gum trade was carried on with Senegal, that the sugar trade was carried on with Cuba, that coffee was exported from Caracas, the hides and indigo from South America.

From Vera Cruz, from Cartegena, from La Plata, from the French colonies in the Antilles, from Cayenne, from Dutch Guiana, from the isles of Mauritius and Reunion, from Batavia and Manila, great fleets of American merchantmen sailed to the United States, there to neutralise the voyage and then to go to Europe. They filled the warehouses at Cadiz and Antwerp to overflowing. They glutted the markets of Emden, Lisbon, Hamburg and Copenhagen with the produce of the West Indies and the fabrics of the east, and, bringing back the products of the looms and forges of Germany to the New World, drove out the manufacturers of Yorkshire, Manchester and Birmingham.

Many of these colonial goods (together with others carried in British ships) would then be smuggled into Napoleon's realms, directly undermining his Continental System. His motives for annexing more and more of Europe's mainland coastline can easily be understood; justification for such high-handed actions is a little harder to find.

So the United States of America saw an economic opportunity and grasped it; small wonder that relationships with Britain became strained as British exports met increasing competition there.

On 4 November 1810 Napoleon wrote:

> The colonial produce placed on the market in Leipzig fair was conveyed in seven hundred carts from Russia; which means that today the whole trade in colonial produce goes through Russia, and that the 1,200 merchantmen were masked by the Swedish, Portuguese, Spanish and American flags, and that, escorted by twenty English men-of-war, they have in part discharged their cargoes in Russia.

Frankfurt and Leipzig blossomed throughout the Napoleonic wars until 1813, when the desperate campaign in Saxony wrecked the economy of that state for some years.

Even during the early stages of the Napoleonic wars, the British government took action – often controversial among their own commercial community – against French trade. This was done through the use of Orders in Council, which offered a shortcut through the democratic process.

An Order in Council was an order issued by the sovereign on the advice of his Privy Council, or of a few selected members of that council and by virtue of the royal prerogative. This differed from statute law, since an Order in Council did not require the approval of both Houses of Parliament. They would seem to have been independent of parliamentary authority, but in practice they were

CHARLES JAMES FOX

only issued on the advice of ministers of the Crown, who were, of course, responsible to Parliament for their actions in all such cases. Such orders did, however, avoid much parliamentary debate, and were thus used to speed controversial legislation through both Houses and avoid a possibly embarrassing defeat for the government of the day.

At the outbreak of war between Britain and France, both nations demanded that neutrals should not trade with each other's enemies, and that if their vessels were freely to submit to their enemy's restrictions, this would violate their neutral status. Despite these restrictions, by the end of the wars of the French Revolution the United States – as we have seen – had already grown to be the world's largest neutral carrier, genuinely profiting from the disputes of the warring parties.

In 25 April 1795, American grain shipments to France had been seized by the Royal Navy under an Order in Council which remained unpublished until the twentieth century, when it was discovered buried in the files of the Foreign Office. With the Order in Council of May 1806, all continental ports from Brest to the river Elbe were placed under blockade by the Royal Navy. This order, known as Fox's Blockade after the foreign minister of the day, sealed off the great Hanseatic ports of Bremen and Hamburg. Napoleon responded with his Berlin Decree (see Appendix B, p. 220), which was a much more rigorous policy than France had previously employed. The British retaliated with new Orders in Council in November 1807 banning neutrals from trading with France and her allies. Spencer Perceval, later to become prime minister, summed up the aim of these new Orders in Council: 'Either the neutral countries will have no trade, or they must be content to accept it through us.'

This action was not universally popular in Britain; the parliamentary opposition was against the actions of the government. As the historian Walter Fitzpatrick wrote:

> Canning and his colleagues seem to have believed that their Orders in Council would give British merchants a monopoly of commerce on the high seas. The leaders of the Opposition, especially Lords Grenville and Auckland, who had learned political economy from Adam Smith, denounced them as founded on an immoral principle, and furthering the policy of Napoleon, with disastrous consequences for Great Britain.

Napoleon's Continental System, the response to Britain's Orders in Council, began – as mentioned above – with the promulgation of the Berlin Decree of 21 November 1806 and the first Milan Decree of 17 December 1807(see Appendix C, p. 223). Napoleon had declared *une croisade contre le sucre et le café, contre les percales et les mousselines* (a crusade against sugar and coffee, against percales – calico – and muslin). Interestingly enough, this was to give a great spur to the development of the European sugar beet industry.

To his brother Louis, King of Holland, Napoleon wrote that his aim was to *conquérir la mer par la puissance de la terre* (conquer the sea with land power). Britain was placed under blockade; all trade with Britain was to cease, British goods on the continent were subject to seizure and no ship – of any nation – could enter any French or allied port if it had previously visited a British port. The effects of this trade war on Holland were disastrous: 1,349 merchantmen entered Amsterdam in 1806; this dropped to 310 in 1809.

The *Moniteur* of 25 September 1806 gave another reason for the promulgation of Napoleon's Continental System: *La prohibition des marchandises de côtes étrangères que vient d'ordonner le Gouvernement ne contribuera pas peu à nous faire obtenir le résultat si désirable de fabriquer nous-mêmes la totalité des articles dont nous avons besoin* (the prohibition of goods from foreign shores ordered by the government will go a long way towards achieving the highly desirable aim of our producing ourselves all items which we need).

The British Orders in Council of November 1807 dismayed not only the neutrals, but even the merchants and manufacturers of London and Liverpool, who petitioned Parliament for their repeal in March 1808. The petitioners complained that the Orders were 'productive of . . . fatal consequences to the interest not only of the petitioners, but of the commerce and manufactures of the empire at large; and . . . likely to interrupt our peace with the United States of America, our intercourse with which, at all times valuable, is infinitely more so since we are excluded from the continent of Europe.' In Parliament, Lord Erskine said in March 1808:

> Up to the very date of your Orders in Council . . . every advantage flowed into your lap. America . . . continued to smuggle your goods into France, for her own interest, and France contrived to buy them for hers. The people huzzaed their emperor in the Tuileries every day, but they broke his laws every night. This was our condition before 11 November: England had the trade of the whole world, whilst France had only an empty label stuck up on the p[issin]g posts of Paris.

Renewed resistance to these Orders arose again in the British economic recession of 1812, by which time a Luddite movement had broken out in northern England, the great centre of the cloth-manufacturing industry. Machines in the mills were smashed and the militia was called out to restore order.

But France was suffering too in this bitter trade war. One of the last major pieces of French legislation in this trade war was the Fontainebleau Decree of 18 October 1810, which introduced new penalties for smuggling, including ten years' severe penal servitude and branding for the worst offenders. Contraband colonial goods and other smuggled items were to be burned in public, although there is evidence that many confiscated goods were recycled, to the profit of the customs officials. Special customs courts (*cours prévôtales des douanes*) were established in France and her satellites to enforce these new penalties.

As no law was promulgated in France without Napoleon's personal intervention, we have evidence here of just how badly he perceived the scourge of smuggling to be. But he was spectacularly unable to stop the flood into his own realm of goods that so many of his people wanted so badly. The international trade wars had hurt everyone; the main direct beneficiaries were the smugglers.

Contraband goods were freely available throughout Europe, including Paris itself, where members of Napoleon's court openly went on shopping expeditions for them. In Parliament on 3 March 1812, Henry Brougham laid out the case against the Orders in Council, attacking them as harmful to Britain and ineffective against France. In 1810 Napoleon had introduced a system of allowing French and other European merchants to buy permits to trade in British goods and to export continental produce to Britain. Overnight, Britain became one of France's best customers. As Brougham said:

> In the year 1810, a sum of between nine and ten million of the property of British merchants was transferred to the French treasury. Here was the secret of Buonaparté's relaxations of the Continental system.
>
> A sum exceeding by two or three million the whole amount of the Droits of Admiralty, accumulated in a period of eighteen years by the plunder taken from Spaniards, from French, from Danes, from our Dutch allies, from Toulon . . . etc. was, as it were, in a moment added to the funds of our enemy . . .

On 4 August 1810 Champagny, the Duke of Cadore, sent to the American ambassador to France, General John Armstrong, a note (largely written by Napoleon) declaring the revocation of Napoleon's Berlin and Milan Decrees if either Britain revoked its Orders in Council or the US Congress resumed its policy of non-intercourse with Britain. Issued on the same day as the Champagny Letter, an expanded system of licences and the Tariff of Trianon continued the economic warfare on another front. The tariff, which affected only twenty-one items, all colonial products prohibited under the Napoleonic Continental System

– cottons, sugar, coffee, spices, etc. – raised duties to an exorbitant rate. The duty on raw sugar rose from fifty-five francs per metric quintal (one hundred kilograms) in 1806 to three hundred francs under the Trianon regime. The duty on raw cotton from South America and the United States rose from sixty francs to eight hundred francs. The practical effect of the new tariff was to retain the blockade no matter what the apparent intent of Champagny's letter. The American author, Frank Edgar Melvin, observed that

> The Trianon tariff of 5 August was actually a public evidence that the old Continental System of rigid exclusion, of a commercial crusade against England, had failed, and while nominally it had not been abandoned, really it had given place to a new system of regulation, to navigation acts, and to a continental protective tariff system directed against English and colonial wares.

In the autumn of 1811 the United States government received Napoleon's Saint-Cloud Decree, backdated to the 28 April, formally repealing his Berlin and Milan Decrees. The Saint-Cloud Decree gave Britain a (welcome?) justification to revoke her Orders in Council, which she did on 23 June 1812.

The historian Peter Mathias wrote: 'During the Continental System in 1807–8, British exports to Europe were running at some £9 million p.a. When the ports of Europe opened again to trade in 1814, goods worth £28 million, much of it derived from re-exports of colonial goods, were sold.' The immense market existing for these British goods in Europe was clearly evident.

As Appendix A (p. 218) illustrates, Britain was also a major importer of French produce when permitted so to do. The volume of French goods smuggled into Britain in the years prior to 1810 may only be guessed at.

In conclusion, Napoleon may have been able to dictate his will militarily to the rest of mainland Europe for years, but neither in the military nor in the commercial sense did he exercise a leading or dominant role at sea, and his control of commerce was a sham. In every way, he was forced to dance to Britain's tune or publicly to accept humiliating defeat.

His reaction to the Britain's Orders in Council and their treatment of international maritime trade – to declare a tit-for-tat boycott on British trade – was forced upon him, even though he surely understood the real impotence of his position. To have done nothing would have been utterly unacceptable, as this would have laid bare his helplessness for all in France to see, resulting in irreparable damage to the reputation of his regime and the rapid end of his reign; but he was merely staving off the inevitable. By galvanising France and her satellites into applying, however ineffectively and unwillingly, the draconian measures of his Continental System, he was merely distracting their attention from his inability to deal with this threat.

Some in Britain, it is plain, knew in advance the full negative effects that the trade war would have on *all* nations involved in maritime commerce. It was a desperate measure brought in to deal with a desperate ill – Napoleon.

The trade war was just like the land war; it was a case of who could – and would – stand the hard pounding longest before buckling financially. In the event, Britain's creditworthiness with international financial institutions won the day. Napoleon was forced to back down first.

Another symptom of Napoleon's unaccustomed position of being forced to play catch-up with Britain during the trade war was the increasingly frantic string of mainland European invasions and annexations which he felt forced to undertake from 1807 onwards. The invasion of Portugal in November of that year was a direct consequence of Portugal's refusal to apply Napoleon's new Continental System of 21 November against Britain. He had moved with lightning speed, Junot's invasion force having been carefully put into position weeks beforehand. The seizure of Spain in mid-February 1808 – apart from placing his brother Joseph on a more prestigious, if less secure, throne – was aimed at removing another Bourbon family and at closing the entire coastline of the Iberian peninsula to British troops and British goods.

Much of the Italian coast was already under his control; following his defeat of Austria in 1809, the Treaty of Schönbrunn of 15 October of that year stripped his future father-in-law of all his possessions on the Croatian and Dalmatian coasts (among much else), thus theoretically sealing more hundreds of miles of the Adriatic coastline against Britain. The French also occupied Corfu and regularly raided other islands in the Adriatic to destroy smugglers' depots of contraband.

In July 1810 Napoleon annexed the Kingdom of Holland, exasperated by Louis's abject failure – or stubborn refusal – to reduce the flood of British contraband into mainland Europe. In December of that year he declared the annexation of the German North Sea coast from what had once been the Kingdom of Holland, across the base of the Danish peninsula and including the Grand Duchy of Oldenburg and the Hanseatic port-cities of Hamburg, Bremen and Lübeck. The motivation for this unilateral step was – again – his frantic need to try to stop the continued influx of British goods.

This process culminated in Napoleon's disastrous invasion of Russia in 1812, caused once more by the obsessive need to force the Tsar to reapply the boycott of the importation of British contraband. This Alexander was unwilling to do, as adherence to the Continental System had brought the economy of

Russia to the brink of collapse and he feared that if he allowed the internal situation to deteriorate any further, he might face another palace coup, such as that in which his father, Tsar Paul I, had died in March 1801.

Thus, Britain's economic warfare gradually forced Napoleon either to capitulate or to overextend himself again and again, finally with catastrophic consequences for the Emperor. In short, the trade war with Britain was one which was outside Napoleon's control and one which he was doomed to lose.

Napoleon's financial treatment of the Kingdom of Westphalia was blatant robbery. He burdened the artificial state with debts of thirty-four million francs, drew seven million francs p.a. from it for his own purse and confiscated estates worth a further five million francs p.a. from it to be distributed as awards to faithful members of his government and army. He also stationed 12,500 French troops in the kingdom, whose upkeep amounted to a further ten million francs p.a. On 14 January 1810 the Emperor gave the old Electorate of Hanover to

LOUIS BONAPARTE

Jerome. Among the attached strings were that a further six thousand cavalry would now be paid for by his pliant brother; this raised the cost of supporting the French military forces in the kingdom to twenty million francs p.a. He burdened Hanover with debts of 180 million francs. In addition to this, Marshal Davout, commanding a corps in Westphalia, ignored King Jerome utterly and requisitioned all that he wanted without reference to him.

On 13 December 1810, the northern part of Westphalia was annexed by Napoleon in another futile attempt to combat the smuggling of British goods. To survive, the unfortunate King Jerome (known to his subjects as the 'merry monarch') had to sell off most of the Crown estates. There was no public interest in investment in the kingdom at all and the burden of taxation on the inhabitants grew continuously. The ex-Prussian provinces of the kingdom were subject to extra heavy tax levies. Property owners enjoyed the special attention of Jerome's tax collectors, so much so that in 1810 there were over three hundred houses standing empty in Magdeburg; the owners had emigrated to avoid paying punitive taxation.

Westphalia was financially ruined. The national debt rose from forty-seven million francs in 1809 to 220 million francs in 1813; but Westphalia was squeezed dry to benefit Napoleon. It was the star fiscal performer of his empire.

The following letter shows Napoleon's complete grasp of the mechanics of the trade war and his determination to keep fighting, regardless of the concerns of the French commercial community:

TO COUNT FOUCHÉ, MINISTER OF POLICE, HOLDING THE PORTFOLIO OF THE MINISTER OF THE INTERIOR.[*]

Schönbrunn, 28 July 1809.

I have received a farrago, which you have sent me, on the subject of the corn trade, and which is perfectly ridiculous. I do not know why you begin there. I wonder you did not begin by teaching me the alphabet. It is merely political economists' chatter. Who is there in France who objects to the corn trade? Who opposes exportation? Not the law of the country. It is the English who prevent neutral nations from entering our ports and carrying off our vessels [sic]. These arguments are pitiful in themselves, but they have one great drawback – that of encouraging the commercial community to lecture the Government, to open discussions, and to disturb men's minds. The Administration has nothing to do with political economy. The principle of the corn trade is unvarying. Exportation

---

[*] *Correspondance* CXCVIII.

begins as soon as there are outlets. There is no exportation without foreign trade. This channel for trade is blocked by England. I have endeavoured to replace it by licences, and if these are used, the evil may be remedied.

As far as I am concerned, I request you will not send me such idle tales; I have no need of the twaddle, nor the advice, of M. Dupont de Nemours and a few merchants.

I have read the letter from the Chamber of Commerce. You did wrong to receive it, and I regret to see the direction you are giving to the internal government of the country.

We do not need any advice from the Chamber of Commerce, and if we did, it would not be M. de Nemours who should bestow it. Some conversations with certain well-informed merchants may be useful, but the deliberations of the Chambers are invariably valueless, and have certain serious drawbacks. The Chamber of Commerce must be very ignorant indeed if it is unaware first, that the Americans have not raised their embargo for France, and second, that I have never objected to the Americans entering my ports. It is the English who have objected to that. The embargo has been raised for Holland. The king thought it his duty to accept it. I have ceased to allow the introduction of Dutch merchandise into France, and I called upon him to revoke the step that he has taken, as I desire France and Holland shall act on the same principle. And certainly, if England is willing to allow American vessels to come to France, I shall be the first to approve her action.

The Chamber of Commerce knows nothing at all, and only chatters theories. I beg you will not expose me to the annoyance of receiving such memoirs. I see you have no experience whatever of internal government. We do not require any fresh legislation on matters of trade. France is suffering greatly, I know, not on account of legislation, but on account of the English blockade. This is because the Danish, Russian and Prussian flags, being those of England's enemy, cannot move about, and because the Americans have laid an embargo on their own ports, and after that have proceeded to publish an act of impeachment.

There is no outlet. I have endeavoured to supply it by patents or licences. Let me know the effect of these measures, and do not disturb the commercial mind by foolish and unseasonable discussions. There will be a world of chatter, and nothing worth saying will be said. They have not even the most elementary notion of the question.

The importance of the economic side of warfare to Napoleon is shown in this instruction to Fouché to print counterfeit Austrian banknotes with the aim of destroying confidence in the currency:

To Count Fouché, Minister of Police.[*]

Schönbrunn, 23 September 1809.

Maret is sending you what you ask for. I repeat that, whether in peace or in war, I attach the greatest importance to having one or two hundred million's worth of notes. This is a political operation. Once the House of Austria is shorn of its paper currency, it will not be able to make war against me. You can set up the workshops where you please – in the Castle of Vincennes, for instance, from which the troops would be withdrawn, and which no one would be allowed to enter. The stringent rule would be accounted for by the presence of state prisoners. Or you can put them in any other place you choose. But it is urgent and important that your closest attention should be given to this matter. If I had destroyed that paper money, I should not have had this war.

The Emperor's relaxation of certain aspects of his Continental System to aid the supply of American cotton for his factories is evidenced in this letter of 1810. It also reflects the shortage of domestic grain supplies and the fact that Russian articles for his fleet were in short supply, but were piling up in Poland. It is clear that Napoleon was very pleased with this raft of measures:

To the Count of Montalivet, Minister of the Interior.[†]

Rambouillet, 16 July 1810.

I have decided on the system of our trade with the Americans, and I conclude you will lay the thirty permits for the cotton trade before me, at the Council. If there should be any difficulty as to the necessary association with factories, you can dispense with that. You may content yourself with the promise, which may or may not be worth anything. But I see no objection to your proceeding further. When these thirty permits are exhausted, you will issue thirty more, so as to have some sixty or eighty persons licensed for the American trade. By this means, my factories will be fully supplied with cotton.

The corn trade in France is forbidden, as a measure of public

[*] *Correspondance* CCXXV

[†] *Correspondance* CCLXXII.

safety. As soon as I am satisfied about the harvest, I shall reopen my ports, and exportation will be allowed along the whole frontier. I conclude that at the present time, in those places where the export of corn is permitted, no ship is allowed to sail without a licence, and that, as my decree provides, no ship is allowed to sail as an adventurer. If I should be mistaken, you must revise the law, so as positively to forbid this, and prevent any ship from sailing for the merchant trade without being licensed.

I suppose you will submit the licences for Bordeaux, La Rochelle, and those ports from which exportation is allowed, for my signature, tomorrow – so that trade may not be checked; and I suppose you will also submit the licences for the Mediterranean ports, so that trade with the Levant and Africa may be carried on.

Having thus provided for the most pressing needs of the export trade of the Empire, we must attend to that of the allied countries. Submit the draft of a Decree which will set forth the arguments on both sides, and will grant licences for Hamburg and Bremen. According to these licences, the ships actually belonging to that country, and no others, will be sent away laden with corn: you will let me know whether these ports contain much wheat. They will be sent to the ports of Dunkirk, with Customs permits. These ships, properly numbered and registered, like those in the American trade, and each bearing on its licence a sentence in cipher (which the Consul will also mention in his letter to Paris) can go to England and anchor there, and unload their corn. But (1) the return cargo must be timber, or matters needful for my fleet, which must be landed at Dunkirk; (2) at Dunkirk a fresh cargo must be shipped of wine, silk stuffs and other French goods, which must be discharged at Hamburg; (3) the licence must be paid for at so much per ton, and I desire the charge shall be a heavy one, quite equal to the double duty imposed in France on exported wheat, so that I may draw considerable benefit from it. This course will bring me three advantages: (1) heavy navigating dues; (2) the exportation of French goods; (3) timber, tar and other supplies which my navy may require. I shall follow the same course for Danzig. This will rejoice the heart of Poland, which country is overflowing.

From the date of the issue of my edict, no vessel will sail from Hamburg, Bremen or Lübeck without a licence.

This Decree, of which you will bring me the rough draft, will be to this effect:

That the ships may put in at Dunkirk or Nantes.

That part of their cargo must be in timber.

That they are to carry a certain proportion of wines and goods, produced and manufactured in France, out of the country.

That there are to be French Customs-house officials at Hamburg, Bremen and Lübeck, who will send out the ships, with licences and permits, number them, notify their sailings to the Director-General of Customs, and take further precautions usual in the American trade.

As to Italy, I will grant licences for exporting corn from Venice and Ancona. This corn may go out of its waters and be taken to Malta and even to England. Apart from the corn trade, I will allow the exportation of cheese and other products grown in Italy. My Consuls will take the same precautions for these ships as for the others. Those which go to England must call and discharge cargo at Nantes on their way back. Those going to Malta must return by Genoa, Toulon or Marseilles. Permission will be given (either direct or by Venice and Ancona) for the exportation of cloth, silk fabrics and other raw and manufactured goods, both French and Italian. And I shall also authorise the issue of licences for the export of oil and cotton goods, on board Neapolitan boats. The origin of the cotton goods would have to be certified, and the vessels would have to load with French goods in my ports.

You will perceive that this huge system will help to feed my ports, will make this trade an exceptional one and will bring me in a considerable revenue. The plan is therefore advantageous, from every point of view. It replies to the English Naval tax by a continental one, it pays back injustice with injustice, and answers one arbitrary act with another. Thus it is no piece of folly which I here undertake.

Russia did not react to this decree by applying for licences; she had no need, for she was already trading busily with Britain and re-exporting colonial and manufactured goods to Prussia, Austria and thus to the rest of mainland Europe. As can be seen from Appendix A (see p. 218), French exports to Russia throughout the period were negligible.

The Tsar had financed the wars against France by issuing paper money; a certain degree of inflation followed, but it was not disastrous. It was certainly nothing compared to that which hit Germany after the First World War, or which ravaged Russia after the fall of Communism in the 1990s.

Following the annexation of Holland in July 1810, Napoleon at once tightened the screws on that unhappy country to wring maximum financial benefit from it. These following letters illustrate his methods and his ruthlessness.

To Prince Lebrun, Grand Treasurer of the Empire, the Emperor's Lieutenant-General in Holland.[*]

Saint-Cloud, 19 September 1810.

I have your letters of the 16th and that of the Director of Customs at Amsterdam. You might have sent my Decree into East Friesland without delaying six days. A courier would have conveyed it there in twenty-four hours. My Decree was founded on your letters, and on the claims of the Dutch. It seemed to me absurd that, after I had given them such immense advantages, they should request me to put off the dates of payment – that is to say, I should let them wait until their correspondents in England send them funds; for the goods they have in Holland are not their own, they only have them on commission, and on current account. Since receiving information on the subject from London, I am half sorry I did not confiscate them all.

The Ministry of Finance is giving orders to facilitate the payments. By payment we mean an undertaking to pay – then no blame can be attached, if the sums cannot be levied.

I am sorry the Dutch mind should be full of terror. Make them aware that I am not King Louis, and that I know how to insure obedience to my orders. There must be no listening to improper claims.

I do not know how a man of your experience can believe these people are terrified, because they cannot pay. Terror is only for those who have no means of paying. Well then, let such persons make a declaration that the goods do not belong to them.

To Prince Lebrun, Grand Treasurer of the Empire, the Emperor's Lieutenant-General in Holland.[†]

Paris, 25 September 1810.

You speak of the complaints of the people of Amsterdam; of their alarm and discontent. Do these Dutchmen take me for their Grand Pensionary Barnevelt? I do not understand such language. I will do what is best for the good of my Empire, and the clamour of the madmen who will insist on knowing what is right better than I do, only fills me with scorn. Really, one would fancy you had never known me! At all events, you must have swiftly

---

[*] *Correspondance* CCLXXXVII.

[†] *Correspondance* CCLXXXVIII. This letter was first printed in the *Correspondance*, No. 16497, but Napoleon had cut out all of the end. We now give it as it was originally drafted.

forgotten me! I have not undertaken the government of Holland to consult the populace of Amsterdam, and do as other people like. The French nation has been willing, at various times, to put its trust in me. Who knows it better than you? I hope the Dutch will be good enough to show me the same respect. If anyone speaks in a different tone before you, you must use language which befits my Lieutenant-General. 'The Emperor is doing that which is best for the good of the Empire, and whatever he plans, he sets his whole soul upon.' The silly talk you credit seems all the more pitiable to me, because I spend my time, here, among the most enlightened men in the country, and I consult no interests but theirs. Let this, then, be the last occasion on which such remarks are heard in your presence.

To Prince Lebrun, Grand Treasurer of the Empire, the Emperor's Lieutenant-General in Holland.[*]

Fontainebleau, 26 September 1810.
I have your letter of the 20th. The Minister Secretary of State sends you the decree I have issued. (You will see I am far from approving of your conduct.[†]) What is the object of showing any special interest in the family of a man killed in any insurrection of which he was a member? Was it right of you to cause one of my Customs officials, who had been wounded in the performance of his duty, to be arrested? (My Decree will inform you of my will.) The inhabitants of Amsterdam must know (that I am not afraid of them, that I am strong enough to break up any plots, and) that I am stronger than the smugglers. Your duty is to give the law active assistance, and not to let yourself be overawed by a few smugglers. Any other behaviour would mean ruin. You will not lead the populace by coaxing it. Call together the municipal authorities (and make them aware of my intentions). They themselves should point out the hidden stores; there are many remaining. You must start on the principle that I mean to know them all; that my Customs-house officers must be supported, and that if the Amsterdam magistrates desire to escape the discomforts consequent on a different line of conduct, they must cause domiciliary visits to be made, and must discover the whereabouts of the forbidden merchandise. Energy is what is wanted. No

---

[*] *Correspondance* CCLXXXIX.

[†] The passages in parentheses have been struck out of the draft.

people which begins by revolt can justify itself. My Customs officers have been ill-treated, stones have been cast at them; it would be a terrible thing for those men, and a disgrace for the Administration, if it forsook them. The burghers do wrong when they resist armed force. The reason given for running down Customs-house officials is quite inadmissible. You will soon see them casting stones at my Customs officers as a matter of honour, and honest principle! If the Superintendent of Customs employed a person of bad character, complaint might fairly be made, but that was no reason for rising in rebellion. The fault, therefore, lies entirely with the town. Make the magistrate aware of my views, and inform them, that if they desire to deserve my favour, and avoid the occupation of their town by thirty thousand of my soldiers, they had better obey me. I will have it thus – do you understand? And you will let them know it clearly.'

Napoleon found sufficient time in 1810 to concern himself with economic affairs that surely by this time should have been delegated to the minister concerned with commerce; it seems that almost everything, however trivial or routine, landed on the Emperor's desk, as is shown by these letters:

TO M. DE CHAMPAGNY, DUKE OF CADORE, MINISTER FOR FOREIGN AFFAIRS.[*]

Fontainebleau, 21 October 1810.
Herewith you will find a letter from General Rapp. Here is my decision, which you will communicate to the Prussian Minister. I demand that all these ships[†] shall be allowed to enter the Prussian ports and then confiscated; that agents of the two courts shall make an independent valuation of the cargoes; that the property shall be mine, but that the amount of the contributions due by Prussia shall be included in the sum confiscated.

On 31 December 1810 Tsar Alexander published a ukase taking Russia out of the Continental System. Economic war had just been openly declared on Napoleon: he could not but pick up the gauntlet.

He recalled Caulaincourt, his ambassador, from Russia and replaced his foreign minister, Champagny (who favoured a negotiated settlement with the Tsar) with a pliant clerk, Hugues-Bernard Maret, the director of his personal

---

[*] *Correspondance* CCCIV.

[†] Vessels laden with English merchandise.

cabinet office. Caulaincourt attempted to warn Napoleon that Russia could – and would – be prepared to fight a long, hard war. Napoleon would have none of it: 'One good battle will see the end of Alexander's resolution – and his sandcastles as well.'

On 25 August 1811, at a reception in honour of St Louise – his wife's patron saint – the Emperor took the Russian ambassador, Prince Kuriakin, to task in public and at great length, to convince him that Russia's only choice lay between reinstating the Continental System or a war of destruction. These were the same bully-boy methods that he had used on the Austrian Chancellor, Prince Metternich, at Saint-Cloud in 1808.

The year 1811 was not a good one for the Empire's economy. Banking houses in Amsterdam and Lübeck failed and thirty-nine investment firms collapsed in Paris itself. Commercial activity in Bordeaux, Lyons and Rouen was almost non-existent; cotton was in very short supply. The smuggling of British goods blossomed everywhere. For the last two years there had been poor grain harvests, but Napoleon forbade the bakers to increase the price of bread. The unemployed in the capital were organised into labour battalions and put to public works – the forerunner of Hitler's Organisation Todt.

The economies of his vassal states were actively managed in order to place France in the best possible economic position. As Napoleon said: 'My object is to export French manufactures, and to import foreign specie.'

The Continental Decrees increased the prices of all colonial produce such as chocolate, coffee, indigo, saffron, silk, spices, sugar and tobacco. The legal commerce of major ports on the Italian peninsula such as Genoa, Trieste and Venice withered and died. The smuggling of British contraband blossomed. Malta became an important depot for such items, as did several islands in the Adriatic. Among the more exotic items banned from the continent were mother of pearl and cashew nuts.

Napoleon biased the economic mechanisms of his mainland European empire in favour of France, at the expense of his vassal European 'colonies' in the same way that Britain (and other European colonial powers) did with their own colonies in the East and West Indies, North and South America.

The Kingdom of Italy was a major market for French exports; ranking fourth after the Confederation of the Rhine. Initially, the import duty on French manufactured goods entering the Kingdom of Italy was 5 per cent, as was the duty on raw Italian goods entering France. The tariffs between the states were 'renegotiated' in 1808; import duties on French goods were reduced to 2½ per cent. In 1810 new restrictions were placed on Italian industry and commerce; cotton cloth, gauze, linen, silk, velvet and wool cloth and all articles made from these fabrics, could only be imported from France.

Raw Italian silk was allowed into France duty-free, where it was processed. Most domestic Italian silk weaving was forbidden. In 1809 Italian silk exports were valued at 42.56 million francs and this rose to 47.12 million in 1811. The Italian silk industry survived largely by producing specialist gauzes and crêpes, for which only they possessed the manufacturing secrets. The export of such secrets and the machinery to produce the fabrics was forbidden, just as Britain forbade the export of industrial techniques and machinery. Some export of Italian cloth products was carried on to the Middle East, Russia and the Confederation of the Rhine.

Finished goods, made in France and imported into Italy, undersold locally produced items; this ruined Italian industry. Napoleon had learned from Britain's example, but his COMECON[*] existed only if protected from outside competition and this he could not ensure, as human greed made the illegal British items more attractive. The French European 'colonies' were allowed to levy duties against one another as well. In 1811, Bavaria placed a duty of 20 per cent on Italian-made cloth.

Italy turned to growing its own cotton where possible, to compensate for the British commodity which fell victim to the trade war. Wheat, rice, wool, hides, olive oil, citrus fruits and wine were all valuable Italian exports into the rest of Napoleon's empire, but Britain's control of the seas severely limited the volume of trade. Overall, Italian commerce continued to generate sufficient funds to allow the country to meet the demands of Napoleon for funds and armies, although the years of 1810 and 1811 were a time of recession, as the economy of France staggered.

In Naples, at the southern tip of the Italian peninsula, economic conditions were less favourable than in the Kingdom of Italy. Social conditions were more primitive and secret societies flourished, as did ignorance, malaria, superstition, corruption, brigandage and feudalism. King Joseph abolished, or at least started to abolish, feudalism in 1806, but the long process of dismantling all its ancient, ingrained structures took years. The strict control of coastal trade by the hostile Royal Navy forced a new canal- and road-building programme, which swallowed up scarce funds and labour.

Napoleon encouraged Naples to produce cotton, olive oil, tobacco, marble and sugar, but the arable land was limited and of poor quality. Smuggling of British contraband was a major branch of Neapolitan commerce, which benefited the criminals more than the state.

* Council for Economic Assistance; a communist economic system set up after the Second World War.

The British victory of Maida on the toe of Italy on 4 July 1806 threw the Kingdom of Naples into a panic for months, wrecking Joseph's economic policies and unleashing widespread lawlessness which took a long time to repress. Britain missed a great opportunity here to stir up even more trouble for her enemies.

The subversive activities of British commercial agents on the continent also caught the Emperor's eye:

TO MARSHAL DAVOUT, PRINCE OF ECKMÜHL, COMMANDER-IN-CHIEF OF THE ARMY IN GERMANY.*

Rambouillet, 17 May 1811.
I have your letter of 12 May. I am glad to see you are going to arrest a large number of English agents. Show no mercy. Keep these people in prison, and if there are any prominent agents among them, have them shot.

Write to M. de St-Marsan, that he is to demand the arrest of the Berlin and Königsberg merchants who are implicated in this correspondence. Write to Kassel to have the Brunswick merchants arrested, and take steps to have those belonging to Swedish Pomerania seized. We must strike terror into these smugglers.

I have given directions that the general in command of the Ems Oriental is to be warned to obey your orders, yet, in ordinary administrative matters, you had better leave him under the orders of the general of his division.

Napoleon's increasing estrangement from Bernadotte (now Crown Prince of Sweden) becomes visible in this letter of July 1811:

TO MARSHAL DAVOUT, PRINCE OF ECKMÜHL, COMMANDER-IN-CHIEF OF THE ARMY IN GERMANY.†

Saint-Cloud, 5 July 1811.
I have carefully read the minutes of the Sitting of the Council of 18 June, and I notice that to General Libert's enquiry as to whether colonial produce from Gothenburg is to be admitted, the Council replied in the negative, 'because Sweden does not belong to the Continental System'. This answer seems to me a strange one, and I therefore write to give you the clear bearings of these questions.

* *Correspondance* CCCXLV.

† *Correspondance* CCCXLV.

Colonial merchandise and produce, coming from Sweden, Prussia or any other place whatsoever, must be seized and confiscated, because it originally comes from England. Send orders to this effect and see they are adhered to. This should direct your action as to Danzig. I conclude my line of Customs-houses has been established on the land side, and that no colonial produce can get through. In consequence of a mistake, Saxony and Westphalia had allowed colonial merchandise from Prussia to enter their country, and had recognised the duty paid in Prussia. But Westphalia and Saxony have changed their procedure. Turn your special attention to this subject, which is of paramount importance. Every article of colonial produce must be stopped, unless it has paid duty to you.

You must quietly stop all communication with Gothenburg. For this purpose, all packets going and coming must be delayed twelve to fifteen days. The letters must be read, and everything for England must be suppressed.

Whenever you are in doubt, write to me, for that gives me an opportunity of explaining my views. Send spies to find out if there is any colonial produce in Holstein, and if the Danes propose to go on receiving it. Speak plainly to the Danish agents, and take measures to have all the produce confiscated.

I expect satisfaction for the insult offered my flag at Stralsund. I shall perhaps decide on giving you orders to occupy Pomerania. You will desire your agents, at the same time, to seize all the colonial merchandise to be found there.

The Emperor's furious attention – and venom – even reached down to the hapless wife and family of a Frenchman who was in British pay:

TO GENERAL SAVARY, DUKE OF ROVIGO. MINISTER OF POLICE.*

Compiègne, 12 September 1811.

Have the wife of Gallet, the pilot who is in English service, arrested, and have that sailor written to, that, unless he comes back to France, or proceeds to some neutral country, so that we may be sure that he is not serving the English, she and her children will be put in prison, into a dark cell, on bread and water. Extend this measure to the wives and children of all pilots in the English service. Submit a Decree on the subject to me, and have full enquiry made, as to the pilots on board enemy ships.

---

* *Correspondance* CCCLXXVIII.

During 1811 the French economy was in poor shape; the Minister of Finance pleaded with the Emperor to maintain peace so that it might recover. Napoleon's response was short and sharp: 'Not at all! It is true that our finances are disordered, but that is why we need war!'

'In affairs of state one must never retreat, never retrace one's steps, never admit an error . . .'

He was apparently pursuing – for him – a coherently thought-out policy; but was he secretly aware that he was losing the trade war and could do nothing at all about it?

And again, before the Chamber of Commerce:

> England has harmed herself far more by her blockade than she has harmed any other country; she has taught us how to dispense with her products. In a couple of years time, Europe will have adapted herself to the new ways of feeding her populations. Soon we shall have more than enough beet sugar and shall be able to do without cane sugar.
>
> . . . Every year I draw only nine hundred million in revenue from my own country; three hundred million I put away, and store in the cellars of the Tuileries. The Bank of France is full of silver; the Bank of England has none. Since the peace of Tilsit, I have received more than a thousand million francs in indemnities. Austria is bankrupt. England and Russia will soon follow suit. I alone have money!

Symptoms of megalomania? Denial of reality?

But there were many – even outside France – who were capable of reading between the lines of the Emperor's much-cherished economic lies, among them the Duke of Wellington. In October 1811 he wrote to Lord Liverpool, then Secretary of State for War:

> I have no doubt but that Napoleon is much distressed for money. Notwithstanding the swindling mode in which his armies are paid, the troops are generally ten and eleven, and some of them twelve months in arrears of pay . . . It is impossible that this fraudulent tyranny can last. If Great Britain continues stout, we must see the destruction of it.

And again, on 24 December 1811, to Lord William Bentinck, commanding British forces in Sicily:

I have long considered it probable, that even we should witness a general resistance throughout Europe to the fraudulent and disgusting tyranny of Buonaparte[*] created by the example of what has been done in Spain and Portugal; and that we should be actors and advisers in these scenes; and I have reflected frequently upon the measures which should be pursued to give a chance of success . . . I am quite certain that the finances of Great Britain are more than a match for Buonaparte, and that we shall have the means of aiding any country that may be disposed to resist his tyranny.

And so, in fact, it proved to be.

Another anecdote, in early 1812, offers another interesting glimpse of the real world of market forces and how they worked despite all the Imperial Decrees, outrage and the armies of customs officials. The Regiment Frankfurt, later to form part of the 34th Division, XI Corps, was in Hamburg in April 1812. Bernays gives us this example of the degree of smuggling that then existed:

Every day the regiment marched out of the city, to drill on the Heiligengeistfelde, which lay outside the customs zone. Before they returned to the city, Danish merchants [the drill ground lay in Danish territory] would fill the barrels of their muskets with coffee beans, cinnamon and the like. When this ruse was finally discovered, the soldiers resorted to hiding the goods in clay busts of the Emperor. The Continental System was so detested, that no one thought to report them.

---

* The Duke loved to refer to the Emperor by his discarded birth name instead of the adopted 'Bonaparte'.

4
1809: The Puppets Fall
⁓ Short of Expectations ⁓

*T*HE FOLLOWING LETTERS DO not cast any doubt on Napoleon's own military competence in 1809. They do, however, illustrate the military limitations of his brother, whom he had placed in command, and call into question his judgement in employing that same brother, in positions of senior command, in 1812 and even in 1815.

In 1809 the newly created puppet state of Westphalia was invaded by the dispossessed Duke Friedrich of Brunswick, aka the Black Duke, with Austrian support. Jerome was thrust into the position of commanding the X Corps of the Grande Armée to combat the enemy. He reluctantly left the luxury of his palace in Kassel, but took the field with a considerable diplomatic retinue and all the mobile comforts that he could load onto a large convoy of vehicles.

In 1809 Austria attacked France while the Emperor was embroiled in Spain. Not only were Spain, Portugal and the Danube valley scenes of desperate conflict, but a carefully planned rash of revolts and invasions of other French-dominated territories took place. Jerome's new kingdom of Westphalia was at once dragged into the mêlée. As ever, his brother was ready with good advice and the usual criticisms. Lacking extensive experience of command in the field (and apparently not having – or not heeding – advice from his generals), Jerome's performance in this campaign was 'poor', as his brother swiftly pointed out:

TO JEROME NAPOLEON, KING OF WESTPHALIA.*

Burghausen, 29 April 1809.
I have your letter of the 22nd; M. Otto sends me one dated the 23rd. I approve of you having kept the Berg regiment. I had sent it orders to come, but you can keep it if you need it. You can send for the

---

* *Correspondance* CLXXIV.

division which is at Hamburg, although it consists of Dutch troops. I am giving Kellermann orders to proceed to Mayence, where he may be in a position to give you such help as circumstances, and his means, will permit.

Your Kingdom has no police, no finances, and no organisation. It is not with foolish display that the foundations of monarchies are laid. What is happening to you now[*] I fully expected. I hope it will teach you a lesson. Give yourself ways and habits suited to those of the country you govern. Thus you will win over the inhabitants, by gaining their esteem, which is always governed by their opinion of your manner of life, and by simplicity of demeanour. However, I feel this is not the moment to preach to you. Make severe examples.

Despite all this excellent advice, young Jerome continued to blunder from catastrophe to another:

To Jerome Napoleon, King of Westphalia.[†]

Schönbrunn, 17 July 1809.

I have seen an Order of the Day of yours, which makes you a laughing stock in Germany, Austria and France. Have you not a single friend about you, to tell you a few truths? You are a King and brother to an Emperor – absurd qualifications in wartime. You should be a soldier, and once more a soldier, and then again a soldier! You should have neither Minister nor Diplomatic Body, nor display. You should bivouac with your advance-guard, be on horseback day and night, march with your advance-guard, so as to secure information. Otherwise you had better stop at home and make your seraglio.

You make war like a satrap. Did you learn that from me? Good God! – from me, who, with my army of two hundred thousand men, lead my own skirmishers, without allowing even Champagny to follow me, leaving him at Munich or Vienna?

What has happened? That everybody is dissatisfied with you! That Kienmayer,[‡] with his twelve thousand men, has made game of you and your absurd pretensions, has concealed his movements from you, and has fallen upon Junot! This would not have happened if you had been with your advance-guard, and had

---

* An abortive revolt in the Westphalian army.

† *Correspondance* CXC

‡ Feldmarschalleutnant Michael Freiherr von Kienmayer, Austrian general commanding a cavalry division.

directed the movements of your army from that position. Then you would have been aware of his movements, and you would have pursued him, either by going into Bohemia, or by following his rear. You have a great deal of pretension, a certain amount of wit, a few good qualities – all ruined by your conceit. You are extremely presumptuous, and you have no knowledge whatever. If the armistice had not been concluded at this juncture, Kienmayer would have attacked you, after having driven Junot out of the running.

Cease making yourself ridiculous; send the Diplomatic Body back to Kassel. Have no baggage and no retinue. Keep one table only – your own. Make war like a young soldier, who longs for fame and glory, and try to be worthy of the rank you have gained, and of the esteem of France and of Europe, whose eyes are upon you. And have sense, by God, to write and speak after a proper fashion!

The receipt of such a crushing torrent of personal criticism would reduce the most irrepressible clown to thoughts of suicide, but there was more to come – and soon.

TO JEROME NAPOLEON, KING OF WESTPHALIA[*]

Schönbrunn, 25 July 1809.
I have your letter of the 20th. The letter you have received from me since that of the 14th will have informed you of my position and intentions. I consider that you have thoroughly misconducted yourself during this campaign. It was no thanks to you that Junot was not well thrashed, and that Kienmayer did not advance against me with his twenty-five thousand men; seeing that, except for the Armistice of Znaim, I should have pursued Prince Charles to Prague.

You have ordered a warship; you have abandoned the sea and left your admiral without orders. You have put forward all sorts of suppositions, which have taken in neither myself, nor my minister; but one ship is a small matter, and I was willing to overlook that incident. I see you continue to carry on the same system: you think other people are deceived, but you take in nobody. During the whole of this campaign you have constantly been just where the enemy was not. You say the Duke of Abrantes's retreat on the Danube forced you to take up a position at Schleitz, and to cease acting on the offensive.

---

[*] *Correspondance* CXCIV.

The Duke of Abrantes's retreat was brought about by your absurd manoeuvres. If you had moved to your right, as I ordered you, to join the Duke of Abrantes, if, after having driven the enemy out of Bayreuth, you had marched on Dresden, this would not have happened. If, instead of remaining three or four days in the same place, instead of being slower and more irresolute than the Austrians themselves, you had marched with the alertness and eagerness befitting your age, the enemy would not have masked his movements, and concealed them from you. This, as to your first observation; and now, as to the second. You were at Schleitz when you received the news of my great victories, and you add that, from that time, you had no reason to fear the enemy would attack you. But you should have feared that it might attack Junot; you should have feared its falling on me; and are twenty-five thousand men, more or less, a matter of so small importance in a battle?

You should have feared the reoccupation of Dresden by that corps. Instead of all that, you break up your own, you content yourself with declaring that Kienmayer's corps is dissolved, and finally, you run away in shameful fashion, and bring disgrace on my arms, and on your young reputation.[*]

As regards the future, I do not desire to disgrace you by relieving you of your command; but nevertheless, I do not intend to risk the glory of my arms, for the sake of any foolish family considerations. One warship more or less was a trifling matter, but twenty thousand men more or less, well handled, may change the fate of Europe. If, therefore, you intend to continue as you have begun, surrounded by men who have never made war, such as d'Albignac, Reubell and Fürstenstein, without a single good adviser, following your own fancy, and not carrying out my orders, you may stop in your seraglio. Be assured that, as a soldier, I have no brother, and that you cannot hide the real motives of your conduct from me, under frivolous and absurd pretexts. I should be glad, so as to save you from the danger of such results, to see you make over the command of your troops to the Duke of Abrantes. You are a spoilt young fellow, although you are full of fine natural qualities. I very much fear it is hopeless to expect anything of you.

If you continue in command of your troops, you are to proceed at once to Dresden. I will send you a chief of staff possessed of common sense. Mass the Saxon and Dutch troops, those of the

---

[*] After this word the following sentence in the rough draft is struck out, by Napoleon's own hand: 'Your tactics do not deceive me; you are too young for that.'

Grand Duchy of Berg, and all those under your orders, at Dresden. Have the fortress rearmed and put in a thorough state of defence. The Saxons will reorganise there. Withdraw the 22e Regiment from the Oder fortresses; but have it replaced by the 1,200 French conscripts you have at Kassel. Let the Duke of Abrantes occupy Bayreuth. Let the Staff have news of you once every day. Do away with your court and your retinue, and make war as befits a man of my name, who thirsts for glory more than any other thing. If hostilities are reopened, Bohemia will be the seat of the war, and you will have to play an active part. If the war should not proceed, the presence of a considerable body of troops at Dresden and Bayreuth may facilitate negotiations.

As for the English, you are better placed for marching against them at Dresden, than anywhere else. Their landing cannot be prevented, but I find it difficult to believe that they will come and set themselves between Denmark and the Confederation. They have quite enough to do in Portugal. Besides, they must disembark, before we can know what we should do. The King of Holland's letter is meaningless, and I do not believe a word of it. I receive similar news from my coasts every day. Their having landed two hundred men rather leads me to suppose that they do not intend to land in force, for it would be a mistake to show they intended to disembark at any particular point. If I were to pay attention to such signs as these, my troops would always be marching and countermarching, and would have to proceed to every point on the ocean, the Mediterranean and the Adriatic. The man who could not read, and weigh the value of reports, and took every molehill for a mountain, would have very little common sense.

One cannot but admire the way in which Napoleon's great mind instantly pierced the clouds of obfuscation with which his incompetent brother attempted in 1809 to cloak his bungled conduct of the campaign.

On 29 July Duke Friedrich of Brunswick, eluding the forces which Jerome had sent after him, stormed the town of Halberstadt and scattered the demoralised garrison, the 5th Westphalian Infantry Regiment. On 1 August he then defeated General Reubell (Jerome's Chief of Staff) at Oelpe and escaped to the Weser estuary where his corps was taken off on British ships. As a punishment, Jean-Jacques Reubell was cashiered. In the September of 1809 he took ship to America with his wife, Betty, cousin to Elizabeth Patterson, Jerome's first wife.

~ The Spanish Ulcer Opens Up ~

Perhaps the second-worst military blunder Napoleon made – his decision to invade Russia being undoubtedly his worst – was the invasion and subsequent mishandling of events in Spain.

Charles-Maurice de Talleyrand, his foreign minister, was instrumental in his decision to become involved in a cakewalk of an invasion, which for the next six years turned out to be a horrendous, expensive and bloody quagmire for the Emperor. Total losses of the Grande Armée during the Peninsular war are assessed at about three hundred thousand men killed, wounded, captured, died of sickness and deserted. This massive loss approached that of his Russian adventure, and one must ask the question: did he have any viable alternative to invasion and attempted occupation?

Napoleon's motives for invading Spain and Portugal were threefold: to close Spain and Portugal to British goods, to replace another Bourbon monarch with a Bonaparte, and to extract men and money from the countries to finance his wars.

JOSEPH BONAPARTE

Without doubt, the exclusion of British goods from the continent – an economic motive – was his first priority; the Spanish and Portuguese would not do it themselves, so they would have to be coerced. With his invasion complete, a great section of Europe's coastline, containing many major ports, would be closed to the entry of British ships and goods.

By replacing the legitimate King of Spain with his brother Joseph, he knew that all his wishes would be compliantly – if inefficiently – put into action. Joseph was a reasonably safe pair of hands. But he completely underestimated the resistance that any such regime change would provoke, convinced that the primitive, ignorant Spaniards and Portuguese would accept his political, social, religious, and legal reforms as eagerly as had the French.

The legendary flow of gold from the New World back into Spain convinced him that the place was awash with the stuff; his knowledge of the true state of the country and its wealth was incomplete and coloured by what he wished to believe.

His expectations that he would be able to derive substantial financial income from the conquered country – as he had from all other subject and allied states – is evident in this letter of May 1808 to his brother in law, Joachim Murat:

TO PRINCE MURAT, GRAND DUKE OF BERG, LIEUTENANT-GENERAL OF THE KINGDOM IN SPAIN.[*]

Bayonne, 23 May 1808, 10 a.m.
It would appear, from a letter from Laforest to Champagny, that the Council of Castile has refused to have anything to do with the business, or to ask that the King of Naples[†] may be made king. This behaviour is neither good nor handsome; try and discover its motive.

In Spain's present position she needs money. What are the plate, diamonds, and other Crown valuables worth? They should certainly be worth forty million. There will be no difficulty in pawning them for that sum.

When the Minister of France arrives, I have no doubt I shall find resources in the country itself, but we must get on for another month without that. Meanwhile, money must be found, both for the necessities of the seaports, and to facilitate administration. Pawn the Crown diamonds; and – as the sum will be too consider-able to be procured in the country – borrow sixty million reals, and pawn diamonds and jewels to that amount. This is quite a natural procedure; they will be redeemed later. I am persuaded money can

---

[*] *Correspondance* CXIII.

[†] Joseph Bonaparte, Napoleon's brother.

be had in Spain, but, to get it, we must know how things are situated; I await the arrival of the Minister of Finance for that.

Postscript: I have no money. If I had, I should not hesitate to lend it, but the Bank of France, when authorised by me, will make no difficulty about lending twenty million francs or eighty million reals, receiving part of the crown diamonds in pledge for the amount.

The Crown has a great number of sheep, which might be turned into money. In present circumstances it will be quite correct that all stocks, interest in the Sinking Fund, or on charitable funds, should wait, and that everything should be given to the War and Naval departments.

Napoleon's apparent ignorance of the true state of the economy of Spain, and of the real – if xenophobic and conservative – sentiments of its populace, are shown by all his actions in the Spanish affair, even years after his initial involvement. His operations in the Iberian peninsula were to cost him over three hundred thousand casualties and more than a billion francs in cash injections to prop up his puppet regime in Spain. Without the money, the French military in the peninsula would have been thrown out in short order. Whichever way one views Napoleon's involvement in Spain and Portugal, it was a major disaster in terms of manpower, finance and prestige.

In 1809 continental Europe exploded in efforts – poorly co-ordinated it is true – to throw off Napoleon's yoke. After replacing the hapless Joseph on his throne and ordering the destruction of Sir John Moore's small, isolated British army in the hostile Galician mountains, the Emperor returned to Paris to concentrate his mind on the problem of the threatening Austrian aggression along the Danube valley. This letter to Champagny tells us – incredibly – how he was now deeply involved in details of court protocol. It also reveals how he trivialised the efforts of his enemies. Overconfidence oozes from the paper.

TO THE COUNT OF CHAMPAGNY, MINISTER FOR FOREIGN AFFAIRS.*

Valladolid, 7 January 1809.

I have received your letter, and that of Mons. de Caulaincourt. You can reply that the two Russian vessels at Toulon will be paid for, the crews paid, and all supplies given. There will be no difficulty of any sort about that. As regards the Grand Duchess, my intention is that Mons. de Caulaincourt should do what is agreeable to the Emperor. My Ambassador must not, and cannot yield precedence to the

---

* *Correspondance* CLV.

Hereditary Prince of Oldenburg;* but he must yield it, without any difficulty, to the husband of the Emperor of Russia's sister, whenever he is recognised as such.

Mons. de Cauliancourt may even notify, that if the Prince and Princess came to Paris, they would be treated the same as in St Petersburg, that is to say, they would be seated in the court circle, etc. Yet, to make things correct, the Emperor should give his brother-in-law the title of Imperial Highness. The Emperor of Austria did this for Prince Albert of Saxony, and I have done it for the Grand Duke of Berg. The whole thing becomes quite simple, once the Emperor gives notice, by a letter to his Master of Ceremonies, that he has bestowed this proof of his regard for his sister, and thenceforward his brother-in-law will be treated as an Imperial Highness, in whatever European court he may visit, without any difficulty being made.

In the matter regarding Sweden, Russia must be left to do as she pleases. Reply that I care very little what she takes from Sweden; that I am ready to make peace; that I am ready to carry on the war; that I approve anything Russia may do.

As for Austria, M. de Caulaincourt must take the correct tone. Be sure he says, 'I am not afraid of Austria, even during the war with Spain.' M. de Caulaincourt must press the Emperor to take measures to close matters at Vienna. He must make him understand, that I have 150,000 men in Italy, without counting my army in Naples; 150,000 men in Germany, without counting the forces of the Rhenish Confederation, four hundred thousand men, in fact, ready to march into Austria; that I am raising eighty thousand more, and all that without withdrawing a single battalion from my armies in Spain. M. de Caulaincourt should tell the Emperor, in confidence, that my Guard is retracing its steps; that it will soon be back in Paris, ready to move on Austria, if this state of things does not end.

Immediately, then, on receipt of this letter, you will send off a courier to St Petersburg. Add that the Duke of Dalmatia is at Lugo, that two thousand of the English rearguard have already been made prisoners, and that part of its artillery and wagons are already in our power.

---

* Grand Duke Peter Friedrich Ludwig of Oldenburg had aroused Napoleon's ire by not reacting strongly enough in the 1809 campaign against the corps of the dispossessed Duke Friedrich of Brunswick, which escaped to England through his territory. Napoleon stored this in the back of his mind and awaited his chance for revenge. The Grand Duke's son, George, married Tsar Alexander's sister Katharina Pavlovna in 1809, forging close links between the tiny grand duchy and Russia. In 1810 Napoleon, still unable to stamp out the rampant smuggling along the north German coast, annexed Oldenburg – among other territories – into France. The dispute over adequate compensation for the Grand Duke of Oldenburg, now a relative of Tsar Alexander, contributed to the war of 1812.

5

⁓ Napoleon, Centre of the Universe ⁓

⁓ In His Headquarters ⁓

*I*T IS TOLD THAT when he was about to leave for the 1796 campaign, Napoleon said to a journalist friend: 'Bear in mind, when writing the narratives of our victories, to speak of me – only of me – always of me, do you understand?'

In a similar vein, the Emperor's instruction to Berthier, his Chief of Staff in February 1806, was: 'Keep strictly to the orders that I give you; I alone know what I must do.' It illustrates just how totally he dominated the operational centre of his army and of his empire. His amazing mental capabilities permitted him to manage the complex mechanisms of both state and army, in great detail and for a long time. It was not until August 1813 that even his great powers began to decline. By that time, his staff and commanders had been so dragooned into being excluded from the planning process and merely obeying the orders that they received, that they had abandoned independent thought.

The rigidity of the day-to-day operations of imperial headquarters is of such importance that it bears closer examination.

Modesty was certainly never one of the Emperor's traits and he was honest enough to admit this:

> I was young when I attained command of armies. My first campaign astonished Europe; the ineptitude of the Directory could no longer support me in the position I had reached. I undertook a gigantic expedition to occupy people's minds and to increase my glory. My former friends disappeared owing to their inactivity or were dishonoured through reverses. When I saw France at the last extremity, I returned and found the path to the throne open in all directions. I mounted it as the last hope of the nation.

Hardly had I been seated than I saw that some had pretensions. Moreau, Bernadotte and Masséna could no longer pardon my successes. It was my duty not to fear but to subdue them, and my plan regarding them was quickly made.

They tried several times to overthrow me or to share with me. As division was less adventurous, twelve generals hatched a plot to divide France into twelve provinces. As my share they generously left me Paris and the suburbs! The agreement was signed at Ruel. Masséna was appointed to hand it to me. But he refused, saying that he would leave the Tuileries only to be shot by my guard. He knew me well. Pichegru and Moreau came to conspire in Paris. We know how their intrigues ended.

My position was not an ordinary one, consequently my conduct had to be in accordance.

Fear and the hope of fortune and favours could alone exist between them and me. I was lavish with both. I have made courtiers; I have never pretended to make friends.

The passage is spine-chillingly revealing as to the personality of this man.

On one occasion, early in the Egyptian adventure, Napoleon heard that several generals, including Murat, were fomenting discontent. He invited them

LOUIS-NICOLAS DAVOUT

to dinner and gave them the following address: 'I know that several generals are dissatisfied and preach revolt. Let them take care. The distance from a general or a drummer boy to me is the same under certain circumstances, and if one of these circumstances presents itself I shall shoot one like the other.'

He certainly knew his generals. After the battle of Auerstädt in October 1806 he showered Marshal Davout with honours. Empress Josephine remarked upon it; his response was: 'Davout is a man to whom I can distribute glory; he will never know how to bear it.'

Napoleon calculated his imperial behaviour for greatest effect. He subjected the selected object of his displeasure to vicious public tongue-lashings. This is known in some modern management doctrines as 'showing anger', and is recommended by experts in that field.

One morning in 1804, General Gouvion Saint-Cyr, then commanding in Naples, unexpectedly appeared at an imperial levee in the Tuileries.

'You doubtless have received the permission of the Minister of War?' asked Napoleon.

'No, sire,' replied Saint-Cyr, 'but there was nothing for me to do in Naples.'

'If, within two hours, you are not on the road back to Naples,' snapped the Emperor, 'you will be shot before noon on the plain of Grenelle!'

His tactics deliberately created a climate of fear, jealousy and servility among all his associates and subordinates.

The Operations of the Headquarters of the Grande Armée: the Flaws

In contrast to the Austrian, Prussian and Russian headquarters, with their defined staff duties and compartmentalised functions, designed to operate under any commander and any composition of officers manning the staff, French imperial headquarters was an organisation entirely devoted to executing the will of one gigantic personality, that of Napoleon. All members of the staff were inspired by and devoted to him: in its way, headquarters resembled an anthill of which Napoleon was the queen.

The losses of the Russian campaign did not have a significantly detrimental effect on the quality of the work of the imperial staff. The system had survived, as had many of the members of the departments.

There was not a document which left headquarters without bearing the office of the originator, running number, location, time and date of dispatch and the name of the courier. Similarly, every document that was received there bore the time and date of receipt and the name of the recipient. The diaries and correspondence registers were all conducted with similar care.

This headquarters was not merely Napoleon's executive tool, it was his spiritual home. He had once said, 'I am a soldier, because I received this special characteristic at birth,' and, 'To be a soldier is everything to me.' Similarly, as Odeleben recorded at the beginning of the 1813 campaign, Napoleon declared: 'I shall fight this war not as Emperor, but as General Bonaparte.'

Whatever his wish, his location – be it a palace or a peasant's hut – was always referred to as *le palais* (the palace), and his massive entourage inevitably included a mini-version of that imperial establishment. Imperial business stole much of the general's time and efforts.

During his time in the artillery school at Brienne, Napoleon had been a solitary figure, possessing – and seeking – no friends. As his astounding career developed, as he became more arrogant and cynical, remote and harsh, so he became more isolated from his surrounding staff. Even Alexandre Berthier, at his side as his Chief of Staff for eleven campaigns over eighteen years, never became personally close to him. Napoleon had become distant even from his veteran comrades in arms.

The corps of his army had to submit status reports (*états de situation*) on a daily basis; these reports contained all the management data which Napoleon needed. Despite this, he frequently sent generals (his aides-de-camp) out to visit formations in the field and give him first-hand accounts of certain aspects of the army – in short, to spy. For example, on 28 June 1813, while in Dresden during the armistice, he sent one of his adjutants, General Lebrun, to the corps of the Duke of Reggio (Oudinot's I Corps of the Young Guard) with the following instructions:[*]

> You will report on his personal state. Has he recovered?[†] Will he be able to take to the field? How are his divisional commanders and where are they? Who are his brigade commanders? You will give me a picture of his entire corps – but just approximately – do not review it. You will only review the cavalry. You will report to me on the status of his infantry, artillery, train, magazines and hospitals and also on his intelligence gathering in his corps area. In a word, you will report anything that could be of interest to me.
>
> You will go as far as Baruth, inspect the outposts there, see what is going on and gather intelligence about the road to Berlin. You will send all official reports to the Major General [Berthier] but you will report everything else directly to me.

---

[*] *Correspondance* 20190.

[†] Oudinot had been wounded on 29 November 1812 at the Beresina.

Any of Napoleon's corps commanders who received such a visit knew full well that the Emperor's critical spotlight was shining mercilessly down upon him.

Strange to say, his charisma was such that, even after having been thrown out of Russia in 1812 with the loss of some 90 per cent of his army, every review of new regiments, largely made up of young conscripts, that he held in 1813 to present eagles, culminated in rapturous choruses of Vive l'Empereur! The problem was that, as Napoleon was the only person permitted to develop strategic thoughts, his staff and his subordinate commanders would now only take action if ordered to do so by him.

Prior to the Revolution, the French army had a corps of staff officers just as in other armies and navies. This was disbanded as being elitist. However, it was Napoleon's responsibility alone that the general staff of the French army had not been re-established, not developed or improved in any way since 1792. To offer the excuse that he was too busy doing other things is to accuse him of failing to recognise the importance of such an organisation to the Grande Armée. He created his 'management organisation' just the way he wanted it. He could not have been ignorant of the staff training and organisations set up by his enemies; he simply chose to ignore them. He could cope without them. The lack of trained staff officers in imperial headquarters was compensated for by having civilian officials deal with the paperwork.

After his victory at Dresden on 26–7 August 1813 he wrote a *Note sur la situation générale de mes affaires*,[*] in which he stated: 'In my situation no plan is acceptable in which I am not personally at the centre. Any plan without me will lead to a war in which the superiority of the enemy in cavalry, in numbers and even in generals, will lead to a complete defeat.' He was absolutely correct. He had made himself the heart and soul of the army, of the Empire, of France. He so motivated Berthier that, despite severe attacks of gout and rheumatism in late September and early October of that year, the latter still stuck to his grinding job throughout. Napoleon had this effect on the entire army, although the loyalty of the German contingents was beginning to wane.

Armand-Augustin-Louis de Caulaincourt, Duke of Vicenza and Grand Master of Horse, left this pen-picture of his master and of the French nation:

> The Emperor pampered neither officer nor man. But he was no stickler for discipline and closed his eyes to certain matters. He did not like people to mention such matters to him, as long as they did not extend beyond eating and drinking. He admitted that his method of making war did not permit of strict discipline as we lived

---

[*] *Correspondance* 20492.

without magazine supplies. If he was generous in times of plenty, he kept the men on a short rein when things were in short supply. He did not let complaints be heard and quoted the Roman legions as his ideals. In the campaign in East Prussia these models were a constant theme during the winter. He wanted to convince us that one could do without everything. He tried to mould us into the form of these ideals from that heroic period, tried to raise our spirits with their great memories. The Frenchman fights well, even without such exhortation; he knows how to bear hardships, yes, even to die of hunger as long as fame marches alongside danger. But if the guns have fallen silent, if the withdrawal has been sounded, if one must depend on one's legs instead of one's courage, then these heroes are also just humans.

The Emperor had altered the character of the nation. The French had become serious. Their attitude was one of dignity. The great questions of the age engaged every mind. Narrow interests waned. The attitude was – one could say – patriotic; one would have blushed if another had said it. The men close to the Emperor took pride in the fact that they did not flatter him. Some of them went so far as to make a point of telling him the blunt truth even at the risk of incurring his displeasure. That was the character of the age.

It is certain that this opposition, if I look at my own case, sprang from a desire to keep what had been achieved and thus to serve the Emperor's fame. Who could then have foreseen all that which was going to happen? Which feeling, which personal interest could have allowed one to affect us all in the midst of this unanimous dedication? I may assure you that we were all motivated solely to do the best for the interests of France, by the thought of maintaining the famous miracles which the Emperor had achieved. It was only these interests that one was able to hold up in the face of a gigantic military fame, whose perils seemed to conceal a secret instinct. Doubtless, this obsession of the Emperor's with his ideas, this ambition, the love of which drove him to accept such monumental risks so far from France, had moved much more into the foreground of everyone's minds since events had made his success seem doubtful. So each condemned his own conduct, but the fact that England still refused to grant the peace that the Emperor stated was the aim of all his undertakings, justified this in the eyes of a nation which would allow itself to be overwhelmed for a long time yet by the delirium of power and by its imagination rather than by reason and experience . . .

The Emperor needed a lot of sleep; but he could sleep

whenever he wanted to, by day or by night . . . The Emperor got up every night at eleven o'clock, by midnight at the latest, because the first reports from the corps came in about then. He worked for about two or three hours, often longer, to compare the reports, to check the troop movements on the map and to give his orders. He dictated them to the Chief of the General Staff or to a clerk, and the Prince of Neuchâtel then took them to the clerks. Sometimes he would write them himself if they contained important points which he wished to bring to the attention of the corps commanders. Despite this, the official part of all correspondence went via the General Staff.

He concerned himself with the smallest details. He wanted to breathe the thrust of his genius into everything. He called me to him every day to give me the orders for the headquarters, the orderly officers, the officers of his staff, for the correspondence, the couriers, the post, etc.

The commander of the Guard, the intendant general, the surgeon general, the fine Larrey, they were all called to him at least once a day. Nothing escaped his attention, no triviality was too small for him. Everything which could contribute to success, to the benefit of the soldier, seemed to be worthy of his daily attention. One could not say that the Emperor ever rested on his laurels; a victory may have been however great – the moment he had achieved it he busied himself with all the contingencies that he

DOMINIQUE-JEAN LARREY

would have to have implemented in the case of a failure. He may have been so tired, or even in the midst of a hot pursuit after a most obvious success; the Emperor reconnoitred the terrain to identify positions which would be useful if he should suffer a reverse.

He possessed an amazing memory for places. The map of the countryside seemed to have been engraved onto his mind. Never has a man with such a magnificent memory been gifted with such creative genius. He could have conjured men, horses and guns out of the air. The numbers of his divisions, his regiments, his provision columns, his train battalions all fell into wonderful order in his head. His memory, in short, could master anything. He knew where everyone was, when they would move, when they would arrive. One could say that his memory threw the staffs of his commanders into embarrassment. But this organising spirit, that could co-ordinate everything to work towards one goal, that inspired and organised in order to bring it to the predestined point – could not change it. For him, the entire campaign had to culminate in victorious battles. He commanded his great chessboard so well that he would surely have won them. But this creative genius did not comprehend the concept of maintenance. Always improvising, he consumed, ruined and destroyed in a few days that which his genius had just created. If a campaign did not bring him the results of a whole year within thirty days, then his calculations were mostly ruined by the losses he had incurred; for everything went so fast, his commanders were so inexperienced, so careless and – most of all – so spoiled by the earlier successes, that everything dissolved into confusion.

The Emperor's genius had always worked such miracles, that everyone relied on him for success. Arriving at the right time on the battlefield seemed to be all that was required. For they were all sure that they would be able to relax afterwards and have the time to reorganise their troops, so they did not worry about things that they lost or left behind on the way, and anyway, the Emperor seldom required them to answer for such losses. The rapid victories in the Italian and German campaigns, the rich resources which these countries offered, had spoiled everyone, including the corps commanders. This familiarity with victory was paid for heavily in Russia and in the following campaigns. The glorious habit of always advancing had transformed us into beginners in the art of retreating. As the Emperor was used to having his troops at hand all the time and of resuming the offensive at any moment, he filled up the roads. He literally piled the columns up one upon another. In this manner, men and horses were destroyed.

In this hymn of praise, the points that strike one as truly singular about Napoleon are his amazing mental powers and memory, and his ability to command sleep and to ration it out to suit the needs of his command function. A rare instance of his being exhausted is in the latter stages of the battle of Leipzig, where he fell asleep on a chair near the tobacco mill. It is recorded that Bernadotte had developed similar sleep patterns by 1813, but how many modern army commanders would have the ability to discipline their bodily needs to such a degree?

In 1812 the organisation of Napoleon's military headquarters was redefined. It was divided into three sections:

1 *le petit quartier général* (Small Headquarters)
2 *le quartier général du major-général* (Berthier) (Headquarters of the Major General)
3 *le quartier général de l'intendant* (Daru) (Headquarters of the Quartermaster General)

This was a retinue of considerable size; on 21 December 1806 it consisted of eight hundred people, excluding the escorts from the Imperial Guard.

~ Le Petit Quartier Général ~

This organ was for Napoleon's personal use, although its name was hardly appropriate when one considers its size. The personnel of this office answered to the Emperor alone. In past campaigns it had included many senior generals – *généraux près de Sa Majesté* – who were at Napoleon's bidding for use as he saw fit, but the heavy losses of the Russian campaign had seen these all redeployed as corps commanders. The last one, Soult, had left to take over command of the crumbling Spanish front in July 1813. The resulting loss of their experience and efforts was keenly felt.

In this headquarters Napoleon planned his campaign and his battles; commander and chief of staff in one. It contained the following components.

~ The Emperor's Cabinet ~

This was always set up in the largest available room and contained Napoleon's archives and maps. Almost always present were four people: the Emperor's two secretaries, Colonel Bacler d'Albe, Director of the Topographic Bureau and Rustan, his Mameluke.

Bacler d'Albe had been at Napoleon's side in this capacity for several years; he was very industrious, possessed extensive geographical knowledge and was an accomplished artist and cartographer. He was absolutely dedicated to his master; when headquarters moved, he was the last one to be needed in the old location, the first one to be needed in the new location. The loss of his entire collection of maps in Russia was a great blow to Napoleon, and during the armistice in the summer of 1813, Bacler d'Albe worked tirelessly to recreate it and to collect maps of the likely future campaign. He was one of very few who could allow himself an unguarded word with the Emperor.

Napoleon disliked writing and scarcely ever did any himself; his signature was almost always a crude scrawl. He demanded that his thoughts and plans be recorded even if they were just preliminary draughts. He dictated at speed, paying no heed to the requirements of the secretaries; often dictating on different topics at the same time. The two secretaries were so overworked to keep up with Napoleon's dictation speed that they developed their own stenography. This in turn meant that they then had to work extra hours, after the dictation had stopped, translating these encryptions back into normal handwriting. Very often, Napoleon would dictate right up to the moment before changing the location of his headquarters, making this recovery process extremely difficult.

Yet, despite the almost random flow of thoughts which issued from his incredible mind, Napoleon always managed to formulate them so that they were logical, unmistakable, absolutely clear and admitted no misinterpretation.

The barons Fain and Mounier were also relatively close to Napoleon and had worked for him for over ten years. Like Bacler d'Albe, they had no characters of their own or personal lives, existing only to serve him.

In the centre of the Cabinet room would be a large table on which would be spread the best available map of the theatre of war; in 1813 it was the Petri. Needles with coloured heads would be stuck into the map to indicate the latest-known tactical situation of friend and foe. Day and night Napoleon spent many hours studying this map, calculating possible strategic ploys and dictating his thoughts to his secretaries. He carried on this planning function alone. He needed no councils of war and no advice on what to do – until the crisis of March 1814.

His so-called Chief of Staff – who was often in the next room – was almost never party to these deliberations; like the others, he received written orders as to what he should do. These instructions usually started, 'My cousin, give orders . . .', and ended with, *Sur ce je prie Dieu qu'Il vous ait en sa sainte garde . . .* (On that note, I pray God to bless you and keep you).

When on the road, Berthier always shared the Emperor's coach and took notes of the things he should do when they arrived at the next location. If

Napoleon wished that an order be sent off at once, he would halt the coach; Berthier and Caulaincourt would act as his secretaries at the roadside and a courier would clatter off into the distance.

Even on the fateful night of 18–19 October 1813, in the Hôtel de Prusse in Leipzig, he stuck to this system. The Cabinet had already left the city for Lindenau, so Berthier and Maret played the roles of secretaries. After having lost a three-day battle and having had only minimal rest, Napoleon's faculties were still so sharp that an eyewitness recorded: 'The Emperor thinks of everything and we cannot fail to admire his steady spirit and the clarity of his thoughts as, in the midst of the collapse of his rule in Germany, he gives orders to save what may be saved.'

The surviving Cabinet documents from the campaign of autumn 1813 show absolute command of the subject matter, logical decisions, and amazing powers of memory and decisiveness. The more Napoleon was put under pressure by the allies, the better he rose to the challenge, the more creative he became. For instance, on 13 October, at Düben, he issued the following instruction to Berthier:[*]

> As of today, the infantry of the army will form in battalions in two instead of in three lines, as His Majesty holds the fire and the bayonets of the third rank to be ineffective . . . This formation, as it will be adopted on the eve of a battle, will have the added advantage that, as it will be new to the enemy, they will assume the army they have before them to be one-third stronger than it really is.

One cannot resist the temptation to observe that – at last – Napoleon had learned something from Wellington.

There is no hint of pessimism to be found; much seems to have been written more to impress posterity than to address the needs of the moment. Indeed, the question must sometimes be asked: how credible did he believe his own dictated orders to be?

It is often said that Napoleon castrated his marshals and generals mentally; they did not have to think, only to do exactly as they were told. Against this it must be said that his writings present a mine of military information from which any interested commander could learn. They are still applicable today. How many of his commanders had access to these writings in their entirety – and had the time to study them – is another matter.

---

[*] *Correspondance* 20793.

Two factors militated against Napoleon training his immediate subordinates: first, none of them even approached his undoubted genius; second, he decided to devote no time to the matter.

To the first, one must ask why he surrounded himself with such mental midgets (think of Berthier's mediocre performance in the early stages of the 1809 campaign)? He could – and did – pick anyone he wished ('I would kiss a man's arse if I wanted him enough'). But what happened to those who may have been his cerebral equals? Kléber ended up abandoned in Egypt; Moreau was exiled in 1804. Flying too close to the imperial sun could be a dangerous hobby.

In answer to the charge of there being no time to groom his commanders, it might be objected that if Napoleon had wished it to be done, he would have found ways and means. His skill at recognising and maintaining priorities was peerless. This was just not on his list of urgencies.

As regards the domestic side of life, the Emperor required three to four rooms for his personal use, with two more in the same house for Berthier. Two of the duty aides-de-camp (ADCs) spent the night in one of Napoleon's rooms, Rustan always slept across the door of the room in which Napoleon slept.

If insufficient accommodation was available, he would make do with what there was. If no house could be found, which was very rarely the case in 1813, the Emperor's five blue-and-white-striped tents (carried on mules) would be

JEAN-BAPTISTE KLÉBER

pitched. One was for Napoleon, two for his immediate retinue, one for the Cabinet and one for Berthier. Whatever the situation, a regiment of the infantry of the Guard formed a protective square around the tents or surrounded the buildings involved.

The *états de situation* which flooded into Napoleon's headquarters from each corps on a daily basis gave detailed data on their locations, losses and rein-forcements of the last twenty-four hours, the number of sick, reports as to the state of their clothing, weapons, equipment and ammunition, rations, special events, scouts' reports and intelligence on enemy activity. Every five days a summary (*situation sommaire*), devised by Berthier, would be sent in and on the 1st and 15th of each month a *grand état de situation* would arrive.

These reports caused the corps much work and they complained bitterly about them, but to no avail: Napoleon wanted them, Napoleon got them. At least the corps sent them off as directed; as the autumn campaign proceeded, however, they were more frequently delayed or intercepted by enemy activity – the ubiquitous Streifkorps.

Incredible as it may seem, Napoleon claimed to Senator Roederer: 'I have my *états de situation* always in my head; my memory will not allow me to remember one Alexandrine [line of a poem], but I do not forget one syllable of my *états*. I will find them in my room tonight; I will not go to sleep without reading them.'

As we have seen, Napoleon was able to keep up his amazingly high rate of activity with remarkably little continuous sleep. When on campaign he would go to bed at about eight or nine o'clock, rise again at one in the morning, work until four and then have another nap. This rhythm of life was ideal for dealing with the last day's reports and *états*, and for preparing orders to be executed the next morning.

Napoleon paid scant regard to elegant horsemanship; he rode small Arabs and slumped in the saddle, paying little apparent heed as to where he was riding, as his horses were trained always to follow the two orderly officers who led the way. In 1813, however, he almost always rode in a six-team coach which was fitted out as a mobile office in which he could work day or night. Caulaincourt rode at the right side of the coach with Napoleon's personal map folded inside the chest of his tunic, ready to hand it to his master whenever the command *La carte!* rang out.

To the left side of the coach rode General Claude-Etienne Guyot, the commander of the imperial escort. Behind the vehicle rode the duty ADCs and orderly officers and two troopers of the Chasseurs à Cheval of the Guard with large leather satchels, the *chasseurs à portefeuille*. Also in the retinue were

Rustan, a page, the escort and the Emperor's horses. If the Emperor left the coach, four men of the escort at once dismounted, fixed bayonets and formed a tiny square around him, facing outwards. If he moved off to reconnoitre, a page with a telescope joined him and the square expanded and moved with him.

The Emperor's journeys were planned in great detail on the stagecoach principle, with teams of fresh horses – including seven spares – at predetermined points along the intended way. This allowed him to move at relatively high speed. At each staging point there were pages, ADCs, orderly officers and secretaries as well as detachments of the escort, ready to execute any imperial command. If his exact route was uncertain, such teams would be sent to all the possible staging points.

When travelling in the vicinity of a battle, there was a well-defined plan of movement designed to minimise losses due to enemy action. The imperial retinue would be divided into four groups, moving with an interval of about four hundred metres between them. Napoleon's group included the page, two of his duty ADCs, two of his duty orderly officers, two interpreters (for Russian and German), his duty groom and Rustan, Berthier, one of his senior officers and one of his ADCs, Caulaincourt, the duty marshal and General Guyot.

The next group was made up of the rest of Napoleon's ADCs and orderly officers, officials of his court and the other ADCs of the generals who were with the Emperor – except those of Berthier. The third group included Berthier's ADCs, selected officers of his staff and the artillery and engineer advisers. The last group held the other officers of the staff and any attached duty officers.

Although the numbers were limited, General Fezensac once described the Emperor's staff, when seen from a distance, as looking like a considerable army formation.

If Napoleon wanted to get close to an action or to an enemy formation, these groups would halt and he would proceed accompanied only by Berthier or Caulaincourt, a page and Rustan, in order not to attract the attention of the enemy.

Whenever possible, Napoleon reconnoitred in person and used every opportunity to improve his knowledge of the terrain. He studied military history and laid such value on it, that on 14 October 1813 he sent Marshal Marmont an account of the action fought by the Swedish king, Gustavus Adolfus, saying: 'It took place in the same position you now hold.'

Before fighting a battle, Napoleon would tell his corps commanders and staff where he would be during the action; he rarely left the designated spot, which was always close behind the front line and from where he would have a good overview of the fighting. He was utterly calm under fire. The Imperial

Guard would be formed close behind him.

By this time Napoleon was not gregarious; he had no friends, only underlings, minions and tools with which to achieve his ends. Meals were thus not social occasions as they were with Blücher and his staff; they were kept to the minimum of fuss. He breakfasted, simply and alone, within ten minutes. Everything had to be served very quickly. Berthier was his only guest for dinner, and this event usually took fifteen minutes. It consisted of soup, two courses and no dessert. He drank wine with water with the meal and black coffee afterwards. The latter was his favourite drink, but Saxony was so ravaged by the war that in the autumn campaign there were times when even the Emperor had to go without. It seems that even he sometimes felt the pinch of his own Continental System.

The officers and officials of the imperial staff dined at two long tables, one for the senior and one for the junior ranks. The fare was as simple as that which the Emperor enjoyed.

The Emperor had selected each of his own ADCs and orderly officers, on the basis of having seen them distinguish themselves in action. The orderly officers came from all the combat arms of the army, and in 1813 were mostly in the thirty-to-forty-year age bracket. They had to be totally devoted to the Emperor and totally effective in carrying out his commands. It was not difficult to find scores of eager candidates for these tasks.

～ The Aides-de-Camp ～

These were usually marshals or senior generals, heavyweights who could wield power in the name of the Emperor if needed. Of the sixteen ADCs with whom Napoleon had started the 1813 campaign, only eight remained by early September. The others had had to be detached to replace casualties among the corps and fortress commanders. Of the eight remaining only General Anne-Charles Lebrun, Duke of Piacenza, had been in this capacity for Napoleon in a previous campaign, but of the newcomers, General Count Antoine Drouot had already won the Emperor's confidence. Soult was one of the last; he was finally detached on 1 July to take command of the crumbling front in south-western France against Wellington.

The opportunity of obtaining a post as ADC or orderly officer in Napoleon's staff was much sought after; the interesting ambience, the opportunity to gain the Emperor's favour with a dashing exploit, the chance of honours, awards and decorations which were showered upon the favoured few were great attractions. In order to reduce the constant demands from influential relatives for such posts, Napoleon had ruled that only colonels might enter the ranks of the ADCs; they had to reach that rank through service in the line and the Guard.

There was no formal division of work for the imperial ADCs and orderly officers, no job descriptions; neither could there be. They were simply required to orbit idly near the imperial presence where, in a totally random manner, they would suddenly be picked to carry out the next task Napoleon wanted done at that moment. While there were no formal, theoretical qualifications required for entering Napoleon's staff, each successful incumbent had to have certain qualities: personal bravery, caution, diplomacy and the practical ability to get the job done, whatever it might be. Whilst most Austrian, Prussian and Russian staff officers spent their time slaving away in offices (duties carried out by civilian officials in the French imperial headquarters), the ADCs and orderly officers who were their superficial counterparts were galloping hither and thither making things work for their imperial master.

The development of staff officers in the French army was less than it had been in 1793. In that year, General Paul-Charles Thiebault (then a young infantry officer; commander, 40th Division in Hamburg in 1813) had been appointed *adjoint* to François-Xavier Donzelot, *adjudant-général chef de bataillon*; when he asked for the duty manual, Donzelot replied: 'Our theory is the practice.'

~ The Orderly Officers ~

In 1813 Napoleon was operating with two or three armies, which were at times widely separated. This placed a heavy strain on his communicators – his orderly officers.

Apart from Napoleon's favourite, Gourgaud, who was a major, all orderly officers were captains, and many came from the best families of France. They wore light blue, Chasseur, undress-style uniforms laced in silver. Their duties were often hard and dangerous, but they received high salaries and allowances, and their prospects of promotion (if they survived long enough) were excellent.

One of them, Captain Caraman, described what their duties consisted of. In the early hours of 6 October he received an order from Napoleon to ride from Dresden to Marshal Marmont in Taucha 'at once, at a gallop to Meissen'. There he was to carry out certain tasks, and to reconnoitre several points en route, but to be in Wurzen by ten o'clock. This meant that he had to cover the ninety kilometres involved, and do the work in Meissen, within seven to eight hours – a hard target to meet now; almost impossible then due to the state of the roads.

He was also to be back in imperial headquarters by eight o'clock on the morning of 7 October, having covered some two hundred kilometres in thirty hours. This meant an average speed of 7 km/hr if he kept moving all the time. We are not aware if he met this target, but the case illustrates why he needed thirteen horses – and they all had to be thoroughbreds, pumped full of oats. In Saxony in 1813 this was most unlikely to be the case.

One of Napoleon's demands of his 'mobile eyes and ears' was that when they reported what they had observed, he was to be convinced 'that I have seen it myself'.

On 24 August Napoleon was about to take the Army of Bohemia in flank through Pirna, when he received a report from Saint-Cyr which caused him concern for the safety of the Saxon capital city of Dresden. Fain* described what followed:

> At midday on 24 August in Bautzen Gourgaud was sent off with the following message [from Napoleon]: 'Tomorrow, on the way to Pirna, I will stop at Stolpen. You will ride as fast as your horse will carry you to Dresden and you will be there tonight. Find Durosnel, the Duke of Bassano, Marshal Saint-Cyr and the King of Naples. Soothe them down. Go also to the [Saxon] Minister, von Gersdorff . . . At dawn, you will find the commandant of the Genie [Engineers] and will inspect the city walls and the redoubts. After you have carefully done this, you will return to me as quickly as possible in Stolpen where you will report to me on the true state of things and of the intentions of Saint-Cyr and of the Duke of Bassano.

Gourgaud reached Stolpen on the evening of 25 August and reported that Dresden would fall on 26 August without Napoleon's presence. The Emperor at once abandoned his march on Pirna and made for Dresden. Gourgaud – on a fresh horse and with new tasks – galloped ahead of him. On 26 and 27 August, Napoleon defeated the allies in the battle of Dresden.

Each ADC had two or more orderly officers at his disposal, but Napoleon often poached these for his own purposes. Even so, there was frequently a shortage of these officer-couriers, so the staff officers of the various corps who brought in the daily *états* were held back, loaded up with orders and tasks and sent off to different destinations regardless of the repercussions for them or their parent corps.

As Napoleon demanded that all his corps maintain regular and frequent

---

* *Manuscript de 1813*, Vol. II, p. 256.

communications among themselves as well as with him, the number of orderly officers at corps level was very high. As the attrition of the campaign took its toll of them, they became precious assets, and Napoleon's wilful poaching was much resented. On one occasion, Murat wrote to the Emperor: 'I beg Your Majesty to send me my Adjutants [*sic*] back, I am now without officers.'

~ Intelligence-Gathering ~

This was a matter of imperial policy – not to be delegated to Berthier, his Chief of Staff – and it was managed by Hugues-Bernard Maret, the Duke of Bassano. It was he who ran the network of spies and collected the reports submitted by the corps; Berthier was not involved in this function, so vital for correct planning.

Intelligence-gathering was made extremely problematic in 1813 by the lack of French cavalry and the superiority of that of the allies. As we have seen, ADCs, couriers and commanders were all used to try to alleviate this shortage but they were hopelessly inadequate for the job. The introduction by the allies of the Trachenberg Plan discussed below (see p. 156) increased French confusion.

Responsibility for intelligence-gathering in Saxony was given by the Emperor to Chevalier Lelorgne d'Ideville, Imperial Interpreter and Chief of the Secret Police. At Dresden on 22 June 1813, during the armistice, Napoleon took the hapless Lelorgne severely to task because he received no reports at all of enemy troop movements. 'It seems that your department is not properly organised, for you achieve nothing. I have never been so badly served on campaign.'*

Another example of Napoleon's arbitrary use of his staff officers as remote observers is when he poached Colonel Louis-François Lejeune, one of Berthier's ADCs, on 15 February 1810 and sent him on the following mission: 'Set out for Spain. See everything in detail, men, *matériel*, and note everything. Return without loss of time, and act in such a way that when I speak to you I shall believe I have seen things for myself. Go and win your spurs.'

Raymond-Aimery de Fezensac had just reported to Marshal Ney on 11 October 1806 as his new ADC; he tells us of the sort of shop which Ney ran. His account borders on the farcical:

> I was on duty at Schleiz. Hardly had I arrived there than the marshal handed me a movement order to carry to General Colbert.† I wanted to ask him in which direction I should go. But he replied: 'No remarks, I don't like them.'
> We were never told of the position of the troops. No movement

---

* *Correspondance* 20174.

† General August-François Colbert de Chabanais commanded the cavalry brigade of Ney's VI Corps.

order or report was communicated to us. We had to find out as best we could, or rather guess.

In my particular case – ADC of a general who did not reflect for a moment whether my horse was in a condition to support such fatigue, or whether I understood my new duties – they entrusted me, at dead of night, when everything was of great importance, with an *ordre de mouvement*, and would not allow me to ask even where I was to go.

They did not enquire, when it was a question of going at full gallop, whether our horses were in a condition even to walk, whether we knew the country, or whether we possessed maps, which we were always without. The order had to be carried out and they did not trouble themselves about the means.

This method of attempting everything with the most feeble resources; this determination to regard nothing as impossible; this boundless confidence in success, which at first had been one of the causes of our superiority, ended by becoming fatal to us.

⁓ Le Quartier Général du Major-Général ⁓

This was Berthier's staff; it was for the most part a copy of Napoleon's own, with a duplicate of the operational map on a table as well. The major difference was in the nature of the work: while plans and decisions were made in the Emperor's, in Berthier's these were translated into executive orders and distributed. Berthier's Cabinet processed all operational orders and associated correspondence and all communications with the marshals. Apart from showing the current locations of the fighting formations, Berthier's map also indicated the activity on the lines of communication and the locations of the magazines.

Napoleon's verdicts on Berthier are contradictory. On St Helena, on one occasion the ex-Emperor called him a 'goose that I made into a sort of eagle'. At other times he admits that Berthier was a priceless treasure who could have been replaced by no one. He also remarked: 'Nature has evidently designed many for subordinate situations; among these is Berthier.'

To have functioned as Napoleon's 'Chief of Staff' – even though many would define him as merely his head clerk – Berthier needed to have a total understanding of his master's personality, his habits and his thought processes, his manner of speech and his method of giving orders. He also had to subordinate himself entirely to the Emperor.

Berthier possessed all these qualities. In addition to this, he was an ardent admirer of Napoleon and utterly dedicated to him. Like Napoleon, Berthier had a tremendous memory for detail; Napoleon called him his *état de situation ambulant* (walking status report).

Berthier never lusted for power or sought to usurp his master's command function; he could take minor decisions on topics which had no effect on operational matters, but that was the limit of his meagre powers, and he was happy with the situation. The Emperor dictated, Berthier copied and distributed – such was the rule.

Despite being sixty years of age in 1813, he was full of energy and healthier than the forty-four-year-old Napoleon. He was often in constant attendance upon the Emperor, and would then work right through the night to complete the necessary orders for the following day.

He was also an accomplished diplomat in his dealings with the marshals, a very prickly bunch to deal with. Berthier was much more humane as a manager than Napoleon and took personal interest in his staff. His adjutant of many years, General Louis-François Lejeune, confirmed that 'he was always in the same mood, simple, polite and modest; however severe his reprimands, he was never insulting or injurious'.

Lejeune only saw Berthier furious on two occasions; once when he found an officer from a marshal's staff sporting the same smart, red riding breeches that were the exclusive signature of his own staff, and on another occasion when an officer visiting imperial headquarters had the audacity to try to use one of his ADCs to hold his horse.

Berthier's Cabinet with his private staff was always co-located with that of the Emperor, and Napoleon often visited it to give instructions to him. Berthier's staff, however, would be located some distance from the Cabinet, which his ADCs were forbidden to enter.

In 1807 Berthier had thirteen ADCs; their duties were exactly the same as those of Napoleon's – they lounged about idly until required to gallop off to some corps or other. The brain-work (secretarial work) was done by the civilian officials in the Cabinet.

Berthier was a shining example to his subordinates; Napoleon often quoted him to his ADCs as the model that they should follow. As Grabowski wrote, one day Napoleon said to his assembled generals: 'I wish you gentlemen would be like him for just twenty-four hours!'

In contrast to his Prussian counterpart von Gneisenau, who preached that the Chief of Staff must be relieved of all detail work, Berthier wrote in his *Dispositions provisoires pour le service de l'état-major de l'armée des Alpes* of 1796: 'Everything in the staff must come from the Chief; he is the central pivot of every action. All correspondence goes through him.' This was Berthier's theory, but, as we have seen, the most vital functions of a modern Chief of Staff (intelligence and planning) were in fact carried out by Napoleon in person, with no reference to Berthier at all. History has proved that von Gneisenau was correct in principle; Berthier's belief that 'everything must come from the Chief' stemmed from his incredible capacity for work, which would destroy most normal human beings within a short time.

One secret of his being able to manage so much work lay in the personalities of his Cabinet staff, who were, in many respects, extensions of his own personality, just as Berthier was an extension of Napoleon's. This staff was made up of civilian officials and invalid officers. Personally selected by Berthier, they were among the best in their field in France and had been with him for many years. Their dedication and loyalty to Berthier mirrored his to the Emperor.

Berthier had three Assistant Chiefs of Staff (ACS). The duty of the 1st ACS (also confusingly entitled the Chief of the General Staff) was to oversee the processing of the work. He communicated with Berthier in writing. He also communicated with the Chiefs of Staff of the various corps. He organised the communications and rear of the army, the movements of convoys and troop reinforcements and evacuations.

The 2nd ACS was also entitled the Quartermaster of the Army. He was in charge of camps, marches and cantonments. He was responsible for allocating 'route cards' for all formations and even for the marshals if needed. For this task he had a staff of five; he communicated directly with the equivalent quartermasters in each corps.

The 3rd ACS was responsible for the topographical department; he had a staff of ten officers and geographical engineers. Each day he had to draw up a tactical plan of the locations of the corps and divisions of the army; he also had to direct reconnaissances, collect topographical data, survey positions and draw up maps on conquered areas. All this data was duplicated: one copy was required in Napoleon's Cabinet, the other in the topographical office of Berthier's General Staff.

Colonel Bonne was the new 3rd ACS in 1813, having replaced General Nicolas-Antoine Sanson who had been captured during the retreat from Moscow. Napoleon laid great value on having accurate, up-to-date maps. In 1813 he had cartographers attached to all advanced guards; they were to sketch the terrain, correct existing maps and collect statistical data. Their maps and reports were sent to Berthier's topographical office, where they were incorporated into new maps.

As we have seen, there was no corps of officers trained for staff duties in the Napoleonic army. Instead, each corps commander had his own retinue of proven friends and followers, frequently relatives, who assisted him in managing his commands. This led to a high degree of continuity in the commanders' working environments, but it also led to a multiplicity of management methods, and years of trial and error until a system was found which worked well in all circumstances. This was extremely wasteful, as each commander spent much time reinventing the same or similar wheels.

Soult, for instance, arrived at imperial headquarters in 1813 with his own 'staff', and took them with him when he left for Spain. When Ney left the Army of the Bober on 23 August, he took his retinue with him to the Army of Berlin. While this system preserved a team, it also meant that in such a transfer both the commander and the entire staff were strangers to the terrain, to the tactical

NICOLAS SOULT

situation and to their own troops when they arrived with any new command.

That Napoleon did not bother to create a staff corps is probably due to the fact that in all campaigns hitherto (Spain excepted) the armies were so concentrated that his gigantic personality and his imperial staff could influence all events within the theatre of war. Ney and Oudinot were each given command of armies during the campaign, but each was still left in command of their own corps. This placed increased loads on their own staffs, which were scaled to handle a corps and not an army.

Berthier insisted that nothing should disturb the quiet of his Cabinet. As we noted above, even his ADCs were forbidden entry. As soon as an order from Napoleon entered Berthier's Cabinet, he read it, issued a few rapid instructions and passed it on for action. It was read by all present, each underlining any parts for which they would be responsible. They would then get to work, the only sound being the scratching of the pens. The finished documents would be passed to Berthier, who compared them with Napoleon's original before signing them off. The orders would then be sent off at once by the orderly officers, several of whom were on duty outside the Cabinet day and night.

We have no exact idea of the size of Berthier's staff in 1813, but it was almost certainly larger than in earlier campaigns. In 1809, for example, it had consisted of ninety officers and twenty senior officials. But if the numbers had increased, the quality of the new, younger officers had suffered; without a staff college this is hardly surprising. Frequently without any knowledge of the theatre of war or of the German language, they often got lost or delayed for hours, or were captured by the Cossacks and Streifkorps which infested the French lines of communication.

Apart from Berthier's Cabinet there was the Office of the General Staff (*bureau de l'état-major général*); an essential figure in this organisation was Berthier's Chief of Staff, General Count Bailly de Monthion, who ran the internal business of the organisation. This office handled all matters which were not dealt with by the Cabinet.

They supplied Berthier's secretaries with the data they needed to collate the *états de situation* for the Emperor. Each of the *adjudants commandants*, in the rank of a colonel, was responsible for a particular topic, which might change according to the strategic situation. Most of these officers and their assistants (the *adjoints*) had been in the staff for years, and had no recent field experience – a most unusual exception to the otherwise very high turnover rate among French army officers. This was because Napoleon regarded his staff as being the one thing that must function efficiently. Once an officer had proved his worth on the staff, he stayed there as if serving a life sentence. There was scant recognition from the Emperor for long and efficient service – a glaring exception and a great contrast to his usual practice of pinching ear lobes and handing out honours and awards.

In August 1813, Berthier proposed one of his *adjudants commandants* for the award of the Legion of Honour. This officer had served for thirty-five years, the last seventeen as a colonel in the imperial staff, and had still not received the decoration that even the youngest orderly officer now wore.

~ Le Quartier Général de l'Intendant ~

The commander of this staff office, Count Daru, was an excellent and experienced administrator. He had served in this function with Napoleon on all his campaigns since 1800. He shared his master's view that the war must pay for itself and thus earned Napoleon's gratitude and the hatred of all the conquered countries. It is in this immensely clever, but totally unrealistic, concept that we can see the causes of Napoleon's failures in Spain, Russia and Saxony.

Daru reported directly to the Emperor and not through Berthier, although the latter sometimes passed Napoleon's instructions to him. His burden of responsibility in 1813 was far heavier than in the past; it included raising money, obtaining ration and forage supplies, and administering the army's hospitals.

On 17 June 1813 Napoleon gave Count Daru a massive, clearly defined and immensely detailed list of his logistical needs, with orders to expedite them. There was little hope – as events so clearly proved – that even 50 per cent of these needs would be met; both men knew this, but at least posterity would have yet another shining example of Napoleon's omniscient mind. He had given the order; Daru, like so many other of his underlings, had failed to deliver.

The failure of the ration and forage supplies in Saxony 1813 had similar causes to the failure of the system in Russia in 1812: the area of operations simply could not meet the demands made on it. In the case of Russia in 1812, Napoleon devoted immense time and energy to planning and implementing a vast logistical system to maintain his army. Unfortunately, the sheer size of the theatre of war and of the numbers to be supported – coupled with the appalling weather at the start of his advance – caused this system to collapse within a few weeks. In turn, Saxony was an empty ruin before the armistice was declared, and remained so for several years after the campaign.

The lessons of Napoleon's failures here and in Russia have not been ignored; no country in the world today would dream of sending off a military or civilian task force without ensuring its logistical resupply beforehand. The North African campaign in the Western Desert of the Second World War was quite obviously won by the most effective logistical supply system. It was no different in 1812 or 1813.

The military-hospital system was also hopelessly inadequate. At the end of the armistice there were ninety thousand sick and wounded requiring care; where a hundred doctors were needed, one was available.

The success of Napoleon's system of waging war rested on the theatre of war being small enough geographically to be capable of being managed by him alone, and the campaign had to be won within a few weeks. Wherever these criteria were not met – Spain, Russia, Saxony – he failed.

It is significant that whereas the general staffs in the allied armies were just emerging into maturity, feeling their way towards the optimum organisation and task-distribution, the French army was led by a commander with a well-rehearsed team of hand-picked experts, some of whom had been working together since 1796. However, this staff – like the army and the Empire – was a one-man band, and this one man had failed – or refused – to realise where the limits of his powers lay.

There are those who maintain that Napoleon's staff structure is the basis of the modern US and NATO staff organisations. Such staffs are organised into five departments:

G1 – personnel matters
G2 – intelligence
G3 – operational planning
G4 – logistics
G5 – co-operation with the civil powers (a new addition to the traditional structure)

All these departments report to the Chief of Staff, who in turn reports to the commander. The Chief of Staff is the pivot of the organisation and a close confidant of the commander. He is directly involved in operational planning.

This differs widely from Napoleon's staff, where Berthier was not involved at all in operational planning, intelligence or logistical matters, and where the Emperor himself would have decided on all personnel matters down to brigade-commander level. Another important difference is that much of the work carried out by modern staff officers (under the direction of the Chief of Staff) was done so in Napoleon's own imperial headquarters by civilian officials entirely divorced from Berthier's organisation.

Modern staff officers undergo specialist training for their tasks; the serving officers of Napoleon's staff received none; they were merely his gofers, at levels of seniority appropriate to the tasks he gave them. As Vachée said:

Napoleon centralised everything – a centralisation, however, which was quite excessive and by no means to be imitated, for it was that which, by suppressing all initiative, contributed to bring about the ruin of the system.

You will understand the reason why, in his command, Napoleon reduced to the role of blind instruments of execution all those men who, by the nature of their duties, ought to have been conscious collaborators in his work.

As Baron de Meneval wrote in his memoirs: 'Berthier, Talleyrand and many others did not give an order or write a dispatch which had not been dictated by Napoleon. He not only took the initiative in thought, but also attended personally to the details of every piece of business.'

Napoleon revelled in the peculiar system of command that he had fashioned: 'In war, men are nothing; it is one man who counts . . . When, at dead of night, a good idea flashes through my brain, the order is given in a quarter of an hour, and in half an hour it is being carried out by the outposts.' The staff in no way participated in the Emperor's intellectual work; it was never taken into his confidence; it had but to obey scrupulously.

Another facet of Napoleon's leadership style which clashes with modern staff practice is that the Emperor hardly ever explained his strategic intentions to his Chief of Staff or his corps commanders. They were merely told to be at a certain place at a certain time; they had no idea what any other corps was doing. He frequently supplemented Berthier's copies of his own orders to corps commanders with letters containing supplementary information which Berthier knew nothing about. The Emperor's so-called Chief of Staff was thus kept in the dark about what was going on; his function was merely that of a chief clerk.

In Vachée's opinion, Napoleon's staff was the weak point of his armies; his genius – and a large helping of good luck – papered over these cracks through 1809. The errors and omissions of this organisation came to the surface from 1812 to 1815, when the better staff methods of the allies proved their worth. Basically, Napoleon's combined imperial / military staff system was adequate for the relatively small wars in which he could oversee and command all his forces in the field at once; when armies became larger, it no longer sufficed.

Interestingly enough, Napoleon III employed his illustrious ancestor's staff organisation and methods in the Franco-Prussian War in 1870, with disastrous results; it was then abandoned.

6
~ Corruption ~

*P*OWER CORRUPTS: ABSOLUTE POWER corrupts absolutely. As First Consul, Napoleon received an allowance of five hundred thousand francs p.a. When he became Emperor, his civil-list allowance increased to twenty-five million francs a year; of this, he claimed to save twelve million. His banker in France was Baron de la Bouillerie; he dealt with another banker in Italy by the name of Torlonia. When he created the Kingdom of Westphalia, he took about half the crown lands of that state – and the incomes thereof – for his own use and to grant rewards to faithful servants of the state. It seems that the full extent of Napoleon's financial affairs will remain a mystery (see further, Appendix H, p. 229).

Corruption in the French state in 1799 – as in many others – was a major problem; it probably had its roots in the pre-Revolutionary French government. The activities of the Jacobins, the Committee of Public Safety and the Directors cannot have improved things. 'What is sauce for the goose . . .'

The habits of Bonaparte as French conqueror of northern Italy in 1796 were on a grand scale, and were certainly not forgotten by his associated generals in their subsequent careers. They led directly, if slowly, to a build-up of anti-French feeling wherever that army trod.

It was in 1800 that Napoleon said: 'But everyone around me is stealing; the ministers are weak. Some people must be laying by vast sums. What is to be done about it? France is corrupt through and through, it has always been like that . . .' In 1806 he became aware that André Masséna, then in command of a corps in Naples, was looting on a grand scale. According to Marcellin de Marbot (admittedly a source to be used with caution), he located a sum of three million francs in a bank account in Leghorn, which had been deposited by Masséna, and confiscated it. The legal background to this affair is unclear, as is what happened to the money following confiscation. Masséna's reputation for being a looter and extorter on a grand scale continued to flourish. The fish, they say, rots from the head: the Emperor condoned what was going on, as was later proved by his reaction to Bourrienne's plundering of Hamburg, which he similarly condoned, leaving Bourrienne with the proceeds.

During his brief presence in Spain in late 1808, Bonaparte confiscated twenty thousand bales of high quality merino wool in Burgos. This was private property, belonging to the owners of the local flocks. He then sold this booty in France for over fifteen million francs.[*] It is not clear where this money went. In committing such blatant theft on such a huge scale, Napoleon sent a clear message to his underlings: 'Fill your pockets, lads; it's all up for grabs!' His generals were quick on the uptake and stripped assets from wherever they could find them. The Church was a prime target, yielding much plate.

Junot (and all other members of his army) had led the way during his invasion of Portugal in 1808. It had been agreed in the Convention of Cintra that the baggage of the French army was to be searched prior to their embarkation on British ships for their return to France. This revealed 'astounding hoards of miscellaneous goods' in the boxes. Junot had used Article 21 of the Convention to send an officer back to France in advance of the main body. This worthy fellow (ADC Lagrave) took with him the most valuable set of books in the Royal Library of Lisbon, fourteen volumes of an illustrated manuscript Bible of the fifteenth century; this was later sold by Junot's widow to the French government for eighty-five thousand francs.

In Junot's other baggage were found £5,000 worth of indigo and a large collection of valuable specimens from the Lisbon Natural History Museum. He had also broken open the Deposito Publico – after having signed the Convention – and stolen £25,000 worth of coinage. This was plucked from his clutches only with great difficulty. General Delaborde had a large collection of sacred pictures looted from Lisbon's churches. Many officers were found to have items of church plate in their private baggage. In the military chest were found gold bars worth a million francs. The paymaster, Thonnellier, was well known as an extremely efficient and rapacious looter.

The French army entered Portugal penniless; when they embarked, they all had advances of pay for the next three months. War really was paying for war most effectively. As the British commissioners reported:

> The conduct of the French has been marked by the most shameful disregard of honour and probity, publicly evincing their intention of departing with their booty, and leaving acknowledged debts unpaid.

---

[*] Sir Charles Oman, *History of the Peninsular War*, Vol. I, p. 426.

Finally they only paid what they were obliged to disgorge. Unmindful of every tie of honour or justice, the French army has taken away a considerable sum in its military chest, still leaving its debts unpaid to a very large amount.

By his decree of 15 February 1810, Napoleon stripped from King Joseph's control all of Spain except the central provinces of Avila and Segovia (both part of Old Castile) and New Castile. The provinces concerned lay between Madrid and France. They were divided into six military governments, commanded by his generals as shown below.

Aragon   – Suchet
Biscay   – Thouvenot
Burgos   – Dorsenne
Catalonia   – Augereau, then Macdonald
Navarre   – Dufour, then Reille
Valladolid – Thiebault

The timing of this decree is interesting; on 18–19 November 1809, Joseph had crushed Spanish General Areizaga's army at the battle of Ocana and returned to his capital, Madrid, in triumphant mood. Now, two months later, his kingdom was ripped from his hands by his brother and his status had publicly been reduced almost to that of mayor of Madrid. Was the Emperor jealous of his success? Could he not tolerate potential competition?

Whatever the motivation, Napoleon's spiteful move, fragmenting civil and military control of the country, certainly made the likelihood of any French victory in the peninsula extremely remote.

These generals commanding provinces were to report directly to the Emperor and to ignore Joseph. They were permitted to keep most of the revenues they could squeeze from their commands for themselves. They quickly decided to squeeze their provinces until the pips squeaked for their own benefits. One of them, Kellermann, had a long history of looting, to which Napoleon usually turned a blind eye, saying: 'Whenever I hear the name of Kellermann, I think only of Marengo.'

That Napoleon was aware of what was going on is proven by these letters, concerning the activities of Kellermann, Barthélémy, Avril and General d'Agoult's nephew in Spain in 1810; these cases were just the tiniest tip of a huge iceberg:

To The Prince of Neuchâtel, Major General of the Army in Spain.[*]

Saint-Cloud, 16 September 1810.

Strong complaints of General Kellermann reach me from all quarters. Send an officer to make him aware of my displeasure at the vexatious acts committed in his government, and ask him for a categorical statement of all the contributions he has levied. Everything, even to the liberation of prisoners, is sold in that government, and this occurs in other places – even at Valladolid. You will inform him that I hold him responsible for abuses so hurtful to the well-being and interests of the army. You will let him know that I have asked for a report on the subject, that the officer you send has orders to bring back his reply, and that I expect he will report to you, that he has caused the persons guilty of such crimes to be arrested, and tried by court martial. You will tell him that if he does not punish these horrible abuses I shall believe he protects them (as public rumour asserts), and that there are more robberies committed in his government, than in any other in Spain.

Despite this indignant letter, Kellermann was retained in his post and continued to flourish, gaining further honours and accolades.

The sauce for this goose – looting – was also used by many other ganders and goslings in Spain, all keen to feather their own nests as rapidly and ruthlessly as possible:

To The Prince of Neuchâtel, Major General of the Army in Spain.[†]

Saint-Cloud, 16 September 1810.

Let General Drouet know that serious complaints are brought against General Barthélémy at Santander; that I intend he shall be dismissed, and replaced by another General, and that an enquiry shall be held as to the embezzlement committed. The same thing is to be done with regard to General Avril. Write him, also, that great complaints are made of General d'Agoult's nephew; that it is urgently necessary that severe examples should be made; that corruption is carried to such lengths, that the freedom of prisoners is sold; and that I desire he will be most energetic in his enquiries. Embezzlement is also going on in the province of Biscay. Desire him

---

[*] *Correspondance CCLXXXV.*

[†] *Correspondance CCLXXXVI.*

to seize the stores of Colonial merchandise, cotton goods, coffee, sugar etc, on the French frontier of Biscay and Navarre. All these goods are intended to be smuggled into France.

General Nicolas-Martin Barthélémy was in fact recalled to France and cashiered for embezzlement in September 1810. He was reinstated in 1811 and continued to serve until the end of 1815. In view of the continuance of widespread looting by almost all French generals in Spain right through 1813, these threats of action by Napoleon must be considered as being mere window dressing.

In March 1811, as Ney's column was retreating from Portugal, he apparently ordered the great historic monasteries of Alcobaca and Batalha to be wrecked in a show of spiteful vengeance. In 1812 Marshal Suchet squeezed two hundred million reals (£2.8 million) out of Valencia – over and above taxes – all on Napoleon's orders. He went to work with a will; the silver statues of the apostles in the cathedral were stolen, as was the ancient jewelled robe of Our Lady of Pity. Churches were forced to buy back their bells for sixty thousand dollars.

The other Spanish provinces, Galicia and those to the west, south and east of Joseph's rump state, were occupied by the French armies of the North, of Portugal, of the South and of Aragon. The commanders of these were under the theoretical command of Joseph in Madrid, but in fact ignored him and attempted to respond to the outdated orders that Napoleon sent directly to them from Paris, Vienna, Erfurth, Wilna, Smolensk, Moscow, or wherever else he happened to be.

Transmission of these orders was by courier. This worked well enough in central Europe, which enjoyed a relatively well-developed road network and lay prostrate under Napoleon's power. In the wild, desolate mountains of Spain, seething with hostile guerrillas, it was a very different situation. Many couriers were captured and killed; their dispatches were often handed over to the British, providing Wellington with an invaluable stream of reliable, up-to-date intelligence on the aims and state of his enemies. Transmission times for those dispatches which did get through could be as long as a month, and it was common for whole French or allied battalions to be detailed to escort such couriers on their perilous ways.

Napoleon of course knew of the operational conditions in Spain and of the difficulties of communication there. He chose to ignore the unpleasant fact that his armies – however large – were constantly engaged in random fire-fighting expeditions in desolate terrain, expeditions which sapped the energy and morale of men, animals and commanders alike, and which always resulted in more and more casualties. This was not all; no sooner was one area allegedly pacified than a new uprising broke out elsewhere. The weary troops had scarcely left the pacified area, than the fires broke out anew.

～ Distractions of the Flesh ～

Perhaps the most serious error that Napoleon committed in the domestic sphere, which slopped over into his conduct of military affairs, was his increasingly obsessive search for a legitimate male heir to succeed him and thus finally to give his dynasty the same kind of pedigree enjoyed by those of his rivals. To date, he had not sired a legitimate child.

In early 1809, having just taken Vienna, Napoleon wrote to one of his mistresses, Countess Maria Waleska in Poland, to come and join him. She arrived in the Austrian capital just after the armistice of Znaim and took residence in a villa in the suburb of Mödling. Almost every evening until the end of September of that year (according to Napoleon's valet, Constant) she arrived at the palace of Schönbrunn to spend the evening with the Emperor. At the end of September it was confirmed that she was pregnant; there was little doubt as to who was the father of the child.

Maria Waleska gave birth to a son, Alexander, in April 1810. This confirmed that Napoleon was not impotent, as Josephine had often implied.

EMPRESS JOSEPHINE

The decision to divorce his great love was swiftly taken. He returned to Paris on 26 October and on 31 November told Josephine of his decision; the legal deed of separation was dated and signed on 14 December in front of the entire imperial court and family. There was no corresponding religious document on the matter. Napoleon was a free man again.

As usual, his fertile brain had been searching through various European royal pedigrees for months already, looking for the most suitable new bride, or 'womb' as he termed her. Metternich, the Austrian chancellor, heard of the imperial intent and, keen to end the bloodshed between his empire and that of the Corsican, offered the hand of the Grand Duchess Marie-Louise, daughter of Kaiser Franz I of Austria. This suggestion was received and placed in the 'Pending' tray. Marie-Louise was the grand-niece of the hapless Marie-Antoinette, victim of another political match, who had lost her head as the wife of Louis XVI.

Following discussions on the topic with Fouché, Murat and others of his court circle, Napoleon chose the Grand Duchess Anna Pavlovna, sister to Tsar Alexander. This request was vetoed by the girl's mother, on the grounds that she was too young at fifteen for such a venture. The Austrian second-choice candidate had prevailed. Diplomatic feelers were stretched out, entwined, writhed and a marriage agreement was worked out. A proxy marriage took place in the Augustiner Church in Vienna on 11 March 1810, with Alexandre Berthier representing Napoleon.

Marie-Louise, a virgin of nineteen years (almost a Lolita figure), set off for Paris; at Compiègne (about eighty kilometres north-east of Paris) on 27 March, Napoleon, impatient to plant his seed, met the convoy of the new empress and rushed her up to bed to complete the act. Years later, on St Helena, Napoleon told Gourgaud 'She liked it so much that she asked me to do it again.' So keen was the Emperor to found his dynasty, and so inviting and so compliant was his new bride, that his top priority absorbed relatively large amounts of his time. The Spanish ulcer was left to fester.

This is not to imply that the Emperor ignored the world outside his bedroom door; from 1810 to early 1812 he concentrated his energies on improving domestic aspects of Parisian and French life. Road-building, grand construction projects, marsh clearance, canals, improved administration and laws, annexation after annexation; it was certainly a busy time. But had he not been intensely involved with his new wife, he may well have thrown himself into solving the Spanish problem.

The strategic military situation in 1810 was that all of Europe – except Britain and the Iberian peninsula – was either allied to France or, like Prussia, under her heel. Although there was a small British army in Portugal, Napoleon convinced himself that with over 230,000 French and allied troops in Spain, they were more than adequate to manage without him being there. Indeed, in the early part of the year, his armies racked up a comforting string of victories against the Spanish: Vic, Astorga, Margalef, Hostalrich, Lleida, Mequinenza, Ciudad Rodrigo, Villa Garcia, Almeida.

But then, as Marshal André Masséna's confident army rolled westwards into Portugal to 'throw the leopards into the sea', as Napoleon predicted, it was given a bloody nose by Wellington at Bussaco on 27 September.

Annoying? Yes, but Masséna turned Wellesley's formidable position within a few days and strode confidently on to put an end to this nuisance. On the morning of 11 October 1810, his advanced guard was brought up short by Wellington's secret weapon: the impregnable lines of Torres Vedras, which blocked the French advance and gave a safe haven to the Anglo-Portuguese army. The area before the lines had been cleared of all inhabitants, shelter, food and forage. Masséna's army was stuck in an inhospitable desert and winter was rolling in.

News of this was sent back to Napoleon; he at once countered the bad publicity of the defeat at Bussaco, which leaked into France in the foreign newspapers despite all his efforts, by issuing declarations of French victories and omnipotence in the peninsula. Masséna's army sat and starved in great discomfort before the lines until 8 March 1811, when they withdrew northwards, back into Spain.

The Spanish ulcer festered on undramatically, with victories and defeats for both sides, but Wellington's forces were slowly growing ever more strong, and the Spanish guerrillas were tying down more and more French troops in isolated garrisons and grinding patrols in force through the mountains and plains.

To finance this campaign of French oppression, money began to flow in large amounts from Napoleon's coffers into Spain – an unprecedented event, definitely not part of the imperial plan. Despite this increasing drain of men and money, Napoleon refused to go down into Spain and finish off the business that he had so lightly started. In the initial planning stages of the invasion of the country he had exhibited a tendency to minimise the attendant difficulties, and his unwillingness to become thoroughly involved in curing the Spanish ulcer after 1809, something he could easily have done, was a big factor in his eventual defeat. His unwillingness to appoint an effective overall supremo in the peninsula and his insistence on managing affairs there from afar, using outdated intelligence, rather than adopting his normal up-close and hands-on approach, are inexplicable.

On 3 December 1809 Napoleon, having just returned from Spain, had boasted to his Legislative Assembly: 'I have only to show myself beyond the Pyrenees . . . to force the English to take to the ocean, in order to avoid shame, defeat and death.' Did he perhaps really see, at an early stage, that Spain was a dangerous mega-blunder, in which he did not want to be involved? If it would be such a bagatelle, why did he not make the quick trip and do the job?

To add to the distractions of his new wife (she was twenty-two years younger than her husband, lusty and willing to please him), economic affairs in the struggle with Britain were not going well. This was due to Russia's refusal to adhere to the Continental System, and Napoleon determined – even before 1810 was out – that he would have to go to war with Alexander to force the issue to a satisfactory conclusion.

On 20 March 1811, Marie-Louise gave birth to Napoleon François Joseph Charles, the King of Rome. Napoleon was ecstatic; his dynasty seemed assured.

EMPRESS MARIE-LOUISE

7

~ 1812: Russia - The Great Blunder ~

I HAVE DECIDED ON A great expedition. I shall need horses and transport on a large scale. The men I shall get easily enough; but the difficulty is to prepare transport facilities.

I shall need an immense amount of transport because I shall be starting from the [river] Niemen [Russia's border with the Grand Duchy of Warsaw] and I intend to operate over large distances and in different directions . . . do not let the question of expense check you.

So stated the Emperor to Lacuée Cessac, head of the imperial ordnance department, in June 1811.

On March 7 1812, Napoleon received one of Marmont's ADCs, Colonel Jardet, who had been charged with explaining to the Emperor the many difficulties of the Army of Portugal. During the interview, Napoleon said: 'Marmont complains that he is short of many resources – food, money, means etc. Well, here I am, about to plunge with an immense army into the heart of a great country which produces absolutely nothing!' Then he fell silent for some minutes, before asking the nonplussed colonel: 'How will it all end?'

General Philippe-Paul, Count Ségur, accompanied Napoleon into Russia, recorded what he witnessed in imperial headquarters and later published his account. When some of Napoleon's quotations are assembled, they reveal a commander and an emperor in uncharacteristically vacillating frame of mind.

Ségur tells us of the contents of some of the Emperor's orders: 'For masses like these, if precautions be not taken, the grain of no country can suffice.'

In another: 'It will be requisite for all the provision wagons to be loaded with flour, bread, rice, pulse and brandy, besides what is necessary for the hospital service. There will be nothing for them to expect from the country and it will be necessary to have everything within ourselves.'

Again, all that he wrote was true.

At a dinner in Danzig, prior to crossing the Niemen, Berthier, Murat and Rapp were with him. The Emperor suddenly asked Rapp: 'How far is it from Danzig to Cadiz?'

'Too far, sire!' Rapp replied.

'I can see, gentlemen, that you no longer have any taste for fighting. The King of Naples would rather be back in his pretty kingdom; Berthier would like to be playing the sportsman in Grosbois; Rapp would fain be enjoying the sweets of Parisian life!' retorted the Emperor.

There was silence – Napoleon had put his finger on the spot; war weariness was infecting even his most senior commanders. He was a giant alone among mere mortals. Or a megalomaniac detached from reality?

At the end of July Napoleon's patience – ever in short supply – had all but evaporated in the absence of real success or of any response from the Tsar. He looked at Witebsk and was unimpressed. Ségur furnishes some revealing imperial quotations, all dated 28 July in that town:

> 'Do you think I have come all this way just to conquer these huts?'

> 'How many reasons have I for going to Moscow at once? How can I bear the boredom of seven months of winter in this place?'

> 'Am I to be reduced to defending myself – I who have always attacked? Such a role is unworthy of me . . . I am not used to playing it . . . It is not in keeping with my genius.'

But then, in answer to a request that they stay in Witebsk, Napoleon said: 'Of course I see that the Russians only want to lure me on. Nevertheless, I must extend my line as far as Smolensk, where I shall establish headquarters . . .'

Somewhat later he stated: 'How far must we pursue these Russians before they decide to give battle? . . . shouldn't all this make us decide to stop here on the border of old Russia?'

Also among the Witebsk quotations, Napoleon said: 'We must take possession of it [Smolensk] so that we may march on the two capitals simultaneously. In Moscow, we'll destroy everything; in St Petersburg we'll keep everything. Then I'll turn my arms against Prussia and make her pay the cost of the war.' Ségur also reports:

> In the presence of Berthier only . . . Napoleon asked his minister [Pierre-Antoine Daru, Minister for War] his opinion of this war; the

latter replied: 'It is certainly not a national matter. The importation of some English goods into Russia, even the creation of the Kingdom of Poland are not sufficient reasons for waging war with such a remote country. Neither your troops nor ourselves see the object or the necessity for such a conflict. Everything warns us to stop where we are.'

But then came another mood swing: 'Peace awaits me at the gates of Moscow . . .'

According to Ségur, Daru said to the Emperor before the battle of Smolensk: 'Your army has already diminished by one-third, either through desertion, famine or disease. If supplies are scarce in Witebsk, what will it be like further on?' This seemed to decide the matter. Shortly afterwards the Emperor said: 'Here I remain. Let us rally our forces. The campaign of 1812 is at an end.'

Ségur also reports comments made to him by Joachim Murat at Smolensk on 18 August, in which he related his attempts to make the Emperor see reason: 'I threw myself on my knees before my brother-in-law and implored him to stop. But he could see nothing but Moscow. Honour, glory, rest – everything was there for him. This Moscow was going to be our ruin!'

So the battle was fought and 'won', and the chase eastwards went on again. The Russians withdrew before the Grande Armée in a most professional manner, leaving behind nothing of value. Their version of events was radically different from that of the invaders, doubtless moulded by the needs of public relations as much as any bulletin. On hearing that Te Deums were being sung in St Petersburg to celebrate alleged Russian victories at Witebsk and Smolensk, Napoleon burst out indignantly: 'What! Te Deums? Then they dare to lie to God as they lie to men!' The Emperor was obviously annoyed that anyone else had dared to infringe his copyright.

After the Russians left, General Rapp asked the Emperor whether the army was to advance or retreat; the answer was: 'The wine is poured out; it must be drunk to the last drop. I am for Moscow . . . Too long have I played the Emperor; it is time I became the general once more.'

As the terrible logistical situation became ever clearer, Napoleon burst out one day: 'The staff is useless; not one of the officers does his duty properly, not the provost-general, nor the quartermaster.'

To quote Ségur, during October in Moscow, Napoleon, with astoundingly accurate foresight, said: 'Oh, I know that from a purely military point of view Moscow is worthless. But Moscow is not a military position, it is a political position. You think I am a general, while I am really an Emperor.' Those hearing this must have felt that his grasp of affairs was slipping.

But then, as if to justify his inaction, Napoleon uttered the famous statement we have quoted above (see p. 60): 'In affairs of state one must never retreat, never retrace one's steps, never admit an error – that brings disrepute. When one makes a mistake, one must stick to it – that makes it right!' Those hearing this now knew that their suspicions were confirmed. Thus over the long period of the Emperor's vacillation, which had extended for months, he had sleepwalked into a fearful trap.

The preparations for this fateful campaign were made with great care and attention to detail, taking over a year to bring to near-fruition; but they would never be fully completed and were totally inadequate for the envisaged task – the invasion and subjugation of Russia. Just as Napoleon had underestimated (or ignored) the geographical difficulties in Spain and the character of its inhabitants in 1808, so he committed exactly the same blunders in 1811 when planning to invade Russia.

This is all the more amazing when one considers that he had already fought one campaign in Poland in 1806–7 and must have known of the hopelessly inadequate infrastructure of the region and the primitive stage of development of its agriculture and roads. He did not lack for Polish officers and officials with knowledge of the intended theatre of operations; his ambassador to the Tsar, General Armand-Augustin-Louis de Caulaincourt, would have been able to give him up-to-date insights into the conditions between St Petersburg and Moscow and the scale of distances involved.

So, was he reliably informed of the true scale of the impending difficulties? If so, he appears to have ignored them, which seems to have been his usual modus operandi, whereby uncomfortable truths were ignored or swept aside.

His immense energies were now thrown into overdrive as he planned this monumental folly of an invasion; he spat out order after order to move men and materials into the desired constellation. One general received no fewer than six dispatches from him in one day.

The entire French Empire and her satellites were cranked into action for the invasion; Europe buzzed with activity from one end to the other. As Bernays tells us in his account of the fate of the Frankfurt contingent:

> Other convoys carried tools of all sorts and apart from furniture, namely ovens, also building materials, prefabricated sections of wooden houses with windows, collapsible windmills – in addition there were whole battalions of artisans, not only bakers, butchers, tailors, cobblers, but also masons, carpenters, gardeners . . . also numerous fire engines, as if one had foreseen the burning of Moscow.

Also trekking eastwards from France were 'disproportionately large numbers of beardless novices, the bad horses of the national French cavalry and the wagonloads of young lads clapped into irons for desertion'.

In December 1810 some eighty thousand young Frenchmen were called up for military service; one year later Napoleon withdrew all the cavalry and artillery of the Imperial Guard that were in Spain. In January 1812 he pulled out the two Young Guard divisions and all the units of the Grand Duchy of Warsaw. Thus twenty-seven thousand veteran soldiers were withdrawn from Spain; this still left an amazing 232,500 French and allied troops in the country, struggling to hold their own and getting nowhere.

In the spring of 1812 the Grande Armée began to form within the borders of the Grand Duchy of Warsaw. The government there were, of course, called upon by Napoleon to provide massive amounts of food and fodder, and the troops were billeted upon the townspeople.

Estimates of the march-in strength of this multinational army vary; Chambry gives a total of 610,000 men, 182,000 horses and 1,372 guns. David Chandler gives figures of more than six hundred thousand men and two hundred thousand horses and oxen, of which eighty thousand were the finest cavalry mounts.

For the supply of some of the troops marching eastwards that spring on what for most of them would be a one-way trip, great magazines had been established with supplies and equipment gathered from all over the Empire. Ségur tells us of the great magazines which were formed in major strategic cities such as Danzig, Königsberg and Thorn. Supplies from here were sent by boat up the Baltic coast, then into the Pregel river to Vehlau and Insterburg, then by land again to Labiau on the Niemen. From here the supplies were to be shipped eastwards along that river and the Vilia to Kowno and Vilna. Unfortunately, due to the drought of early 1812, the Vilia was no longer navigable. Another negative factor was that the type of wagons used by the French in 1812 were far heavier than the local carts, and this was to be a major factor in the disaster which was soon to come.

On the diplomatic front, Napoleon gave orders that the Ottoman Empire should be encouraged to step up the war with Russia on their common borders. Unfortunately for him, Alexander's diplomats were more effective and concluded the Peace of Bucharest on 28 May 1812 with Turkey, thus freeing up Admiral Paul Vasilievich Chichagov's twenty-five-thousand-strong Army of the Moldau, which was sent north to attack the French later in the year.

Prior to Napoleon leaving France, the young Marie-Louise was acclaimed regent. In this capacity she presided over sittings of the Senate. Of course, the

Emperor carefully stage-managed the entire system to ensure that she was never asked contentious questions or to decide on anything of real substance, but it was a considerable mark of his affection for and trust in her. He wrote to her almost daily from the field, frequently asking her to write to her father in Vienna to influence Austrian decisions in Napoleon's favour.

Napoleon's plan for 1812 was to leap across the Russian border and fall upon the two enemy armies before they could unite, and to defeat them in detail. It was the usual plan that had worked so well in 1805, 1806 and 1809; success against the bumbling Russians was a foregone conclusion. Peace would then be dictated, the Continental System reimposed and Britain strangled. Success depended upon the Russian armies obliging by staying put, divided and up against their western border.

There certainly was confusion and disunity in the Tsar's high command at this point; General of Infantry Prince Mikhail Barclay de Tolly, commanding the 1st Army of the West (one hundred thousand men), wanted to adopt a strategy of falling back before the superior invaders, buying time with space, until campaign attrition reduced the Grande Armée to a suitable size for a successful battle to be fought. The commander of the smaller 2nd Army of the West (thirty thousand men), General of Infantry Prince Piotr Ivanovich Bagration, an aggressive and very competent general, hated Barclay and wished to dispute every inch of Mother Russia's holy soil. The Tsar was showered with various plans from his many advisers, many of them foreigners, unpopular with the native Russia officers. Luckily for him, Barclay won the day. The rest is history.

The supplies in the magazines created by Napoleon's orders were available for the Imperial Guard and other guard troops only during the invasion. All other formations were told to collect rations and forage from the countryside.

The population of the Grand Duchy was about 3.6 million; the state had been sucked dry financially since its creation in 1807 and the harvest of 1811 had been far below average. The extra supplies demanded by Napoleon for his 'Golden Horde' were just not to be had. As a result, the unfortunate line troops, barred from the magazines, were faced with a stark choice: take what was needed by force – for the peasantry would not willingly surrender their few supplies, cows, sheep and poultry – or starve.

The resultant chaos was unspeakable. Farms, villages and towns were repeatedly looted, houses were torn down to provide building materials for bivouacs and fuel for the fires. Anything that would burn went into the fires. The foraging parties from the leading regiments in the immense column of invaders returned loaded to excess with everything that they could find; perishables that were not rapidly consumed rotted and were thrown away. The following regiments found nothing near the line of march and were forced to send foragers ever further away to find enough to survive. The inhabitants starved.

Apologists for Napoleon have accused only the foreigners of having looted; this was far from the truth. The German contingents were used to being supplied with rations and forage from magazines; they were now forced to steal to survive. And they were still in 'friendly' territory.

The cavalry were reduced to feeding their starving horses on green grain crops or even thatching straw; colic swept through the horse lines. And this was before the invasion had even begun.

Up until the crossing of the Niemen on 23 June, the weather in the region had been extremely hot and dry. Streams and wells had run dry, and there was a serious shortage of clean, safe drinking water for the men and horses of the Grande Armée. This rapidly became so severe that many men were reduced to drinking their own urine; many cases of suicide among the troops were reported and the proportion of stragglers grew to frightening levels.

A sudden change of weather took place on 29 June; a period of unseasonal cold coupled with violent rainstorms began, which lasted until 4 July. The roads of the area were not metalled; the soil was light and sandy. In hot weather the marching columns were permanently shrouded in clouds of dust. But as soon as it rained, these same 'roads' were quickly turned into knee-deep quagmires which stalled progress, trapped all vehicles up to their axles in mud and exhausted men and horses. The heavy wagons from western Europe just sank into this morass. Some ten thousand of Napoleon's precious horses died in this brief wet spell.

The logistical theory of the invasion was that the supplies in the wagons would be eaten, then the draught animals would be slaughtered and cooked on fires built from the vehicles. As it was, the horses died, the food rotted and the wagons remained mired, blocking the 'roads' of the advance.

But how did the Russians manage to evade Napoleon's great leap forward at the start of the campaign? The Grande Armée was divided into three groups and confronted the weaker Russian defence forces as shown below:

> The X Corps was at Tilsit to the north-east, with the task of guarding the northern flank of the main body. TOTAL: *28,100 men, 100 guns.*
>
> They were opposed by the Army of Finland of Lieutenant-General Count F. F. Steinheil.   TOTAL: *26,000 men, 78 guns.*

The Emperor commanded the main body, which was concen-

trated between Danzig and Thorn and consisted of the Imperial Guard, I, II and III Corps and the I and II Cavalry Corps.   TOTAL: *180,986 men, 528 guns.*
Prince Eugène commanded the IV and VI Corps and the III Cavalry Corps around Plock, to the south of Napoleon's main body.   TOTAL: *85,850 men, 150 guns.*

These two groups were opposed by Barclay's 1st Army of the West, between Grodno and Vilna, with Wittgenstein's independent corps to the north.

TOTAL: *104,290 men, 488 guns.*

King Jerome of Westphalia was to the south-east again around Warsaw and Lublin with the V, VII and VIII Corps and the IV Cavalry Corps.   TOTAL: *75,155 men, 232 guns.*
They were opposed by Bagration's 2nd Army of the West between Bialystock and Brest Litovsk.

TOTAL: *47,910 men, 180 guns.*

Far to the south, below the Pripet marshes, was Schwarzenberg with the Austrian corps at Lemberg.

TOTAL: *49,313 men, 130 guns.*
They were facing General of Cavalry A. P. Tormasov's 3rd Army of the West at Lutsk.   TOTAL: *44,850 men, 164 guns.*

Readers will have noticed that the third-largest of Napoleon's armies was commanded by his brother, Jerome, whose ineptitude as a military commander of a much smaller force had been so clearly recognised and condemned by the Emperor in 1809. Once again the question arises: why did the Emperor continue to tolerate the antics of his siblings, who distracted him so frequently and failed him so utterly?

Not only was Jerome given four corps to toy with, he was also given a key role to play in the crucial initial phase of the invasion; his aim was to catch and destroy Bagration's 2nd Army. For some reason, the position of Jerome's group, spread out from Warsaw in the north-west to the area of the river Bug 160 kilometres to the south-east, in order to facilitate foraging prior to advancing eastwards, was wrongly assessed by Napoleon in relation to the speed of the 'lunge' that they would have to make in order to catch and destroy Bagration's 2nd Army.

As the Westphalian General von Ochs's biographer, Leopold, Freiherr von Holzhausen, recorded in his work:

On 14 June the king received orders to cross the River Niemen at Grodno. As the right wing of the Grande Armée had previously been designated to operate against Wolhynia,* most of the troops were located in this direction and needed several marches in order to reach their new line of operations.

By 17–18 June the Westphalian Corps was concentrated around Pultusk[†] and set off by forced marches behind V (Polish) Corps via Ostrolenka,[‡] Sczyczyn and Augustowo towards Grodno.[§]

Napoleon and the main body of the army crossed the River Niemen at Kowno on 23–4 June and the advanced guard entered Wilna 28 June. Napoleon's aim was to prevent the unification of the 1st and 2nd Russian Armies . . . this gave the King of Westphalia the task of catching up with Bagration's 2nd Army and bringing him to battle while Davout, with forty thousand men, raced for Minsk, to turn Bagration's northern flank and cut him off from Barclay de Tolly's 1st Army.

Jerome tried to fulfil the Emperor's wishes by pushing on at full speed by more forced marches but, despite all the efforts of his men, his advanced guard reached Grodno only on 28 June. The Russians had broken the bridges; General Allix had them rapidly rebuilt and the VIII Corps entered Grodno that same day. There was a minor brush with some of Platov's Cossacks who lost about a hundred men.

King Jerome entered the town with his guard cavalry and a Polish division on 28 June; the Westphalian infantry[¶] came in on 2 July.

Napoleon made Jerome entirely responsible for Bagration's escape, forgetting that on 14 June his V and VIII Corps were still in cantonements on the Vistula and the Bug. Jerome now allowed his shattered troops two days' rest so that the stragglers could catch up.

If Napoleon's judgement of Jerome's martial skills in 1809 was correct – and it is quite clear that it was – then why on earth did he let him loose again in such a senior position only three years later? And why did he allocate such a key role to his bungling brother's command?

---

* The present-day Ukraine.

† Fifty kilometres north of Warsaw.

‡ On the river Narew.

§ From Pultusk to Grodno was a distance of about 250 kilometres; marching at a rate of twenty kilometres per day – as in the Nijmegen Marches today – this would take about twelve days on good roads with ealthy, well-nourished men. In Lithuania in 1812, none of these criteria applied.

¶ Those that had not fallen out with exhaustion or died of fatigue.

There were violent rows and recriminations between General Dominique-Joseph Vandamme, the commander of the VIII Corps, and King Jerome in Grodno on 30 June; Jerome removed Vandamme from command. Both men wrote passionate letters of self-justification to the Emperor. Napoleon appointed General Junot, probably mentally unstable at this point, to take Vandamme's place as corps commander. Vandamme's departure was deeply regretted by all members of his corps; they were less worried that the Merry Monarch would soon depart. Junot's erratic actions at the critical battles of Smolensk and Valutina Gora were to cost his men dear.

Already, in this early stage of the campaign, the Emperor was becoming very uneasy at the military conduct of his brother – and others.

JEROME BONAPARTE

TO JEROME NAPOLEON, KING OF WESTPHALIA.[*]

Wilna, 4 July 1812.

I have received your packet sent from Grodno, at four o'clock yesterday afternoon. I was exceedingly glad of its arrival, as I hoped you would have sent the Major General[†] news of Bagration's Corps, of the direction in which Prince Poniatowski had pursued it, and of the movements of troops in Volhynia. What was my astonishment at learning that all the Major General received, was a complaint of a General!

I can only express my dissatisfaction at the small amount of information I have from you. I know neither the number of Bagration's divisions, nor their names, nor where he was, nor what information you obtained at Grodno, nor what you are doing. I have five or six columns in motion, to intercept Bagration's march. I cannot think you have so neglected your duty, as not to have pursued him, the very next morning. I hope, at all events, that Prince Poniatowski has followed him, with the whole of the 5th Corps. My operations are stopped for want of information from Grodno. I have had none since the 30th. The Chief of your staff does not write; Prince Poniatowski does not write. It is impossible to make war in this fashion! You never think to speak of anything but trifles, and I am distressed to see how thoroughly small-minded you are. If General Vandamme has committed acts of brigandage, you did well to send him to the rear, but in present circumstances the question is such a secondary one, that I regret you have not sent me information which might have been of service to me, nor explained your position by your courier.

I do not know why Prince Poniatowski does not correspond with the Major General twice a day. I certainly ordered him to do so.

Postscript. You are jeopardising the whole success of the campaign, on the right; it is not possible to carry on the war in this way.

On 16 July Marshal Davout arrived at Jerome's headquarters in Nieschwitz and, with great satisfaction, handed him a letter from the Emperor; it was to tell Jerome that he was sacked and should return to his seraglio in Kassel. Davout took command of the right wing of the Grande Armée.

However, this failure in the southern sector of the central front was not the only thing which went wrong in the Great Plan. The main group of the Grande Armée to the north of Jerome's, which Napoleon led in person, were also unable

---

[*] *Correspondance* CDI.

[†] Alexandre Berthier, Napoleon's invaluable Chief of Staff.

to bring their prey, Barclay, to battle when they rushed across the Niemen on 23 and 24 June.

Jerome had failed his brother again, but so had all the other commanders in the Grande Armée in 1812. Perhaps the goals that the Emperor set them were simply unattainable given the weather, the distances to be covered, the state of the roads and the tactical agility of the Russian armies.

Despite the almost total lack of contact with the enemy, the cost of the pursuit to Jerome's group had been high, and would continue to be so, as can be seen from the parade states shown below:

Corps	23 June	20 July	28 July
V (Poles)	30,000	23,000	22,000
VII (Saxons)	17,000	14,000	13,000
VIII (Westphalians)	18,000	14,000	10,000
IV Cavalry Corps	10,000	6,500	5,000
Totals	**75,000**	**57,500**	**50,000**
Deficit		17,500	25,000

So, in less than a month, Jerome's army had lost one-third of its strength, and the only action it had fought was on 9 July at Korelitchi, where their advanced guard had lost 356 casualties to Hetman Platov's Cossacks. These losses were reflected in the other French armies as they straggled forwards. If the chase was to extend for any distance, it was obvious that the Grande Armée would evaporate from a raging torrent to a pathetic trickle, even without fighting any battles.

If Jerome was late at Grodno on 28 June, Prince Eugène's central group was even further behind. They reached the Niemen at the village of Preni (about thirty kilometres south of Kowno) only on 2 July, Novi Troki on 12 July and were reviewed by Napoleon at Wilna two days later.

So both main Russian armies escaped intact to the east to fight another day. True, their initial attempts to join up were frustrated at Mir on 10 July and at Saltanovka (Mogilev) on 23 July, but their critically important junction took place at Smolensk on 16 August.

Napoleon's plan had been overambitious and had misfired; once again, he had underestimated his enemy. What was he now to do?

Even before the invasion he had been – not surprisingly – confused in his own mind as to how to tackle the challenge of the immense Russian Empire. At one point he explained that his initial aim was only to liberate Poland. But

Poland had once been a vast kingdom, stretching down into south-western Russia; what did he mean?

On another occasion, he said that he would only go as far as Smolensk. 'There or in Minsk', he told a member of his entourage, 'the campaign will end. I shall winter in Vilna, organise Lithuania, and live at Russia's expense. If then peace cannot be secured, I shall, next year, advance into the centre of the enemy's land, and stay there until the Tsar becomes pliable.'

When he was in Vilna, with the Russians still fleeing before his armies, he again appraised the strategic situation:

> If Monsieur Barclay imagines that I am going to run after him to the Volga, he is making a great mistake. We will follow him to Smolensk and the Dwina, where a good battle will provide us with quarters . . . It would certainly be destruction, were we to cross the Dvina this year. I shall go back to Vilna, spend the winter there, send for a troupe from the Théâtre Français, and another to play opera. We shall finish off the affair next May, unless peace is made during the winter.

He then wrote a conciliatory letter to Alexander, proposing negotiations; it was delivered, but never answered.

Meanwhile, the troops of the Grande Armée, lashed ever forward, ever faster by their master, had outrun the surviving, lumbering, wallowing supply vehicles. The retreating Russians applied a scorched earth policy to the land that they left for the invaders; stocks of forage and food were eaten down, evacuated or burned, as were the towns and villages. Wells and streams were defiled with dead animals and refuse.

The chase went on to Smolensk, where, on 16 August, the armies of Barclay de Tolly and Bagration finally united. Napoleon, expecting a battle, exclaimed: 'Here I remain. Let us rally our forces. The campaign of 1812 is at an end.'

Murat advised advancing further; the Emperor responded: 'In 1813 I shall be at Moscow; in '14 at St Petersburg. This war will last three years.'

But next day, just prior to the battle of Smolensk, he said: 'Russia cannot continue this sacrifice of her towns. Alexander can only begin negotiations after there has been a major battle. No blood has yet been spilled. Even if I have to march as far as the holy city of Moscow, I am determined to force a fight and win!'

In the battle of Smolensk on 17–18 August the Grande Armée lost over 8,560 men; the Russians lost some six thousand and slipped away to the east. The city was destroyed by fire; no quarters here.

At the same time, away to the north, Marshal Oudinot with the II and VI Corps had fought General Count Wittgenstein's Russians to a bloody draw; no resounding French victory here either.

On 19 August another opportunity for Napoleon to catch the Russians at the defile of Valutina Gora was missed, largely due to Junot's blatant – and expensive – mishandling of his VIII Westphalian corps.

Again a captured Russian general was asked by Napoleon to carry a message of peace to the Tsar; the plea was mixed with numerous threats of what destruction would be wreaked on Russia if no peace ensued. The letter was written and delivered; it was never answered. Alexander had learned to play poker with the big boys very well.

After the Russian left, General Rapp asked the Emperor whether the army was to advance or retreat, receiving the answer quoted above (see p. 143), that it was time Napoleon 'became the general once more'. At long last, the fateful die had been cast.

However, the months of uncharacteristic, querulous indecision on Napoleon's part betrayed the changes that were taking place in his thought processes – or was it just that luck was turning against him? This indecision was to surface again in the 1813 campaign.

So the army trudged on eastwards, getting weaker, smaller and further from its bases with every weary step. The drain of manpower became obvious to the Emperor. On 2 September he ordered Alexandre Berthier to write to the corps commanders on the subject:

> My Cousin:
> Order the King of Naples, the Prince of Eckmühl, the Viceroy, Prince Poniatowski, the Duke of Elchingen, to take a day's rest, to get in their stragglers, to have a roll-call at three in the afternoon, and to let me know precisely the number of men they can place in line.
>
> The staff is useless; not one of the officers does his duty properly, not the provost-general, nor the quartermaster. You have my order for the baggage. See to it that the first baggage wagons I order burned are not those of the general staff.

The last sentence is most revealing, considering that he had just condemned the lot of them as being 'useless'. As he had selected all the senior staff officers personally, what does this say about his acumen for selecting the right men for the right jobs?

Next day, again to Berthier, he stated:

Write to the officers commanding the army corps that we lose so many men daily because there is no system in the supply service; it is urgently necessary that they should take measures in concert with their colonels to put an end to the state of things that threatens the army with destruction. Every day the enemy pick up several hundred prisoners. During the twenty years in which I have commanded French armies, I have never seen the commissariat service so hopelessly bad; there is no one; the people sent out here have no ability and no experience.

So, in just two days the scales suddenly fell from his eyes regarding the efficiency of his general staff and commissariat, and the extreme strategic attrition that his army was suffering deep in hostile Russia. But why only now? Was he so insulated from what had been happening to his army even since before he crossed the Niemen on 23 June? Did he not see the thousands of corpses of his men and horses lining the route of his advancing columns? Did he receive no daily and weekly parade states? Did he not read them and notice the dwindling numbers of men and horses day after day, week after week? Or did Berthier fudge all the figures?

The truth is that the welfare of his army only became a topic of interest to him when it was painfully obvious that it was falling apart, and thus endangering the fulfilment of his own personal aims.

On 7 September the bloody slogging match that was perhaps Napoleon's worst battle was fought at Borodino, seventy miles west of Moscow. By this time, the cunning old General of Infantry Prince Mikhail Illarionovich Golenischev Kutusov had taken command of the Russian army in place of Barclay de Tolly, and the honour of the nation demanded that a battle be fought to save Moscow.

Prior to this battle, Napoleon received a dispatch from Spain reporting Marshal Marmont's defeat by Wellington at Salamanca on 22 July. Perhaps the news caused him to be a little careful at Borodino.

On the eve of the action, Davout suggested a right-flanking manoeuvre. The Emperor dismissed this as being too risky; he was all for a head-to-head confrontation. As the day progressed, his generals called for the pampered Imperial Guard to be committed to break the enemy; Napoleon refused.

On St Helena Napoleon said of Borodino: 'No other battle cost me so much and brought me so little.' He was right. Allied losses were twenty-eight thousand, including many of Napoleon's veteran generals. The Russians lost about forty-four thousand – the exact figures will never be known – but their army withdrew towards Moscow, otherwise intact.

Napoleon was now far, far out on a limb, his army dangerously weakened, his foe implacable, the theatre of war immense. All reason would have told him that the game was lost; but Napoleon had stopped listening to reason years ago. It was now a case of 'I want; I *will* have!'

He should have stopped at Smolensk. He should have wintered in Vilna once he had ventured to bully Alexander into submission. Indeed, perhaps he should not have tried to bully the Tsar of all the Russias in the first place, but then, as Napoleon himself had said, he had poured the wine in the first place, and now had to drink it to the last drop.

So he blundered on into Moscow, entering a half-empty city on 15 September. The abandoned city was yet another witness to Alexander's steel reserve and the implacable resistance of the whole Russian nation. As he saw the city for the first time, Napoleon said: 'Moscow! It is time!' Time for what?

Napoleon (perhaps like President George W. Bush in Iraq in 2003) simply lacked an exit strategy from the disastrous cul-de-sac into which he had thrust himself – and over half a million innocent conscripted souls. He had never contemplated failure in his months of meticulous planning; it was merely a case of victory in 1812, or 1813, or 1814. Defeat? Never!

So he lingered in Moscow, which was soon to be largely reduced to ashes.

Yet again a letter, a fragile olive branch, was sent by Napoleon to the Tsar; yet again it was delivered, and yet again it received no answer. The Emperor had misjudged Alexander's character, never suspecting that the man whom he had dismissed as being putty in his fingers had the resolve to challenge him. For five weeks Napoleon waited in Moscow, as the season drew towards winter; still there was no answer.

What was left of the Grande Armée, by now only one-third of the march-in strength, idled its way around what was left of Moscow, looting, drinking, surviving. No coherent contingency plans for the future were decided, nothing done to prepare for an advance, a withdrawal or a stay through the winter in the ruined city. It was as if Napoleon has reached his final goal and did not know where next to go, what next to do. Then, on 18 October the Russians attacked Murat at Winkowo (Tarutino), sixty-seven kilometres south-west of Moscow, inflicting a sharp defeat on him.

At last the Emperor snapped awake. On 19 October he ordered his few remaining troops to evacuate Moscow. But even now, his sense of reality seemed to be impaired; he ordered the great golden cross on the Church of St John, inside the Kremlin, to be taken down and hauled back to Paris as a trophy. The remnants of the Grande Armée trudged out of the ruined city, laden with loot of all descriptions and accompanied by a great throng of refugee French expatriates who had been living in Moscow and now feared the vengeance of their hosts.

Knowing only too well the devastated condition of the corridor through which he had invaded Russia, he sensibly went south from Moscow to return to the west through lands unravaged by warfare and potentially able to offer food, fodder and shelter.

The Tsar, however, was ready for this. On 24 October, at Malojaroslawetz on the river Luscha, some 103 kilometres south-west of Moscow, the Russians stopped this movement and the dispirited invaders were forced to head for their old route.

It is not our task to wallow in the misery of the retreat from Moscow, but misery it was and on a vast scale, not to be seen again until the Second World War, when the hapless Wehrmacht were to give a repeat performance of this senseless tragedy.

Back in Paris – where none yet knew of any reverses in Russia – General Claude-François de Malet mounted a coup against the Emperor on 22 October. A committed republican, Malet had opposed the introduction of the Empire and had been committed to a mental institution in 1807. In the October of

The retreat from Moscow

1812, he escaped from his asylum, gathered a few friends, commandeered a National Guard unit, announced that Napoleon had died in Russia, and attempted to seize power. For several hours he was very close to his goal: many of Napoleon's officials were taken in. Just in time he was arrested, tried and shot, together with fourteen co-conspirators.

On 6 November news of the failed plot reached Napoleon, fifty-five kilometres east of Smolensk. After slipping through the Russian armies converging on the French crossing point of Borisov on the Beresina, and thanks to the heroic efforts of General Eble and his sappers in building two bridges over the river at Studianka on 28 November, Napoleon handed over command of the remnants of his army to Murat at Smorgoni, eighty kilometres east of Vilna, and left to return to Paris as quickly as possible.

This was undoubtedly the correct decision in the circumstances, even if it recalls his abandonment of another army in Egypt in 1799. There was nothing for a head of state and head of government to do in Russia now. His presence in Paris was vital, before another Malet popped out of the woodwork.

Late at night on 18 December, he re-entered the Tuileries, one day after the notorious 29th Bulletin gave Parisians his version of how he had squandered the lives of half a million of his countrymen, to say nothing of the countless Austrians, Germans, Italians, Poles, Spanish and Russians (military and civilian) who had also died:

> *29th Bulletin, 3 December, at our Headquarters at Molodetchna.*
> Until 6 November the weather was perfect and the movement of the army was carried out with complete success. On the 7th the cold set in; from that moment we lost several hundred horses at each night's bivouac. On reaching Smolensk we had already lost an immense quantity of cavalry and artillery horses. The cold became more intense, and between the 14th and the 16th the thermometer fell to zero. The roads were covered with ice, the horses were dying every night, not in hundreds but in thousands. More than thirty thousand horses died in a few days; our cavalry was dismounted, our artillery and transport had no teams. Without cavalry we could not risk a battle; we were compelled to march so as not to be forced into a battle, which we wished to avoid because of our shortness of ammunition.
>
> The enemy, marching in the footsteps of the frightful calamity that had overtaken the French army, tried to profit by it. All our columns were surrounded by Cossacks who, like the Arabs in the desert, picked up every cart or wagon that lagged behind. This contemptible cavalry, which only knows how to shout and couldn't ride

down so much as a company of light infantry, became formidable from the force of circumstances!

But the enemy held the passage of the Beresina, a river eighty yards wide; the water was full of floating ice, and the banks are marshy for a distance of six hundred yards, which made it a difficult obstacle to overcome. The enemy had placed four divisions at four points where they supposed the French army would attempt to pass. After having deceived the enemy by various manoeuvres on the 25th, the Emperor marched on the village of Studienka at break of day on the 26th, and, in the face of a division of the enemy, had two bridges thrown across the river. The army was crossing all through the 26th and the 27th.

It may be concluded from what has been said that the army needs to re-establish its discipline, to be re-equipped, to remount its cavalry, its artillery, and its transport. During all these events the Emperor constantly marched in the midst of the Guard, the cavalry commanded by the Duke of Istria, the infantry by the Duke of Danzig. Our cavalry was so reduced that it became necessary to form all the officers who were still mounted into dour companies of 150 men each. Generals acted as captains, and colonels as corporals. This Sacred Squadron, commanded by General Grouchy, and under the orders of the King of Naples, kept the closest watch over the Emperor.

His majesty's health has never been better.
NAPOLEON.

Napoleon, in the best of health, at once set to work, with his usual furious energy, to secure his dynasty and to build yet another army.

8
~The Errors of 1813~

*A*S VACHÉE SAID, NAPOLEON was an unrestrained gambler; in 1813 he
still thought that his luck would hold.

Back in the east, Prussian General Hans David Ludwig von Yorck,
commanding the Prussian corps in Courland, concluded an armistice with
General Ivan Ivanovich von Diebitsch (German name Hans Karl Friedrich
Anton), a Prussian officer in Russian service, in December 1812. This unau-
thorised step was to take Prussia from the detested French camp and into that
of Russia. The weights in the scales were shifting.

Napoleon, meanwhile, had managed to conscript over two hundred
thousand new men, put them into some sort of uniform, give them some sort
of training and equipment and pack them off to the east. A further ninety-one
thousand men were placed into the National Guard for territorial defence. On
11 January the Senate agreed that these men should form the new 135e–156e
Line Infantry Regiments, which were thus available for use in Saxony.

The navy provided a further four regiments of 'Naval Artillery' (actually
they were infantry) with eight thousand sailors, who fought with great valour
at Leipzig, and a further ten thousand Gardes d'Honneur (a copy of Prussia's
Volunteer Jägers) were raised from the better-off classes to swell the cavalry.
These measures provided a stunning 656,000 new troops. A further thirty
thousand conscripts were called up in August and 240,000 more in October.

This was a truly magnificent achievement on the part of the Emperor, of
his government machinery and – not least – of the French nation itself. But the
nation was beginning to grow weary of coming to the Emperor's rescue all over
Europe, and each time paying the bloody price.

It goes without saying that Napoleon's enemies were also working frantically;
British gold was flowing and British agents scurried busily across Europe, cobbling
together yet another coalition against Napoleon; this time they scented blood.

The dreadful experiences of the Russian campaign had shaken the resolve and loyalty of many, even high-ranking officers. Junot, Duke of Abrantes and an old friend of Napoleon's, had been wounded in the head years before. His conduct in Russia was erratic to say the least, and it seems that his behaviour in early 1813 was no longer acceptable to the Emperor; his dismissal was communicated with brutal brevity:

To Prince Eugène Napoleon, Viceroy of Italy, in Chief Command of the Grande Armée.*

> *Paris, 28 January 1813.*
> I have your letter of 21 Jan. You can dismiss the Duke of Abrantes – that will be one encumbrance the less for the army; and indeed he is a man who would not be of the slightest use to you. Let him know that he is no longer employed with the army.

Junot died on 29 July 1813 by jumping out of a window.

Others of high rank were also feeling the strain:

To General Clarke, Duke of Feltre, Minister of War.[†]

> *Paris, 31 March 1813.*
> The Viceroy informs me that General Reynier has started without leave, and I see from the Travellers' Report at Mayence, that he has just arrived in that town. Send an officer to meet him, with orders that he is to turn back at once. Make him aware of my displeasure at his having left his post, without leave from the Viceroy, who has made a complaint to me on the subject. Your officer will tell him that if he pushes forward, and does not at once return to his post, he will be arrested.
>
> You are to have General Loison put under arrest at once, and you will then have him questioned as to the reasons he left his post. You will ask him why he was not at the head of his division when it came upon the enemy at Wilna – a fact which caused the loss of that fine division.

General Count Jean-Louis-Ebenezer Reynier went on to command the VII Corps (the Saxons) through the 1813 campaign; he died in Paris on 27 February 1814, worn out by years of campaigning.

---

* *Correspondance* CCCXVI.

† *Correspondance* CDXXIX.

As the letter above shows, General Loison also felt the Emperor's displeasure for sloppy command habits that spring. Napoleon was to pursue the matter:

To General Clarke, Duke of Feltre, Minister of War. [*]

Paris, 8 April 1813.

Have the enquiry into General Loison's conduct proceeded with. It is time to make an example. The greatest insubordination exists among the generals; it is affecting the lives of my soldiers and the glory of my arms. Make General Loison answer the following questions:

Did he receive information at Königsberg that he had been placed in command of the 34th Division?

Did he consequently make a bargain to buy horses and teams for his artillery?

Did he get orders to start with the 34th Division?

Why did he allow it to start without him?

The affair concluded as follows:

To General Clarke, Duke of Feltre, Minister of War. [†]

Saint-Cloud, 14 April 1813.

I return you the documents relating to General Loison. You will express my displeasure to him. Make him aware that I have read his answers very attentively, and that they are very far from justifying him. Tell him, that once his division reached Kowno, it was before the enemy, and that, from that moment, he should have marched, if not with the leading battalions, at all events with the bulk of his troops; that I therefore still think the loss of the division confided to his care, must be attributed to him; that, in spite of this, I am willing not to forget the service he has rendered me on other occasions, but that I hope this will be a lesson to him, and that he will come to a better understanding of the importance of the duty of a general commanding a division for which he is answerable. Give orders for him to be released from arrest, and let him be at his own home within twenty-four hours. You will then let him know his ultimate destination.

---

[*] *Correspondance* CDXXXI.

[†] *Correspondance* CDXXXIII.

General Count Louis-Henri Loison was released from arrest on 14 April 1813, commanded the 3rd Division from then until the end of the campaign and died on 30 December 1816.

Another of Napoleon's generals, François-Joseph-Pamphile Lacroix, incurred the Emperor's displeasure, and was tried and cashiered on 22 July 1813. He was reinstated under the Bourbons, rose to high rank and died in Versailles on 16 October 1841.

One of the Emperor's more contentious decisions was to throw over fifty thousand men of the Grande Armée into the fortresses of Danzig, Glogau, Küstrin, Modlin and Thorn as his army withdrew westwards in the early days of 1813. He just could not bring himself to let all these strategically important fortresses, with their stores, weapons and equipment, fall into allied hands. He was convinced that he would be back in the spring to relieve these garrisons, and their presence would force the allies to detach blockading forces to watch them, so weakening their thrust westwards.

In the latter calculation Napoleon overestimated the value of this tactic. As the weeks passed, the veteran troops of the blockading forces were replaced by second-line troops and militia, and the veterans moved westwards to join the front line. Meanwhile, the garrisons in these fortresses lingered on, gradually wasting away, until they surrendered or until peace came in April 1814.

On 6 April 1813 Napoleon told Charles Lebrun, his treasurer, that he felt no worries at all about the future fidelity of his Austrian father-in-law. 'From Austria there is no cause for anxiety; the most intimate relations exist between the two courts.' If he wanted to believe something was so, it was just so.

On Thursday 15 April the Emperor left Paris to return to the front in Saxony. Once more, as in 1812, he needed a crushing victory to settle the campaign quickly. However, although he had been able to create and arm an army of over half a million men in a short space of time, he had been unable to find enough horses for his artillery, cavalry and train. On 2 May 1813 the battle of Lützen was fought; it was a French victory, but lack of cavalry meant that it was incomplete.

Austrian foreign policy was largely managed by Prince Clemens Wenzel Lothar von Metternich-Winneburg-Beilstein, whose feudal estates in the Rhine valley had been swallowed up by the Revolution. He was a politician of formidable skills and subtlety, no warmonger, but neither was he a friend of Napoleon. His policy was to reassert Austria as a major player in European politics. Metternich was also wary of Russia and Prussia, both old enemies from the past.

During May, Napoleon was in Dresden, the Saxon capital. He received intelligence that an Austrian army of some sixty-four thousand men was forming in Bohemia, to the south; smelling a rat, he wrote to Marie-Louise telling her to warn her father against breaking faith with his son-in-law. The result was that the Austrian general Graf Ferdinand von Bubna appeared in Dresden, with Metternich's proposal that Austria would act as mediator between France and her enemies with the aim of brokering an honourable peace, acceptable to both sides. In return for their services to Napoleon, the Austrians suggested the return of French enclaves on the eastern bank of the Rhine, renegotiation of their borders with Bavaria and Italy, influence in the affairs of the Confederation of the Rhine and another partition of Poland.

Boosted by his recent victory, the Emperor rejected these demands out of hand. This was a mistake. His appetite for yet more conquests – and his arrogance – had been rekindled; they were to lead to his downfall.

On 20 and 21 May the battle of Bautzen (or Würschen), again a French victory, again incomplete, followed.

If Napoleon was now bullish, Berthier and Caulaincourt were more cautious; they were also scared when the Emperor advanced to Breslau, deep in Silesia, in pursuit of the Russo-Prussian army. At last he heeded their advice, and on 4 June agreed to the Armistice of Pläswitz, which was to last at least until 20 July, while peace negotiations continued. Both sides – and Austria – worked feverishly to improve their field armies and their political alliances.

The Napoleon of 1796, of 1805, of 1806 would have been most unlikely to have agreed to such an armistice. True, his army was battered, but so were those of the allies. Continued pressure on his part may well have caused the coalition leaders to lose their nerve, to crack – as coalitions had so often in the past – and fall away into their separate homelands.

Metternich met with Alexander in mid-June; the Tsar wanted total victory over the French and did not trust Metternich; King Friedrich Wilhelm of Prussia was burning for revenge for all the damage the French had caused his realm and was also for total victory.

Metternich then went to Napoleon in the Marcolini Palace outside Dresden; there the famous interview took place in which, according to Metternich, the Emperor threw his hat to the floor, accused Metternich of being in British pay and uttered the infamously revealing remark: 'What are the lives of a million men to a man such as me?'

Metternich also reported that, when told that France was becoming war-weary, Napoleon said: 'France has no reason to complain. To spare France I have sacrificed Germans and Poles. In Russia I lost three hundred thousand men, but only one-tenth of them were Frenchmen!' History proves that his grasp of mathematics was a little fuzzy.

Apparently he then said: 'It was exceedingly stupid of me to marry an archduchess. I was trying to weld the new with the old, to make Gothic prejudices square with the institutions of my own century. Now I can see the whole extent of my error! The blunder may cost me my throne, but I will bury the world beneath its ruins!' As there were no others present, we shall never know the truth of these assertions, but they certainly ring true.

Negotiations dragged on in Prague. Napoleon was willing to surrender Danzig, Dalmatia and the Grand Duchy of Warsaw – so much for all the faithful service of his Polish allies – but Germany and Italy were sacred to him. He was well aware of the tensions in the alliance, and sought to drive wedges between his opponents.

On 21 June the Duke of Wellington defeated King Joseph of Spain at Vitoria; it was the death knell for the French presence in Spain.

The Prague conference broke up on 8 August; four days later, Austria joined Russia and Prussia and declared war on France. So much for the secure familial ties.

At this point the allies could command about eight hundred thousand men in the field in Saxony against Napoleon's seven hundred thousand. On all sides, these were mainly young, hastily trained soldiers with poor equipment, often marching barefoot and ill-clothed. As General Raymond-Aimery de Fezensac wrote of the Grande Armée: 'At Wagram Napoleon complained that he no longer had the soldiers of Austerlitz, and in 1813 we certainly did not have the soldiers of Wagram.' Many of the French commanders were no longer the men who had forged the Glory Years either; this applied equally to the Emperor. His physical condition had deteriorated quite badly, and Russia had shown him indecisive and unable to grasp and hold the initiative.

On the allied side, however, it must be said that the military qualities of most of the monarchs and their senior commanders had improved markedly since 1805 in the harsh school of Napoleonic war. Another not inconsiderable factor was that the average age of the French commanders had increased since 1805, while that of their opponents had been reduced considerably as fading personalities were ruthlessly retired. It was no longer a case of 'teenagers fighting geriatrics', as it had been at Austerlitz and Jena.

This said, the French still enjoyed three great advantages over their opponents in Saxony. First, they held the central position and thus enjoyed interior lines of communication; the allies, by contrast, were spread around them in three separate armies in a vast arc. Command, control and co-ordination would be a time-consuming business and the different languages and calendars increased the confusion. Second, the French enjoyed unified command under one of history's greatest commanders. Third, the allies – as usual – were politically divided and suspicious of one another. Bernadotte (commanding the Army of the North) in particular was a totally unreliable ally and extremely ineffective, if not downright treacherous, throughout this campaign.

During the armistice however, the allies devised the so-called Trachenberg Plan. It was simple and very effective. The allied army which found itself confronted by a French army commanded by the Emperor would withdraw and inform the other two, who would close on the enemy's flanks. The aim was to avoid a battle against the Master until his forces had been worn down by constant marching and countermarching. This plan worked beautifully.

Hostilities resumed and Napoleon took the offensive, sending Macdonald after Blücher, who had crossed the agreed demarcation line before the end of the armistice. At the river Katzbach in Silesia on 26 August, Blücher's Army of Silesia severely mauled Marshal Etienne-Jacques Macdonald's Army of the Bober, inflicting about thirty thousand casualties and taking 105 guns.

It was becoming clear that for as long as Napoleon could exercise immediate, effective command over all his forces, he was still extremely dangerous. When his armies were so large that they had to be given independent commanders, the Master's touch was lost and the detached marshals often proved to be mere mortals, like their enemies.

French spirits rallied when Napoleon won a resounding victory at Dresden on 26 and 27 August, exploiting allied timidity. The allies lost some twenty-three thousand men and forty guns, but withdrew into the Bohemian hills, otherwise intact. General Vandamme was charged with pursuing them, but at Kulm on 29 and 30 August he was taken in rear and his army lost fifteen thousand men and twenty-one guns. Vandamme himself was captured.

ETIENNE-JACQUES MACDONALD

Napoleon now tried a familiar ploy – a thrust at an enemy's capital, in this case Berlin. He gave the job to Marshal Ney; on 6 September Ney was badly defeated by the Prussians at Dennewitz (Jüterbog), losing twenty thousand men and fifty-four guns. Bernadotte hovered in the wings, constantly trying to sabotage Prussian efforts.

Some people have criticised Napoleon's choice of Marshal Davout to command in Hamburg in 1813 instead of giving him a command in the field. Davout was possibly the most capable commander the Emperor had; was it truly an error to leave him in the rear area, while other, less effective marshals blundered into allied traps? It must be remembered that from 1810 Hamburg and the other Hanseatic cities formed Departments of France itself. The reason for their annexation was that for years they had been used as entry points for contraband English goods that had made a mockery of Napoleon's Continental System. Annexing them placed them under tight control and stemmed the flood of smuggled produce. From January 1813 General Carra Saint-Cyr was in command of Hamburg; on 12 March a small force of Cossacks under Colonel Tettenborn approached the city and Carra Saint-Cyr fled to Bremen. The joyful citizens of the mighty port-city of Hamburg quickly renounced their French nationality and welcomed the Cossacks in.

The Emperor was livid. Not only contraband, but also allied forces could be thrown into the city and cause havoc in his rear; the whole house of cards might come crashing down behind his back. It was essential that a safe pair of hands re-establish French command of Hamburg and ensure that it was quickly placed into a state of defence. The selected man would have to be capable of operating on his own initiative in an isolated position for maybe months on end. Davout was that man.

On 30 May he re-entered the city, exacted a terrible revenge on the citizens for letting the Russians in and at once began to fortify the place. He was to hold it against all allied efforts until the end of the war in 1814.

In this case, Napoleon's choice was correct; for this role Davout was a perfect fit. The fact that Macdonald, Ney and Oudinot were each to be decisively beaten – almost under the Emperor's nose – in no way justifies criticism of Davout's appointment to command Hamburg. Davout may well also have been beaten in the field when the endgame of the Leipzig campaign was played out that year. His undoubted talents would, however, be sorely missed in the desperate campaign in France in the spring of 1814.

On 1 September, the Duke of Wellington won the battle of the Bidassoa and invaded south-western France on 7 October.

Napoleon rushed hither and thither in Saxony, like a fly trapped in the web of the Trachenberg Plan, his forces wasting away before his eyes, his marshals blundering. On 2 October, he wrote: 'It would be the best possible news to hear that the enemy are running their heads into Leipzig with eighty thousand men; the war would soon be over then; but I imagine they know my methods too well to take any such risks.' Little did he know that he was soon to have his wish granted.

On 3 October the Prussian general von Yorck defeated General Count Henri-Gratien Bertrand's IV Corps at Wartenburg, causing him two thousand casualties and taking thirteen guns. This action heralded Blücher's fateful advance to Leipzig; Yorck received the title 'von Wartenburg'.

Napoleon's political and strategic situations continued to deteriorate; the loyalty of many of the states of the Confederation of the Rhine began to crumble away. The writing was on the wall.

On the afternoon of the 6 October, Marshal Gouvion Saint-Cyr, commander of Dresden, had a long conversation with Napoleon in that city, during which the Emperor expounded various strategic possibilities, but stressed the vital importance of holding Dresden. It was to be the pivot of his future operations. Saint-Cyr was not convinced of its value, but Napoleon was so adamant about holding it that he did not dare to contradict him.

At midnight the same day, Napoleon sent for Saint-Cyr again. He had received news of Ney and had altered his plans. He now aimed to abandon Dresden, to take the entire garrison with him into the field and to crush Bernadotte and Blücher. Saint-Cyr recorded the Emperor's reasoning behind this sudden and radical change of strategic policy as follows: 'I shall certainly fight a battle. If I win, I shall surely regret not having all my troops under my hand.' The lesson of Marengo seemed to have been well and truly learned. He continued:

If, on the contrary, I suffer a reverse, in leaving you here you will be of no service to me in the battle and you will be hopelessly lost.

Moreover, what is Dresden worth today? It can no longer be the pivot of the operations of the army, which, owing to the exhaustion of the surrounding country, cannot subsist here.

This city cannot even be considered as a great depot, for you would find in it subsistence for a few days only.

There are in Dresden twelve thousand sick who will die since they are the residue of the sixty thousand who have entered the hospitals since the commencement of the campaign.

Add to this that the season is advancing, and that the Elbe, once frozen over, no longer offers a position.

I wish to take up another position for the winter, refusing my right on Erfurt, and extending my centre along the Saale, which is a good position in all seasons, because the heights of my left bank are always excellent for defence.

I shall rest my left on Magdeburg,[*] and that city will become for me of greater importance than Dresden.

After elaborating on the strengths of the defences of Magdeburg, Napoleon continued:

Besides, I repeat, I want to change my position; Dresden is too near Bohemia. As soon as I make the smallest movement from the neighbourhood of the city to approach Bohemia, the enemy's armies, having only a very short distance to cover, will return to it, and I have no chance of cutting them off by moving on their rear.

Finally, by adopting the more distant position I am going to occupy, I wish to give them great blows; to force the allied sovereigns to a solid peace, putting an end to the calamities of Europe.

But twelve hours later, after he had left Dresden for the last time, the Emperor's strategic thinking made another 180-degree turn, tossing overboard all the valid arguments of the previous night. At one o'clock in the afternoon of 7 October, in Meissen, twenty-six kilometres down the Elbe from Dresden, Napoleon wrote to Saint-Cyr telling him that he had decided to hold on to Dresden after all. Convoys of supplies were to be sent there, the defences were to be strengthened, the wounded and sick evacuated. The Emperor hoped for an early battle and was advancing to the north-west. Napoleon thus robbed himself of two corps (I and XIV) for the forthcoming battle of Leipzig, and these two corps were subsequently 'hopelessly lost', as he had so accurately predicted. What of Marengo now?

On 8 October, Bavaria joined the allies by the Treaty of Ried and an Austro-Bavarian corps was formed in Bavaria to operate against Napoleon's lines of communication back through Erfurt and Mainz to France.

Meanwhile, Napoleon had learned of Blücher's Elbe crossing on the 5th, and also of the Prussian commander's successful union with the Army of the North, which had at last begun to move south up the Mulde towards Leipzig. He also heard that Ney had retreated and that the Army of Bohemia was at Chemnitz, only sixty kilometres west of Dresden and a hundred kilometres south-east of Leipzig.

The allied net was closing.

---

* Magdeburg is 192 kilometres to the north-west of Dresden, down the Elbe.

9
~ 1813: Leipzig, the Battle of the Nations ~

FROM 10 TO 14 OCTOBER Napoleon stayed in the moated castle of Düben on the river Mulde, about thirty-four kilometres north of Leipzig. Baron von Odeleben accompanied him, and recounts that they must have been the most irksome days that the Emperor had passed in many years.

> I saw the Emperor there, anxiously awaiting news from the Elbe, sitting idly on a sofa in his cabinet before a great table, on which lay a piece of white paper on which he doodled large, Gothic letters. His geographer, Bacler d'Albe, and another official – also idle – were with him in a corner of the room. Such rare moments of his career deserve to be recorded.

This was clearly no longer the Emperor of Austerlitz and Jena. Then, he would have been up with his outposts, fighting for the vital intelligence, divining enemy intentions and weaknesses, striking like a thunderbolt. Now, he lounges in his suite, doodling, idle, not knowing what to do. His minions have nothing to do either; truly a contrast between day and night.

By this time, the allied ring was drawing closer around its prey, whose possible options were reducing day by day. But still Napoleon was mired in the confidence of the Glory Years: 'They will never dare to attack me.'

For inexplicable reasons he then adopted a battle position to the east of Leipzig, with an almost impenetrable obstacle – the Elster – Pleisse swamp complex – directly to his rear and across his line of communication back to his base at Erfurt. He then ordered all the bridges over this barrier, except one, to be broken. This extraordinary plan might have been hatched by a geriatric Spanish general early in the peninsular struggle, but that Napoleon should have thought of it – and that his obsequious staff did not protest against such madness – is stunning.

There followed the awful bloodbath of the Battle of the Nations from 16 to 19 October.

On 16 October the commander of the II Austrian Corps of the Army of Bohemia, General of Cavalry Maximilian Count von Meerveldt, who was extremely short-sighted, mistook some of the enemy troops over the Pleisse for Prussians (they were in fact part of Curial's 2nd Division of the Old Guard) and thought that the time had at last come for him to cross the river and join his allies. He ordered an infantry bridge to be thrown over the Pleisse just upstream of Dölitz manor and rode over it with a few ADCs and orderlies. He got to within about twenty paces of the 'allies' before they delivered a volley, which brought down his horse. He was captured (the ADC who came back over the river reported that he had been killed), and in his pocket was found a copy of the allied plan of action for 17 October. The omniscient General Wolzogen (a Russian equivalent of the imaginative Frenchman Marbot) recounts that he had pleaded with von Meerveldt to leave this vital document with him before crossing the Pleisse, but that Meerveldt had refused to do so. On reporting Meerveldt's capture to the Tsar next day, Wolzogen was promoted to Major General for his efforts in the allied cause on the 16th. General von Meerveldt was called in to see the Emperor shortly after midday the next day. Meerveldt reported the subsequent conversation as follows:

> At two o'clock in the afternoon of 17 October Emperor Napoleon called me to him. After he had made some complimentary remarks about our attempt to take his army in flank, he told me that, as a mark of his high regard for me, he was going to release me on my word of honour.
>
> After some questions as to the strength of the allied armies, he confessed to me that he had not thought them to be so strong; he asked if we had known that he was with the army and I confirmed that we did.
>
> N: 'So, you intended to fight a battle with me?'
>
> M: 'Yes, sire.'
>
> N: 'You are mistaken as to the strength that I have concentrated here; how many men do you think I have?'
>
> M: 'At the most 120,000.'
>
> N: 'I have two hundred thousand. I think I have underestimated your numbers; how many do you have?'
>
> M: 'Over 350,000, sire.'
>
> N: 'Will you attack tomorrow?'
>
> M: 'I do not doubt it, sire. The allied armies, trusting in their greater numbers, will attack your majesty every day; they hope to

bring about a decisive battle and the withdrawal of the French army.'

N: 'Will this war last for ever then? It's time to end it once and for all.'

M: 'Sire, that is the wish of us all and peace lies in your majesty's hands; it depended upon your majesty to make peace at the Congress of Prague.'

N: 'They were not honest with me, they tried to trick me, they set too close a deadline; such an important matter cannot be decided in ten days. Austria missed the opportunity to set herself at Europe's head. I would have done everything that she asked and we would have dictated to the world.'

M: 'I cannot conceal from your majesty that in Austria we are convinced that you would have dictated terms to Austria.'

N: 'But someone has to make the proposals, even if it is Austria! As far as Russia is concerned, she is under England's influence and England does not want peace.'

M: 'I am not at all informed of the intentions of my government, sire. Everything that I say to your majesty must be regarded as being my own opinions; but I know that the Kaiser, my lord, is totally determined to act in unison with the allied courts and that he expects this union of purpose to bring about a lasting peace. Your majesty knows that the allied courts share the wish that peace should be achieved as quickly as possible.'

N: 'Well then, why do they not accept my offer to negotiate? You must see that England does not want peace.'

M: 'Sire, I know with certainty that we await daily an answer to the offer that your majesty has made [to England] and that we think it will be positive.'

N: 'You will see that she will not agree.'

M: 'England needs peace badly herself, sire, but she needs peace, not just an armistice. A peace based on terms which ensure that it will last.'

N: 'And what do you think these conditions might be?'

M: 'A balance of forces in Europe that would limit France's dominance.'

N: 'Well then, England should give me my islands back and I will return Hanover to her. I am also ready to give up the annexed Departments and the Hanseatic towns.'

M: 'I think, sire, that they will insist on the re-creation of Holland.'

N: 'Oh! It will not be able to exist; no one will recognise her flag; an isolated Holland would fall under England's influence.'

M: 'I believe, sire, that England's maritime principles are merely a product of the war and will be amended when the war is over; if that is the case, your majesty would have no more need to keep Holland.'

N: 'Well, we shall have to negotiate about this independence, but, with England's attitude, this will not be easy.'

M: 'It would be a generous decision and a great step towards peace.'

N: 'I long for peace; I would make sacrifices – great sacrifices – but there are things that are matters of honour for me, which I could not give up in my situation; for example my protectorate of Germany.'

M: 'Your majesty knows only too well what an obstacle your protectorate of Germany is to the re-establishment of the balance of power in Europe and will thus understand that it cannot be reinforced by a peace. Our alliance with Bavaria and other states of the Confederation of the Rhine, the prospect of including Saxony, will rob your majesty of part of your allies and we believe that the rest will follow when they see the power and successes of our superior strength.'

N: 'Oh! Those who do not want my protection may do as they wish. They will regret it; but my honour forbids me from abandoning the protection of the rest.'

M: 'I remember that your majesty once said to me that it was essential for peace in Europe that France should be separated from the other major European powers by a belt of smaller, independent states. Were your majesty to be prepared to return to this reasonable principle, which your majesty formulated in much more peaceful times, the welfare of Europe would be assured.'

The Emperor gave an answer to this which was not negative. There followed a short silence; then the Emperor said:

N: 'Good, we shall see, but this will not bring peace. How can I negotiate with England who wishes to limit to thirty the number of ships of the line I may build in my harbours? The English themselves know how unacceptable this condition is, that's why they don't mention it, but I know what they want.'

M: 'Sire, I was convinced at the beginning of this conversation that the aim of the allied powers in this war was the re-establishment of the balance in Europe. England cannot ignore the fact that the extension of the coastline under your majesty's control, stretching from the Adriatic to the North Sea, would allow you to build a fleet two or three times as strong as that which Great Britain would have. And with your majesty's talent and energy, the obvious outcome may easily be calculated. How else will they try to avoid this imbalance other than by limiting the number of ships that may be built in France's harbours; while your majesty would not return to the agreement that you yourself made when you set yourself at the head of the Kingdom of Italy, that is to say, to give that country independence again as soon as peace was achieved? I am not aware of anything that your majesty has published that has revoked this undertaking that you laid upon yourself. It would contribute much to calm in Europe; Europe would regard this as a great sacrifice which would be much more preferable to your majesty than trying to limit the number of ships which France would be allowed to build. You would have all the credit for this peace and after you have achieved the highest military fame, this peace would give you the time to complete all those magnificent projects which you have started in France and to found the happiness of your empire, which would be so dear to you.'

The Emperor admitted that this would be acceptable to him.

N: 'In any case, I would not agree to anything which would lead to the re-establishment of the old order in Italy. This country, unified under a single ruler, would comply with the general system of European politics.'

M: 'Concerning the Duchy of Warsaw, I assume that your majesty would relinquish this?'

N: 'Of course; I offered it but they did not accept it.'

M: 'Then perhaps Spain would be a bone of contention?'

N: 'No; Spain is a dynastic matter.'

M: 'Certainly, sire, but I assume that the warring parties do not all support the same dynasty.'

N: 'I have been forced to evacuate Spain. This question has thus been settled.'

M: 'It seems, then, that peace is possible.'

N: 'Well, send me someone whom I can trust and we will reach agreement. I am always being accused of proposing armistices, so I will propose none, but you have to admit that the general good would only benefit from one. If it is wished, I would be prepared to retire behind the Saale, the Russians and Prussians would fall back behind the Elbe and you would go back into Bohemia. Poor Saxony, that has suffered so much, would be neutral.'

M: 'Due to supplies and forage we would not be able to relinquish Saxony, even if we did not wish to see your majesty back over the Rhine by the autumn due to our superior strength. The allied armies, I believe, would never agree to your majesty staying on this side of that river if there were to be an armistice.'

N: 'With reference to that, I would first have to lose a battle; that may happen – but it hasn't happened yet.'

An examination of Napoleon's offer of mutual withdrawals reveals just how cunning it was. He was prepared to withdraw behind the river Saale (some thirty kilometres to the west of the trap of Leipzig in which he was now stuck) if the Austrian army would pull back south into Bohemia (over a hundred kilometres away) and the Russo-Prussian armies would withdraw eastwards to the east bank of the river Elbe (sixty kilometres to the east of Leipzig). But it is difficult to judge if Napoleon expected anyone to take his proposal seriously. Any halfwit could at once see that it was advantageous only to Napoleon and must be doomed to rejection by the coalition. It called for the allies to abandon their stranglehold on their extremely dangerous and cunning enemy, to unravel their carefully integrated armies, to give up large tracts of strategically important territory, to place themselves behind geographical obstacles, and to put themselves once again in the perilous situation of being destroyed in isolation, one by one. All the heavy sacrifices of the past seven years would have been thrown away in exchange for a few minor provinces, which would fall into their hands anyway – together with much, much more – if they could only stick together long enough to see the job through.

Spain, which the French had no hope of controlling anyway, had great relevance to the Leipzig situation. The longer the French had to maintain an army there to oppose the Duke of Wellington's advance into southern France, the fewer resources Napoleon could concentrate against the allies in Germany.

After this discussion, Meerveldt was escorted through the front lines and went to Kaiser Franz in Rötha. The Kaiser made it clear at once that he would only discuss Meerveldt's conversation with Napoleon in the presence of his allies. When the Tsar and the Prussian king arrived they quickly recognised the implications behind Napoleon's ploy and made it plain that they would not even answer his offer.

This left Napoleon with only two courses of action: to surrender, or to run for Erfurt and then the Rhine. Surrender was obviously out of the question, which only left flight.

During 18 October many Saxon and Württemberg troops deserted to the allies. Though their tactical impact was minimal, the political consequences were immense: the Confederation of the Rhine had fallen apart.

On the evening of 18 October, Napoleon finally bowed to the inevitable and ordered a withdrawal towards Erfurt. He had been given the battle he so dearly desired, at the spot of his own choosing; his defeat was comprehensive.

There was now one big problem – there was only one bridge for the entire French army to use to escape their vengeful enemies.

Marcellin de Marbot (a source to be used with caution it is true) wrote his account of the drama that was now played out.

> Of course, all these obstacles could have been overcome, had the ditches, minor streams and particularly the Pleisse, the Parthe and – especially – the Elster, which received many tributaries around the town, been provided in good time with an adequate number of wide bridges. The material to build these essential bridges was available in abundance in Leipzig and its suburbs and surrounding villages. And there had been plenty of time and plenty of labour available to build them since we had taken up position at Leipzig. Even on the 17th much could have been done.
>
> Despite this, astoundingly, absolutely nothing had been done in this direction. In a convergence of unfortunate circumstances and irresponsible negligence and omissions by the responsible authorities, no attention had been given to this eminently important aspect.
>
> Nothing can conceal this monstrous fact. Among all the documents that have been preserved for us on this famous battle there is not one, in fact not a single one that could serve as proof that any provision had been made for a retreat if this had been needed.
>
> None of the officers that survived the catastrophe, no historian or any other writer that has described this gigantic battle, has been able to prove that the commanders of this army ordered such preparations, or even thought about the building of such crossing points or of the preservation of existing bridges.
>
> In fact, it is only General Pelet – a great admirer of Napoleon – who, some fifteen years after the battle, wrote that the Commissary General Odier (also Commissary of the Imperial Guard) repeatedly assured him during the morning planning conference (he does not say which day) that he was present when Napoleon ordered a general of the general staff to consider the building of bridges and gave him the responsibility for this task.
>
> General Pelet does not mention the name of the general concerned, but it would be very interesting and important to learn who it was.
>
> In other places, Napoleon's secretary, M. Fain, wrote in his

memoirs that the Emperor had ordered the building of new crossing points in order to ease the crossing of these wide swamps.

I do not know how history will judge the truth of these late claims, but even if we accept their veracity, there are some historians who think that Napoleon should not have placed this vital task in the hands of just a single officer of the general staff, but should have ordered the chief of the general staff to require that all corps commanders ensure that adequate crossing points were built in their sectors in case a retreat should become necessary.

But these are criticisms that are easily said and are not placed at the right doorsteps. They do not alter the fact that no one bothered about the matter. The real cause of this omission is attributable to a situation that was then known only to a few insiders. It was as follows.

The chief of the general staff was Marshal Prince Berthier, who had not left the Emperor's side since the famous campaign in Italy in 1796. He was a very talented man, industrious and reliable in his work, but who – despite this – often had to suffer under Napoleon's outbursts of rage. He had developed such a fear of the Emperor's moods that he finally decided that he would allow it to become a completely one-way relationship. He would never take an initiative, never ask a question, merely execute the written orders which were passed to him.

This system, which maintained the relationship between master and servant, was most harmful to the well-being of the army, for regardless of the genius and industry of the Emperor, it was just impossible for him to see and to attend to everything. His massive workload dictated that certain things would be forgotten and not attended to.

In accordance with this state of affairs, Marshal Berthier had developed a stereotyped answer to the repeated requests from the various corps commanders to order the construction of supplementary bridges that he received in the last few days: 'The Emperor has not yet ordered anything to be done.'

It was notorious that you could not move him from this standpoint. And so, when the Emperor gave the order for the withdrawal to the Saale on the road through Weissenfels on the night of the 18th–19th, only the few existing crossings over the many watercourses were available.

So the imperial camels were forced to try to pass through the eye of a single needle, and that with the allies baying at their heels. To make matters even worse, this single bridge was blown up prematurely, trapping thousands on the wrong side of the river system.

French losses will never be known, but are estimated at about eighty thousand; 325 guns were also taken. The allies lost about sixty-one thousand, the Russians bearing the heaviest casualties. Of these, Bernadotte's Swedes lost 178 officers and men, killed, wounded and missing; eloquent testimony to their involvement – or lack of – in this monumental battle.

Joachim Murat, Napoleon's brother-in-law, left the army after this cataclysmic battle 'to defend his threatened kingdom of Naples' – and to open up clandestine communications with the enemy.

The consequences of this bloodiest battle of the Napoleonic wars were immense. Napoleon was thrown out of Germany, France was invaded on New Year's Day in 1814 and the Emperor abdicated on March 1814. But still more European blood was to be spilled before this abdication.

As a direct result of the battle of Leipzig, Prussia took her place in the first rank of European powers, soon to rise even further as the Prussian Empire. Austria regained her lost eminence and Tsar Alexander became celebrated as the saviour of Europe.

On 10 November 1813 the Duke of Wellington again defeated Marshal Soult at the battle of the Nivelle, and on 13 December he won the battle of Bayonne (second battle of the Nive). Southern France was being wrested from Napoleon's forces and a strange phenomenon was observed. Instead of rising in revolt against the invaders, the French peasants were happily selling them fodder and supplies! This was because Wellington insisted on paying market prices with cash, instead of 'requisitioning' by force as had become the norm with the French army.

In Mainz, in early November 1813, new, generous peace proposals were sent to the Emperor by Metternich. France was to keep her natural borders; the Pyrenees, the Alps and the Rhine. These proposals were interpreted by Napoleon as a sign of Austrian weakness (he was already hard at work in Paris conscripting new young hordes) and he ignored them, proposing instead a new peace conference at Mannheim. This was another, serious, error.

But now there was a new problem – the British refused to agree to France keeping Belgium and thus control of the mouths of the Scheldt. Metternich's all too generous peace plan was vetoed.

JOACHIM MURAT

10

1814: Flashes of Genius, ~Thoughts of Suicide~

*B*ACK IN PARIS, NAPOLEON, on 19 December, sought support for renewed conscription and more war efforts from the Senate and the Legislative Assembly. But by now even these poodles of his own creation had had enough of his relentless ambition, and the accompanying commercial stagnation and rivers of blood that still flowed out of France.

He received grudging permission to do what was necessary, but on 29 December the deputies of the Legislative Assembly effectively denied him a vote of confidence. The French people would henceforth fight only in defence of their own homeland, they told him; by implication, foreign conquest was henceforth unacceptable. They also requested that he grant a charter guaranteeing the citizens' political and civil liberties. His response was in character: he dissolved the Legislative Assembly.

'What are you within the Constitution?' he hissed, 'Nothing! The throne – that is the Constitution. Everything resides within the throne.'

And on 1 January 1814, as Blücher's Prussians poured into France (to Napoleon's complete surprise) across the middle Rhine at Kaub in the middle of an unusually harsh frosty spell, he cried: 'I am one of those men who triumphs or dies. France needs me more than I need France!' This was hollow bombast from a totalitarian dictator who had completely lost touch with the sentiments of his own country and the realities of the world around him.

He could no longer impose his will on all of Europe as in the good old days of the Glory Years. He could have negotiated an acceptable peace; instead he swept the offer contemptuously from the table, hell-bent on his own *Götterdämmerung*. He was living in the past.

The Austrians had already invaded Switzerland in mid-December and turned for Belfort; the other allied armies were pushing into the Low Countries and closing up to the Rhine. Napoleon had utterly underestimated the resilience and steely resolve of the allied coalition; this time they really meant business.

The French government made Herculean efforts to build the defences of their country. On 4 January Napoleon declared a *levée en masse* in the eastern Departments. The young conscripts, responding to patriotic appeals from the Empress, became known as *les Marie-Louises*, and marched off, half-trained, half-clothed, half-fed, to fight and die like veterans in many cases.

In southern Italy, Joachim Murat, King of Naples by Napoleon's grace and favour, and his queen, Marie-Caroline, the Emperor's loving sister, were in treacherous contact with the Austrians and British and had been since mid-1813.

The French tactical situation deteriorated; Napoleon decided to leave Paris to take direct command of the war from his bungling marshals, Macdonald, Marmont, Mortier, Ney and Victor. In Paris he again installed Marie-Louise as regent ('She is wiser than all my ministers'), but felt, correctly, that she needed a reliable military adviser. In particular, this military adviser was to concentrate on the defence of Paris.

QUEEN MARIE-CAROLINE

So, whom did Napoleon select for this critically important post?

None other than that failed King of Spain and proven military nincompoop, whom he had ordered thrown into house arrest on his return to France in 1813 – his brother Joseph! These letters of the Emperor's throw light on his true relationship with his elder brother.

TO JOSEPH NAPOLEON, KING OF SPAIN.[*]

July 1813.

I have thought proper to appoint Marshal the Duke of Dalmatia my Lieutenant-General, in chief command of my armies in Spain and in the Pyrenees. Make over the command to him. I desire you personally will remain, according to circumstances, at Burgos, Vitoria, San Sebastian, Pamplona, or Bayonne, until I further inform you of my intentions. You will put your Guards, and all armed Spaniards, under the command of the Duke of Dalmatia; and I desire you will not concern yourself in any way with the affairs of my army.

How Joseph's self-respect could stomach this insult is a mystery. But more – and worse – was yet to come. Joseph finally left Spain and fled to France. Napoleon dogged his every move from Saxony:

TO GENERAL SAVARY, DUKE OF ROVIGO, MINISTER OF POLICE.[†]

Dresden, 20 July 1813.

I think I have informed you of my positive intention that the King of Spain shall not go to Paris, nor even near it. He is to stay at Mortfontaine. If he were to come to Paris, or to Saint-Cloud, you would take measures to have him arrested, and he must not be left in ignorance of that. My intention is, that no one belonging to my household, no high dignitary, none of my ministers, no President of any section of the Council of State, nor President of the Senate shall see him; and that, in fact, he is to remain in the most complete incognito, until I arrive. He may only receive his wife, Madame, his own family, a few of his intimate friends among the Spaniards, and Roerderer – but that without attracting any remark. As you will have seen by the English newspapers, the misfortunes in Spain are all the greater, because of their absurdity. That is England's own opinion of

---

[*] *Correspondance* CDLII.

[†] *Correspondance* CDLXIX.

them. But there is no disgrace to the army. The army in Spain had a general too little, and a King too much. *When I look at it closely, I cannot help seeing that the fault is mine.** If, as it occurred to me to do, just as I was leaving Paris, I had sent the Duke of Dalmatia back to Valladolid, to take up the command, this would not have happened. Of course, you must not allow anything to be printed about the Prince; but yet it is necessary he should know this is my opinion and should not be able to deceive himself upon the subject.

So there we have it; the fault was all Joseph's.

Yet now, when this deep national crisis demanded the best talents in all the right places, Napoleon chose to place his incompetent brother at the head of territorial defence. Nepotism had blinded his reasoning; there is no other possible explanation.

~ General Bonaparte Rides Again ~

The 1814 campaign shows us the Emperor at his astounding best – in the famous Nine Days Campaign – and at his incredible worst as he then marched away from Paris, leaving it at the mercy of three allied armies and leading directly to his defeat, first abdication and the reinstallation of the Bourbons.

Following some mawkishly sentimental amateur melodramatics in the Salon of the Marshals in the Tuileries on 23 January, in which he committed his wife and son to the protection of eight hundred weeping officers of the National Guard, Napoleon left Paris in the early hours of 25 January for the field.

Four days later, with the Imperial Guard under Ney's command, he threw Blücher's Russo-Prussians out of Brienne. Blücher had his revenge on 1 February at La Rothière and prepared to thrust at Paris along the Marne.

But the allies had seemingly forgotten the lessons of 1813 and the Trachenberg Plan completely. Their movements were poorly co-ordinated, and Blücher threw all caution to the winds and all co-operation with his allies out of the window, so obsessed was he with the destruction of Napoleon and the capture of Paris.

At this point, nearly forty thousand of the shakily new French army had deserted since it crossed the Rhine; the old master's magic was waning. One veteran from the republican past, however, an old opponent of the Emperor, was of great enough spirit to come forward and offer his services in this moment of crisis: Lazare Carnot, sixty-one-year-old organiser of the salvation

---

* My emphasis.

of France in the period 1792–3. He was entrusted with the defence of the strategically important city of Antwerp, which he defended stoutly until the war ended.

On 12 January, Napoleon penned the following note to King Joseph: 'No preparations are to be made for abandoning Paris; if necessary we must be buried under its ruins.'

On 8 February he wrote to Joseph:

> If, owing to circumstances that I cannot foresee, I should move to the Loire, I would not leave the Empress and my son far from me, because whatever happened they would be seized and taken to Vienna . . .
>
> If news should come of a lost battle and my death, you would receive it before my ministers. Send the Empress and the King of Rome to Rambouillet . . . Never let the Empress or the King of Rome fall into the hands of the enemy. I feel that I would rather my son were strangled, than see him brought up in Vienna as an Austrian prince.

Truly paternal sentiments!

On 16 March he was again to send such instructions to his brother Joseph; clearly *l'aiglon* was lucky to enjoy the brief lifespan that he did. With fathers like these . . .

The Nine Days Campaign

In the field, Napoleon was at his best. Recognising Blücher's error in allowing his forces to string out too much, the Emperor pounced on General Nikolas Dimitrievich Olsufiev's isolated IX Corps at Champeaubert on 10 February and effectively destroyed it.

Next day he struck again at Montmirail, this time at the overextended corps of von Yorck and the Russians under Baron Fabien Gottlieb Wilhelmovich Osten-Sacken and Tallisin.

In great elation, he wrote optimistically to King Joseph:

> My brother, it is eight o'clock and before turning in I send you these two lines to inform you that today's work has been decisive. The enemy's Army of Silesia no longer exists; I have completely routed it. We have captured all its guns and baggage and taken thousands, perhaps seven thousand; they are coming in every minute. There

are five to six thousand of the enemy on the field. All this was effected by only one half of the Old Guard engaged . . . Our loss is slight. The infantry of my Guard, my dragoons, my horse grenadiers, performed miracles.

This battle was a masterpiece; the Emperor was justly proud. He had watched, waited and struck when Sacken ignored von Yorck's warnings of allowing himself to become separated.

Napoleon had the Old and Young Guard and VI Corps, some twenty-five thousand men against thirty-two thousand Prussians and Russians. French casualties were some 2,100 killed and wounded. The Prussians lost under nine hundred men; the Russians 2,500 (including a thousand prisoners), seventeen guns and six colours.

On 12 February he followed up his beaten prey and struck them again at Château-Thierry. Two days later, at Vauchamps, he was again victorious, over General Ferdinand Heinrich von Kleist's II Prussian Corps and the battered 9th Division and the X Russians Corps under Olsufiev and Piotr Mikhailovich Kapsevich respectively. With eleven thousand men, the Emperor defeated twenty-one thousand of the enemy, causing 3,350 casualties and taking six guns and a Prussian colour.

In his triumphant letter to Joseph, Napoleon wrote:

> I left Château-Thierry at three this morning just as the enemy were arriving at its gates. I marched straight on the enemy who formed line near the village of Vauchamps. I defeated them, took eight thousand prisoners, three guns and ten colours, and drove them to Etoges. I did not lose three hundred killed and wounded. This splendid result was due to the fact that the enemy had no cavalry, while I had six thousand or eight thousand horse, with which I constantly menaced them and outflanked them, while all the time I crushed them with grape from a hundred guns.

The imperial mathematics were a little fuzzy, but they read well.

Blücher was paying dearly for his over-hasty and sloppy advance. After this defeat, he fell into deep depression and his Chief of Staff, von Gneisenau, effectively took over command and ran the show quite successfully. Contrast this to what happened if Napoleon absented himself from his headquarters: everything froze.

On 17 February Napoleon won yet another, minor, victory at Nangis against General Count Ludwig Adolf Petrovich von Wittgenstein of the Army of Bohemia, and next day he completed this tour de force with yet another victory over the Austro-Württembergers, at Montereau on the Seine.

This amazing string of victories re-established the Emperor's reputation as a fearsome field commander when he could oversee and manage all his forces directly. Allied stupidity also played straight into his hands.

The Austrians were on the ropes. Napoleon commented gleefully:

> At last Prince Schwarzenberg shows signs of life. He has sent an officer to ask for an armistice. It would not be easy to match such cowardice! He has consistently refused, in the most insulting terms, to discuss any suspension of hostilities. The dogs! At the first reverse they are on their knees! . . . I shall grant them no armistice until my soil is purged of their presence.

This rejection of what was to be the final chance of a negotiated peace was a mistake.

But already on 21 February reality had re-entered his mind; Napoleon was making overtures of peace to Kaiser Franz of Austria, suggesting that a treaty

Napoleon at Montereau

be signed immediately on the basis of the terms laid down by him at Frankfurt – that France should retain her natural borders of the Rhine, the Alps and the Pyrenees.

Again, events on the battlefield moved faster than the pens of the diplomats.

~ After the Lord Mayor's Show ~

The brilliant outburst had come to an end; the Emperor's reputation as a fearsome battlefield commander probably never stood higher.

But by now, the allies were closing in on Paris, and the boot was soon to be on the other foot. There was a lull in major actions in the theatre of war as both sides gathered breath and revised their plans.

On 26 and 27 February Marshal Oudinot was caught with his forces divided by the river Aube at Bar-sur-Aube and defeated by the Bavarians of Schwarzenberg's Army of Bohemia under General Karl Philipp von Wrede.

Then on 3 March, a stroke of luck for the allies: General Friedrich Wilhelm von Bülow's III Corps closed up to Soissons on the river Aisne, an important crossing point. The garrison commander, General Jean-Claude Moreau, capitulated and was allowed to march off to rejoin the Grande Armée with his two Polish infantry regiments and a battery of guns. Field Marshal von Blücher now quickly crossed the river at Soissons to unite with von Bülow and Wintzingerode and to escape Napoleon, who was hard on his heels.

Napoleon was livid with rage; on 4 March he wrote to General Henri-Jacques Clarke about his plans for Moreau:

> I am sending orders to the Minister of War to have him arrested, tried by a court martial and shot. He must be shot in the middle of the Place de Grève, and the execution must be made a conspicuous event. Five generals can be appointed to try him. Without any doubt the enemy's army was lost and would have been destroyed. As it is, I shall have to manoeuvre and lose much time throwing bridges.

Moreau was in fact court-martialled and imprisoned at Abbaye, then events saved him. He served under Napoleon in the Hundred Days as commandant of the Department of l'Indre.

The tables now began to turn against the French. Marshal Macdonald was defeated at Laubressel (aka La Guillotière or Troyes) on 3 and 4 March, and the Emperor himself was beaten at Craonne on 7 March by Wintzingerode.

Napoleon fell back, but Marmont was convincingly beaten by Blücher on 9 and 10 March at Laon, 140 kilometres north-east of Paris. Napoleon's arrival saved a total defeat.

Joseph, meanwhile, was becoming increasingly close to Marie-Louise; word of it reached Napoleon from his omniscient agents. He reacted quickly: 'Do not be too familiar with the king, keep him at a distance, never allow him into your private apartments . . . do not let him play the part of adviser.'

Next day he found time to write again on the topic: 'You trust Joseph too much . . . Everyone has betrayed me . . . The king has an evil reputation with women.'

Some days later he wrote again: 'The king is intriguing; he will be the first to suffer; he is a pygmy, swelling with his own importance.'

Perhaps it ran in the family.

Rumbles of events in Paris trickled through to him. On 14 March, at Reims, he found time to reply to a report of events in Paris from Savary, his Minister of Police:

> You send me no news of what is going on in Paris. A Regency is being discussed, an address, and a thousand foolish and ridiculous intrigues that proceed at best from the brain of a fool like Miot.* These people have forgotten that I cut Gordian knots after the fashion of Alexander. They had better remember that I am today the same man that I was at Wagram and at Austerlitz; that I will permit no intrigues in the State; that there is no authority but mine, and that in the case of urgent events it is the [Empress] Regent in whom my trust reposes.

That same day, he wrote to his brother, Joseph:

> I have received your letter of 12 March. The National Guard of Paris is a part of the people of France, and so long as I live I intend to be master everywhere in France . . . Today as at Austerlitz, I am the master. I imagine that they can perceive the difference between the time of Lafayette when the mob was sovereign and today when it is I.

Swaggering overconfidence can be seen in every line.

Two days later he wrote to Joseph again:

> I am going to manoeuvre in such a way that you may be several days without news from me. Should the enemy advance on Paris with

---

* André-François Miot de Melito, a career diplomat and head of Joseph's household.

forces so large as to make resistance impossible, send the Regent and my son in the direction of the Loire.* Do not leave my son's side, and remember that I would sooner know him in the Seine than in the hands of the enemies of France. The fate of Astyanax[†] as prisoner of the Greeks has always seemed to me to be the most unhappy in history.

With such a trivial mention did Napoleon deal with the topics of the fate of his capital and of his son, and this to a man who must be counted as an unreliable ally at best, but to whom he had entrusted the fates of both. This was the second time that the Emperor had issued contingency plans for the murder of his son and heir. The King of Rome – once the apple of his eye – was suddenly expendable.

His letter written in Reims on 17 March gives us a glimpse into the reasoning behind his Delphic thrust to the east:

> There are three possible courses: one is to march on Arcis,[‡] thirteen leagues; we could get there tomorrow, the 18th; this is the boldest [course] and the result is incalculable; to move on Sézanne;[§] the third would be to march straight on Meaux[¶] by the highroad.
>
> The third is the safest because it takes us rapidly towards Paris, but is also the one that has no moral effect, and leaves everything to the chance of a great battle. But, if the enemy have seventy or eighty thousand men, such a battle would be a fearful risk, while if we move towards Troyes and strike in at their rear, while the Duke of Tarento[**] retreats, disputing every position, we may stand a much better chance.

Later that same day, he has made his decision: 'Tomorrow, before dawn, I shall start for Arcis-sur-Aube; I shall be there the day after tomorrow at noon, to strike the enemy's rear.'

We now encounter a cardinal error in the Emperor's strategic thinking. Realising that he was now totally outnumbered, he decided to mount a

---

* i.e. to the south.

† Astyanax was the son of the Trojan hero Hector and his wife Andromache; he was killed by Neoptolemus, son of Achilles, at the fall of Troy.

‡ Arcis-sur-Aube, in Schwarzenberg's rear.

§ South-south-west of Reims and aiming at Schwarzenberg's advanced guard.

¶ On the Marne, just north-east of Paris.

** Marshal Macdonald, confronting Schwarzenberg south-east of Paris.

stunning manoeuvre to throw his enemies into confusion and save the day. He would march to the south-east and throw himself across Schwarzenberg's lines of communication *à la* Ulm campaign of 1805.

This was 'the boldest course and the result is incalculable'. In other words, it was a desperate gamble. There is just one snag in such a plan; if a commander places his army across his enemy's lines of communication, the enemy is then, usually, on the commander's.

The next question which arises is: which party should be most concerned at the resultant situation? The answer in this case was: Napoleon, but he would not yet recognise it.

On 20 March Marshal Augereau allowed himself to be pushed out of Lyons down to the south – many said too easily.

The next major action was on 20 and 21 March at Arcis-sur-Aube, where Napoleon attacked the Austrians; Schwarzenberg's caution let Napoleon escape without too much damage. French losses were some four thousand men and three guns; the allies lost about three thousand. The Emperor now fell back to the east, along the upper Marne, calling Marmont and Mortier away from Paris to join him at St Dizier on that river. He also awaited Macdonald to come up with troops taken from the eastern fortresses.

In his note of 20 March, he wrote: 'During the fight at Arcis-sur-Aube I did all I could to meet with a glorious end defending the soil of our country inch by inch. I exposed myself continuously. Bullets rained all around me; my clothes were full of them; but not one touched me. I am condemned to live!'

It seems that the Emperor was already in suicidal mood; hardly the state of mind of one in control of his affairs.

Napoleon scribbled a hasty note to Marie-Louise on the morning of 23 March, in which he told her that he had decided to head north for the river Marne, in order to draw the enemy's armies back from Paris by attacking their lines of communication. He also called out the Garde Nationale in the eastern region and issued proclamations calling for a general uprising against the invaders. But while the peasantry were willing to take revenge for the depredations of Russian, Austrian and Prussian marauders, they were not willing to leave their homes and start a full-scale guerrilla war.

By rushing off to the east, the Emperor had made a serious error in this vital game of strategic poker. The game now appeared to have become blind man's buff, and Napoleon was wearing the blindfold. Believing that the enemy was too timid to attack Paris, and yet not knowing the exact strengths and locations of their armies due to lack of cavalry for intelligence gathering, he had ended up in a cul-de-sac.

Off rode the courier with the note for the Empress, only to be captured by the Prussians, who delivered the dispatches that he carried to Marshal Blücher. Having read the personal letter, Blücher had it copied, then gallantly forwarded it on to Marie-Louise.

Hearing the contents of the Emperor's note to Marie-Louise in his turn, the Tsar convinced the cautious Schwarzenberg to join with Blücher's Army of Silesia on the lower Marne, in an advance on the enemy capital, leaving only one corps (Wintzingerode's) to watch Napoleon, who was so soon to become irrelevant.

Another factor affecting the decision to advance on Paris as opposed to withdrawing south-east from Troyes was that Lord Castlereagh, visiting the Tsar's headquarters, threatened to end all British subsidies unless Schwarzenberg took the offensive. Money talks.

It was at about this point that Talleyrand, with a sure eye to the future, sent a letter to Alexander, also urging an advance on Paris: 'You venture nothing, when you may safely venture everything – venture once more.'

CHARLES-MAURICE DE TALLEYRAND

It was rapidly becoming a case of the Emperor being the only one in tune.

On 25 March Marshals Marmont and Mortier clashed with the corps of the Crown Prince of Württemberg at Fère-Champenoise, 112 kilometres east of Paris, and were defeated.

Incredibly, Napoleon pushed on to the east. This indicates again that the Emperor had lost his grip on reality. But his relative inaction over the next few days is equally hard to understand. For four whole days Napoleon moved around St Dizier on the upper Marne, some 205 kilometres east of Paris, waiting for something to turn up. Where was his cavalry? Where was the vital information about his enemies? Why the uncharacteristic inactivity? He had knowingly removed himself from the decisive centre of the campaign and thus fatally weakened the defence of his capital, the current abode of his wife and the irreplaceable heir to his dynasty. Napoleon had lost the plot, or the allies had stolen it from him; either way, the outcome was the same.

On 26 March Napoleon clashed with Wintzingerode's corps near St Dizier and realised that he was dealing only with a rearguard and not the main body of the Army of Bohemia. He called a council of war – the first of his life – with Marshals Berthier, Macdonald and Ney.

Not for the first time in his life, Napoleon did not know what to do. It was a telling moment.

During this singular council, Macdonald said: 'Were I in your place, I would go into Lorraine and Alsace, collect the garrisons from there, and wage war to the knife upon the enemy's rear, cutting off their communications, intercepting their convoys and reinforcements. They would be compelled to retreat, and you would be supported by our strongholds.'

Napoleon replied: 'I have already ordered General Durutte to collect ten thousand men round Metz, but before deciding upon anything I must have reports.'

Obviously Macdonald's time in Spain had generated in him great respect for guerrilla warfare, but conditions in Alsace-Lorraine were not comparable to those in Catalonia; the allies – despite certain limited outbreaks of looting and atrocities – had not yet engendered the general deep hatred which the Spanish felt for the French in their country.

They decided – now – that they should make for Paris in a desperate race to get there before the allies, but there was a snag: due to the exhausted state of the country on the direct road from St Dizier through Sézanne to the capital, it was decided to detour deep to the south, via Troyes, Sens and Fontainebleau. Neither Napoleon nor his closest advisers could accept that the war was already over; that all their frantic efforts were to be in vain.

So, not only were they well behind the enemy in this desperate race, they also had further to march. In fact, Napoleon's men marched 180 kilometres in seven days; twenty-seven kilometres a day; a remarkable achievement.

It was not until about midnight on 30–1 March, when the battle for Paris had been lost and Marmont had negotiated a capitulation with the allies, that Napoleon – now at the coaching house La Cour de France, only a few kilometres from the city, met the defeated troops of Generals Belliard and Curial, trudging away from his capital.

On 3 April Napoleon addressed the Old Guard: 'The enemy have stolen three marches on us, and have entered Paris . . .' The allies had stolen nothing; they had found three marches 'lying in the gutter – and had picked them up and used them'. Napoleon had been completely fooled – or, more correctly, he had made a complete fool of himself.

In reality, his prospects of winning on the field of battle in 1814 were extremely slim; right from the start, the wolf packs were closing in for the kill. He would have been much better advised to make a sober assessment of the state of France (and the state of his army and its commanders) and go to the negotiating table to save what he could. But, with his immense ego, each of the stunning tactical victories of his Nine Days Campaign merely encouraged him to throw away the pen and to grasp his sword ever more tightly, thrusting his head further and further into the allies' noose.

As General Charles-François Dumouriez (an ex-French general who had defected to the Austrians in early 1793 and who was at this point in England in exile) wrote in a letter to a friend on 7 April 1814:

> Let us turn to Buonaparte. For a month past all his plans have been marked by a folly. He had it in his power to make the most sure and lasting peace, keeping all his authority over France, and even afterwards carrying out all the plans of his insatiable ambition, if only he would defer them, seeing that his conscience is too elastic to bid him regard treaties of peace as sacred, whenever the allies had departed, or should have disarmed or be in conflict – a contingency easy to foresee by a Machiavellian more profound and less atrocious than he is.

~ The First Abdication ~

The capital was now alive with white cockades and cries of *Vive le roi!* The mob has a notoriously short memory.

Charles-Maurice de Talleyrand, the consummate diplomat, was at once in discussions with the allied monarchs as to the political future of France; on 4

April the rump of the French Senate voted for Napoleon's deposition and elected Talleyrand as head of the government. Napoleon's reaction was characteristic: 'I am one of those men who triumphs or dies. France needs me more than I need France!'

But on 4 April, Marshals Lefebvre, Macdonald, Ney and Oudinot broached to him the subject of his possible abdication. Napoleon angrily rejected the idea, saying that he had decided to march on Paris again; the army would obey him.

Ney responded: 'No it will not. The army will obey its commanders!'

Napoleon had come to the end of his magic; not even the marshals, whom he had made among the richest men in the land, would dance to his tune any longer.

He penned his abdication.

> The allied powers having proclaimed that the Emperor Napoleon is the sole obstacle to the re-establishment of peace in Europe, he, faithful to his oath, declares that he is ready to descend from the throne, to quit France, and even to relinquish life, for the good of his country; which is inseparable from the rights of his Son, from those of the Regency in the person of the Empress, and from the maintenance of the laws of the Empire.
>
> Done at our Palace of Fontainebleau, 4 April 1814. NAPOLEON.

On 5 April Marshal Marmont took his VI Corps of some twenty thousand men, the strongest left in the French army, over to the enemy. The game was finally over.

As soon as the stunning reality of the changed situation dawned on them, a steady and growing stream of officers made their way into Paris to swear allegiance to the new government. When some accused Marmont of being a traitor, Talleyrand replied dryly: 'His watch only went a little faster than the others.' Realistically, not even twenty thousand men more could have saved Napoleon at this point.

Wellington's victory at Toulouse on 10 April was the last major action of the campaign. Alexandre Berthier also abandoned Napoleon a few days later; his absence from Napoleon's side in 1815 was critical.

Napoleon's initial abdication was rejected by the allies; they demanded an unconditional renouncement of the throne. They were now holding all the cards. Alexander proposed the following deal: Napoleon was to retain the title of Emperor, with sovereignty over the island of Elba and a small army and navy; France would pay him a pension of six million francs annually; Marie-Louise and her heirs were to receive the Duchies of Parma, Piacenza and Guastalla; A pension of two million francs from France was to be paid to the ex-Empress and other members of the Bonaparte family.

The desired unconditional act of abdication was signed by the Emperor on 11 April. Next day, in the depths of despair, betrayed by so many of his creatures, Napoleon attempted suicide, using a poisonous powder consisting of belladonna, opium and white hellebore that he had carried since the autumn of 1812 in Russia. Apparently it had lost its potency; for four hours he suffered stomach pains and vomiting, but then it was over. He was 'condemned to live'.

There followed, on 20 April, the legendary farewell of the Emperor to his weeping Guard at Fontainebleau. The Emperor's speech went thus:

> All Europe has armed against me. France herself has deserted me, and chosen another dynasty. I might, with my soldiers, have maintained a civil war for years – but it would have rendered France unhappy. Be faithful to the new sovereign whom your country has chosen. Do not lament my fate: I shall always be happy while I know that you are so. I could have died – nothing was easier – but I will always follow the path of honour. I will record with my pen the deeds we have done together.
>
> I cannot embrace you all, but I embrace your general.

Napoleon at Fontainebleau

Bring hither the eagle.

Beloved eagle! May the kisses I bestow on you long resound in the hearts of the brave.

Farewell my children – Farewell my brave companions – surround me once more – farewell!

There followed a nine-day coach trip to Fréjus, the short sea voyage on the frigate HMS *Undaunted* and his disembarkation on Elba on 4 May at Porto Ferrajo. He was in his new home – for the time being at least.

Marie-Louise had left Paris on 29 March to go to Blois. She would never see Napoleon again. In the convoy which accompanied her were fifteen wagons full of coin and plate from the Tuileries. From here, she and the King of Rome went to Orléans. On 12 April 1813 they were taken from there by Princes Esterhazy and Wenzel Liechtenstein, on Metternich's orders, to be transported to Rambouillet, out of Napoleon's reach.

Four days later, her father arrived there, to convince her to accompany him to Austria. She complied.

By all accounts, Marie-Louise was seduced by her escort, Graf Adam Albert von Neipperg on 24 September 1814 in the guesthouse Zur Goldener Sonne, near Küssnacht, on Lake Lucerne.

In 1821 they would be married.

NAPOLEON FRANÇOIS JOSEPH CHARLES

～ 1815: One Last Throw – The Hundred Days ～

$\mathcal{T}$HE FRENCH IN 1814 WERE humbled; embarrassed before all of Europe, over whom they had so recently lorded it so mightily. Truculence and a repressed longing for revenge characterised their mood.

'Louis the Unavoidable' (Louis XVIII) was invited to return to the throne of France by the Senate, on condition that the existing bicameral system be regarded as fixed and unchangeable, and that those who had acquired properties from the Church or the émigré nobility would retain them. All titles and decorations conferred by Napoleon were also to be respected.

Louis agreed. He returned to France, where he was politely received. He then proceeded to date his first official act as having been given 'in the twentieth year of our reign'; shivers ran down thousands of French spines. The nation feared that it could already hear the painful sounds of the political and social clocks being turned back to 1797. Even in the short time that he was on the throne of post-Napoleonic France, he and his horde of returned Bourbon émigrés and churchmen managed to make themselves incredibly unpopular with the majority of the common people and with the army.

But many of Napoleon's marshals and generals swallowed their pride and prejudice to take service under Louis; a few refused, and some left France, becoming the new émigrés. The proud and famous old regiments (including much of the Guard) which had trampled most of Europe under their boots were disbanded or renumbered on 12 May 1814. Economic measures had thrown thousands of old soldiers onto the streets as the army was reduced to peace establishment. The allies quickly repatriated over 150,000 French prisoners of war who were swelling the ranks of the idle, hungry and discontented. Louis remained on the throne largely with the implicit support of the armies of the victorious powers.

In many respects, these victorious powers treated defeated France with kid gloves in 1814. Apart from certain items repossessed from the Louvre by the Prussians, they left intact the bombastic pictures of Napoleon's legendary victories and triumphs. They did not touch the monuments which commemorated their own defeats, and Wellington even dissuaded Marshal Blücher from blowing up the Pont de Jena in the city. Generous conduct indeed, especially when compared to Napoleon's spiteful destruction in 1806 of the monument to Frederick the Great's victory over the French and imperials at Rossbach in 1757.

In the eyes of the diehard Bonapartists (a not inconsiderable share of the enfranchised populace) Louis could do nothing right. The Legion of Honour was retained as a decoration, but when it was awarded to ex-émigrés, these Bonapartist discontents at once grumbled that its value was being debased.

In an attempt to avoid alienating Napoleon's adherents, Louis appointed very few ex-émigrés to high military rank; within a month of his return to the throne, the ex-émigrés were as discontent as their imperial opponents. Like the modern British Conservative party, the French nation was so deeply divided within itself that the office of leader was a poison chalice.

But perhaps Louis's most important error was that he did not pay Napoleon the annual pension agreed to in the treaty; the Emperor of Elba was running short of cash. News of this popular unrest in France trickled through to him on his island realm in a regular stream.

Even before autumn 1814 had closed, he had sent some two hundred of his guardsmen back to France to spy on events and to prepare the ground for his return. The dispossessed Emperor had primed them to say that he would return to save his nation 'when the violets bloomed again'. He was soon referred to by them as 'Corporal Violet' and his disciples wore small violet ribbons.

So Napoleon, Emperor of Elba, was sitting on a dwindling sack of money and boredom was gnawing at him. He eagerly read and assessed all items of news which reached him, not only concerning domestic French politics but also of the progress of the allies' negotiations in Vienna. He heard of the continued discord and disunity, the plots, the wheeling and dealing at the Congress.

Finally, he called a family meeting; the topic for discussion was: should he return to discontented France and snatch his throne back from the unpopular Bourbon?

With the agreement of those members of his family that had accompanied him to Elba, the inveterate gambler decided to stake all on one last card. He would return to France with his 'Elba Guard' of six hundred men and two guns and attempt to seize power again.

This decision was what the Germans call *Wünschdenken* or deluding oneself into believing that one's decision is right because it seems so attractive. It was true that Louis XVIII was very unpopular and that there was widespread discontent among the population. But Napoleon and his family had underestimated the resolve of the squabbling allies to keep him away from power in Europe at all costs, not only on an international level, but even within France. It was at this latter, modest target that Napoleon aimed his initial – and all subsequent – public utterances.

They sailed on 20 February 1815 on the brig *Inconstant* and several other small vessels. Luckily they evaded the French naval patrols of the area. On 1 March they landed – unopposed – at Cannes, on the eastern Riviera, the Côte d'Azur.

The Congress of Vienna, designed to reconstruct Europe in the victors' mould, had opened on 25 September 1814; the victors, each with their own secret agenda, were still haggling over details of who was to receive what and under which conditions, when, on 7 March 1815, news reached Vienna that Napoleon had left Elba. By this time they had agreed that Russia should take most of Poland, Prussia was to receive the western part of Saxony and certain Rhenish provinces, Austria was to recover the Tyrol, and much of northern Italy, and Genoa, Nice and the Savoy were to go to Sardinia.

Napoleon's return from Elba

Napoleon marched by the modern Route 85, avoiding the pro-royalist lowland areas, through the Alpes de Provence, via Grasse, Digne and Cerenon. The road was so bad that the two guns had to be abandoned. Everywhere he was met either with joy or indifference – there was no open hostility. After five days they reached Gap, still high in the hills; this was in Dauphiny, the 'cradle of the Revolution', and his popular receptions became ever warmer, his retinue increased.

The incredible tale of his personal bravery when confronted by the 5th Infantry Regiment at La Mure, just outside Grenoble, is proof that he had resolved to do or die. The royalist troops blocked the road as Napoleon approached at the head of his small force. The atmosphere was charged; he dismounted and advanced alone.

'Soldiers of the 5th! Don't you know me? If there is one among you who wishes to kill his Emperor, he can do so. Here I am!' And he threw open his grey greatcoat.

The 5th dissolved into riotous joy, surging round him and screaming the inevitable *Vive l'Empereur!*

It was business as usual again.

General Jean-Gabriel Marchand, commandant of Grenoble, had locked the gates of the city and refused to permit Napoleon's force of some two thousand men to enter; two guns were brought up and the gates blown in. There was no fighting and Marchand was allowed to leave.

Here Napoleon published his first proclamation to the army of the campaign, doubtless well prepared in advance on Elba:

> Soldiers! We have not been beaten. Two men, raised from our ranks, betrayed our laurels, their country, their prince, their benefactor.*In my exile I have heard your voice. I have arrived once more among you, despite all obstacles, and all perils. We ought to forget that we have been masters of the world; but we ought never to suffer foreign interference in our affairs. Who dares pretend to be masters over us? Take again the eagles which you followed at Ulm, at Austerlitz, at Jena, at Montmirail. Come and range yourselves under the banners of your old chief. Victory will march at the *pas de charge*. The eagle, with the national colours, shall fly from steeple to steeple – on to the towers of Notre-Dame! In your old age, surrounded and honoured by your fellow citizens, you will be heard with respect when you recount your great deeds. You shall then say with pride –

---

* This is a reference to Augereau and Marmont.

> I also was one of that great army which entered twice within the walls of Vienna, which took Rome, Berlin and Madrid and Moscow – and which delivered Paris from the stain printed on it by domestic treason, and the occupation of strangers.

Stirring stuff! Appealing directly to the jingoism of the Glory Years, with a dash of Shakespeare's *Henry V* thrown in for good measure. Just how many who had fought at Ulm and ridden roughshod over Germany had survived the crushing debacle of Napoleon's Moscow madness, his Leipzig lunacy and the grinding winter campaign of 1814 has never been calculated, but the total cannot be very high. But such speeches are written not to provoke deep thought, but to stir gut feelings.

The intended import of this proclamation was to define his aim to all of Europe, and that that aim was to be master of France alone – no empire, no *cordon sanitaire*, no territorial claims, no vassal states, no more lightning invasions or crushing victories.

But, if this were truly the case, why the challenge to 'foreign interference', to those who dare 'pretend to be masters over us?' Why the references to the 'eagles of Ulm, Austerlitz, Jena and Montmirail'? Why, and in which direction, was the proud Victory to 'march at the *pas de charge*'? Why would the 'eagles fly from steeple to steeple'? Whose steeples? Why the mentions of foreign conquests Vienna, Rome, Berlin, Madrid and Moscow?

Any reader of this message must surely have heard the echoes of the stirring bulletins which followed so many destructions of armies and the fall of kingdoms and capitals. With so much humiliation and bloodshed so fresh in their minds, even the quarrelling allies in Vienna could clearly read between these lines. And none of them liked what they read. This was no mere claim to domestic power; it was a direct threat to them all. 'I'm back! Get ready to run!'

After all the years of bombast in the bulletins, it was just not possible for Napoleon to write anything in clear text. He could write only in bullets and salvoes. And regardless of the possible real aims of the Emperor, that is exactly what the allies read into this example. So this proclamation – possibly genuinely intended to publicise Napoleon's modest aim of helping only his betrayed, depressed, suffering countrymen to stand upright again – put the cat among the nervous international royal pigeons.

And now Europe was treated to the spectacle of unified international military action, the like of which we have so recently witnessed in Iraq: forcible regime change. In 1815, as in 2003, the mad dog dictator had made himself unacceptable to the international community. In 1815, as in 2003, a large section of the dictator's populace remained loyal to him.

It must also be mentioned that Napoleon had submitted himself successfully to an election process in 1815. But this acceptance by France was less generous than in 1804; most eligible voters abstained and instead of four million (or so) yes votes, there were only 1.5 million, against 4,802 who voted no. About 3.5 million of the eligible voters had abstained. They didn't care too much who sat on the throne.

But to return to early March 1815, Napoleon left Grenoble with seven thousand men on 9 March and pushed on to Lyons, the garrison of which city joined him; he stayed here from 10 to 13 March, organising his campaign and issuing proclamations.

Marshal Ney, now serving the Bourbons as a member of the Council of War, was sent off south to stop Napoleon. Somewhat dramatically, he promised his king that he would bring him to Paris 'in an iron cage'. He did not have a hope.

Napoleon, hearing of his approach, sent him a note to 'fly the tricolour and join me at Châlons'. One whiff of the old magic and Ney rolled over; he and his corps joined Napoleon's ranks on 17 March at Auxerre.

The imperial snowball was gathering impetus; the country was again split into Bourbonist and Bonapartist camps. Sensing that another catastrophe was looming, that his very court was falling to pieces under his feet, Louis XVIII left Paris for Ghent. On 20 March 1815 Napoleon re-entered the capital unopposed.

He acted quickly to suppress the various royalist rebellions; first, in May, the Vendée was pacified, then General Clausel was sent south to restore Napoleonic order. Within a few weeks Antibes, Marseilles and Toulon were back under the tricolour.

But while these internal distractions were being dealt with, greater storm clouds were gathering on France's borders. The Congress of Vienna issued the following declaration:

> By breaking the convention which established him in Elba, Buonaparte destroys the only legal title on which his existence depended. By appearing again in France, with projects of confusion and disorder, he has deprived himself of the protection of the law, and manifested to the universe that there can be neither peace nor truce with him.
>
> The powers consequently declare that Napoleon Buonaparte has placed himself without the pale of civil and social relations, and that, as an enemy and disturber of the tranquillity of the world, he has rendered himself liable to public vengeance.

Napoleon was now an outlaw – though it could, of course, be argued that Louis XVIII had also broken the convention by withholding Napoleon's pension.

Meanwhile, back in Paris, Napoleon was courting the organs of government, not with bullets and salvoes, but with honeyed words. Addressing the Council of State on 26 March, he stated: 'I have renounced the notion of a great empire of which I have only laid down the bases. Henceforth the welfare and the consolidation of the French Empire will be the object of all my thoughts.' So, he was no longer the totalitarian dictator that they all knew from the past; he would work within the constitution and wanted to rule only the 'French Empire'. The problem was that this key concept had been left undefined.

On 22 April the Acte Additionnel aux Constitutions de l'Empire (drawn up by Napoleon himself) was signed by the government and by Napoleon. It was only an interim document, but it guaranteed legislative liberties and individual rights such as freedom of speech, equality before the law, the right of individual petition and the freedom of religion. The act also allowed a hereditary monarch, hereditary peers, a house of representatives elected by popular vote at least once every five years, taxes levied by the whole legislature, judges who could not be removed from office by the monarch or government and trial by jury.

The staunch old republican, Carnot, opposed the Additional Act to Napoleon's face: 'Your Additional Act has not pleased the people; it will not meet with acceptance. Promise me that you will amend it. I must tell you the truth, for your and our salvation hangs upon your tolerance.'

Napoleon, unused to contradiction, made a gesture of annoyance.

Carnot responded: 'This word alarms you, sire? Yes, you must show tolerance in the face of the national will.'

'The foe is at the gate,' replied Napoleon. 'First of all, help to chase him away; then I shall have time to occupy myself with your liberal panaceas.'

Despite this rejection, Carnot served him as Minister of the Interior.

The big question was – would Napoleon respect this call for tolerance once his iron grip had tightened on power once again? Or would the carefully concealed, familiar spots then suddenly reappear? Would the sheathed claws slide quietly forth again to shred democracy? Opinion was split, but eventually the legislation was passed, and Napoleon certainly seemed to have been somewhat humbled by the experiences of his fall from power and exile.

The workload of recreating and expanding the army and rallying the divided nation to his cause was immense; the pressure on him was intense and his old energy seemed to be on the wane. The absence of Marie-Louise and his son also depressed him, particularly when a letter fell into his hands, exposing details of her liaison with Neipperg.

Of the marshals, Augereau, Berthier, Gouvion Saint-Cyr, Macdonald, Oudinot and Victor had stayed with the Bourbons. Alexandre Berthier, the legendary Siamese twin of his staff work, was to fall to his death on 1 June 1815 from a window in a building in the Bavarian city of Bamberg. The circumstances of his death remain unclear. He was to be sorely missed during the Hundred Days, but it is doubtful that his absence alone was responsible for the disastrous outcome of the campaign.

Having betrayed Napoleon in 1814, Joachim Murat suddenly decided in early 1815 to attack the Austrians. The first clash of his erratic adventure took place at Modena on 4 April, when he seized the river crossing. But his star was to wane very rapidly; on 3 May his army was decisively beaten at Tolentino. Murat fled to France, anxious to place his sabre at the Emperor's service again. Napoleon refused to see him. He eventually returned to Naples, was arrested, tried, condemned and shot – in somewhat indecent haste – on 13 October of the year.

Among those who returned to serve Napoleon in this last desperate adventure were Brune, Clausel, Decaen, Drouot, Exelmans, Gérard, Grouchy, Kellermann, Masséna, Milhaud, Mouton, Rapp, Reille, Soult and Suchet. Ney was to appear at the eleventh hour, just in time to help snatch defeat from the indecisive bloody mess of Waterloo. Macdonald and Mortier had accompanied the king to Belgium, but Mortier returned to serve his old comrade – until laid low by sciatica.

Marshal Soult, Duke of Dalmatia, had been picked by the Emperor to be his Chief of Staff for the Hundred Days; the task of filling the legendary boots of Alexandre Berthier was to prove beyond him. But then could anyone else have done any better?

And still the well-oiled wheels of Napoleonic nepotism turned. This was a critical period, but, incredibly, out of military oblivion popped the Emperor's brother, ex-king Jerome, clown of the 1809 campaign in Germany and drastic failure of the doomed 1812 adventure. This time he was given command only of a division, the 6th in Reille's II Corps, but it beggars belief that Napoleon would let him anywhere near his army.

Military manpower – the cannon fodder – was also in short supply; Louis XVIII had drastically reduced the army, as much in the interests of his exchequer as anything else, and had removed all vestiges of its proud imperial past. Napoleon issued an appeal to retired veterans – not only in France itself, but also in Belgium and his old German annexations – to return to the colours, promising them immediate retirement once he had achieved the essential victory. Military matters, however, had been relegated to secondary importance for a year, and this neglect, together with the disbanding of the regiments, were not to be reversed in an instant.

On 9 March the tricolour replaced the fleur-de-lis; four days later the Emperor decreed the dissolution of the Royal Guard and the re-creation of the old regiments of the Old Guard and the Fusiliers. On 28 March six regiments each of Tirailleurs and Voltigeurs were also raised. On this same day the 1st and 2nd battalions of all regiments of the line were mobilised, the 3rd battalions formed the depots and officer cadres for the 4th and 5th battalions were established. On 3 April five foreign regiments were raised: 1st (Italian), 2nd (Swiss), 3rd (Polish), 4th (German) and 5th (Belgian). Eight days later the 6th (Spanish and Portuguese), 7th (Irish) and 8th (Italian) joined them. The old imperial regimental numbers 1er–11e were reissued to the ninety royal regiments of the line. The three existing royal foreign regiments were disbanded on 2 May and their men distributed among the new regiments according to their nationality.

ANDRÉ MASSÉNA

The navy, in no shape to act effectively at sea, was converted on 3 May into a coastal defence force of some sixty thousand men. All Departments were ordered to raise National Guard units to garrison the fortresses in their areas.

With all this frantic activity, the French army on 15 June fielded the Guard, with four regiments each of Grenadiers and Chasseurs, eight regiments each of Tirailleurs and Voltigeurs, the Grenadiers and Chasseurs à Cheval, a troop of Mamelukes, 1st and 2nd Chevaux-Légers and artillery; the line infantry, which possessed ninety regiments, the light now at fifteen, each with four battalions; the cavalry, which consisted of two regiments of carabiniers, twelve of cuirassiers, twenty of dragoons, six of Chevaux-Légers, fifteen of Chasseurs à Cheval and seven of hussars; finally, an additional 393 battalions of National Guards, twelve battalions of *fédérés* and various other legions and veteran companies.

He had called for 250,000 men to take up arms; just over sixty thousand responded.

On 1 June 1815 there took place the Convocation of the Champ de Mai in Paris, a solemn ceremony celebrating the remarriage of the French people to their Emperor, to be crowned by their public acceptance of the Additional Act to the Constitutions of the Empire. Present were fifty thousand troops and a great multitude of the public, as well as the imperial family and all the great and good of the Church and government.

For this ceremony, which lasted for hours, Napoleon appeared, not in his famous green coat, but in a faintly ridiculous white silk costume with a hat embellished with great, nodding ostrich-feather plumes.

After celebrating high mass, there was a long address from the government to Napoleon and a response (both in treacly, patriotic terms), followed by the presentation of eagles to the regiments and a march past of the fifty thousand soldiers and sailors. Again, though, the Emperor was fired a warning shot; the spokesman for the two new chambers of government stated in the address: 'Trusting your pledges, the Deputies will sagaciously revise our laws and harmonise them with the Constitution.' This implied that they wanted more than just this Additional Act.

The resultant cheers from the assembled multitude were enthusiastic from the military, but noticeably moderate from the civilians. As one eyewitness said: 'They were not the cheers of Austerlitz and Wagram. The Emperor could not fail to notice it.'

For the Waterloo campaign Napoleon concentrated the Imperial Guard, five corps and four cavalry corps, totalling 135,000 men and three hundred guns under his hand. In all, there were 375,000 men under arms in France.

Masséna commanded at Toulon, Suchet on the Swiss frontier.

Happily for the allies, due to the haggling in Vienna none of them had placed their armies on peace establishment; they were thus able to respond quickly to the sudden emergence of the genie from his bottle. By the end of May, there were almost half a million allied troops at various points along the borders of France.

There were three hundred thousand Austrians (already partly returned to their peace time garrisons), 236,000 Prussians (of these thirty thousand between Aachen, Wesel and Koblenz), 225,000 Russians (in Silesia), 150,000 men of the minor German states, and fifty thousand each from Britain and the Netherlands. The Russian and Austrian main bodies were far off to the east and would take weeks to close up to the border. With Murat now out of the way, the Austrian troops in Italy were free to act against France.

LOUIS-GABRIEL SUCHET

Napoleon's actions were dictated by the military moves of his enemies. They had declared him to be an outlaw; diplomacy had no role to play in this drama; war was inevitable and he was the target.

Those allied formations most ready to take the field, and closest to Paris, were the Anglo-Netherlands army under Wellington around the area of Ostend–Brussels, and Blücher's Prussians (now counting 120,000) away to the east around Liège, but spreading forwards to Charleroi. Once again, even these allies, who were in relatively close proximity to one another, offered a critical weakness to Napoleon: their lines of communication lay at 90 degrees to one another. Wellington's led northwards to Brussels and then Antwerp; Blücher's ran away to the east.

Lines of communication are the arteries, the umbilical cords along which armies receive supplies, instructions, reinforcements. It was – and is – conventional wisdom that a field army must retain contact with its lines of communication; if defeated, an army usually falls back along these lines. If Napoleon struck at the interface between the Prussians and Wellington's allies, and managed to inflict defeats on them, it could be assumed that each would recoil along its lines of communication, thus drawing away from one another, each step making their individual destruction more certain.

If forced into military action – as he was – Napoleon's obvious choice was to strike at the two armies in Belgium before they could combine, and to destroy them one after the other. This quick double victory might well destroy the will of the coalition to continue the war. To wait until the allies completed their military preparations would be disastrous, even though he still needed weeks to complete his own. His decision to make a rapid, preemptive strike was, militarily, correct. Once again, the French army enjoyed unified command and internal lines of communication; it was the 'same old style', as the Duke of Wellington would say. It remained to be seen if it would end in the same old way.

For Napoleon the stakes could not have been higher; this was his last chance. He had made overtures of peace to the allies directly after resuming power, but these had all been ignored; the allies had been through all this in 1813 and 1814, and this time would save their breath for the more serious work.

It is not the aim of this book to offer another, inadequate, description of the battle of Waterloo; other authors have done this very well, many times. Here we will merely comment on Napoleon's decisions in the field and their correctness.

On 11 June, Napoleon left Paris to 'measure myself against Wellington'.

Three days later he reviewed his army at Beaumont and delivered the following address:

NAPOLEON, BY THE GRACE OF GOD AND THE CONSTITUTIONS OF THE EMPIRE, EMPEROR OF THE FRENCH ETC., TO THE GRANDE ARMÉE.

At the Imperial Headquarters, Avesnes, 14 June 1815.
Soldiers! This day is the anniversary of Marengo and of Friedland, which twice decided the destiny of Europe. Then, as after Austerlitz, as after Wagram, we were too generous! We believed in the protestations and in the oaths of princes, whom we left on their thrones. Now, however, leagued together, they aim at the independence, and the most sacred rights of France. They have commenced the most unjust of aggressions. Let us, then, march to meet them. Are they and we no longer the same men?

Soldiers! At Jena, against these same Prussians, now so arrogant, you were one to three, and at Montmirail one to six!

Let those amongst you who have been captives to the English, describe the nature of their prison ships and the frightful miseries they endured.

The Saxons, the Belgians, the Hanoverians, the soldiers of the Confederation of the Rhine, lament that they are compelled to use their arms in the cause of the princes, the enemies of justice and of the rights of all nations. They know that this coalition is insatiable! After having devoured twelve million Poles, twelve million Italians, one million Saxons, and six million Belgians, it now wishes to devour the states of the second rank in Germany.

Madmen! one moment of prosperity has bewildered them. The oppression and humiliation of the French people are beyond their power. If they enter France they will find their grave.

Soldiers! We have forced marches to make, battles to fight, dangers to encounter; but, with firmness, victory will be ours. The rights, the honour, and the happiness of the country will be recovered!

For every Frenchman who has a heart, the moment is now arrived to conquer or to perish!
NAPOLEON
The Marshal Duke of Dalmatia,
Major General.

With these bullets and salvoes, the morale of the French troops rose as in the good old days. But this high morale was now extremely brittle, as events were to show.

~ Ligny or Quatre-Bras? ~

It should be noted that imperial headquarters was at Avesnes, north of Paris, on the modern Route N2. To enemy spies – and commanders – this might be interpreted as a thrust to turn Wellington's western flank. This position had been carefully chosen to create just this impression. When the time came, Napoleon would strike, very fast, north-east through Charleroi at Sombreffe, at the interface between the allies.

In the weeks prior to the battle of Waterloo, the Emperor had ordered a clampdown on the press and complete cessation of postal traffic over France's northern borders; this security blanket worked extremely well. But even if the allies had little reliable knowledge of actual enemy dispositions, it was simple enough to work out that he would attack in the north first, split the allies, defeat them in detail and make a dash to grab Brussels – the same old game.

Another advantage was presented to Napoleon, in that Wellington and Blücher decided to concentrate their armies very close to his Armée du Nord, always a hazardous choice.

There was further confirmation of the real French aims, when the commander of the advanced guard of their right-hand column deserted to the Prussians on 15 June, complete with his staff. This was General Louis-Auguste-Victor de Bourmont, commander of the 14th Division, IV Corps. Bourmont had refused to sign the Additional Act. Although his defection brought the allies no new intelligence, it did confirm their impression of enemy intentions.

Early on 15 June the French cavalry of the Imperial Guard, the III and IV Corps, fell upon the unwittingly overextended Prussians of von Ziethen's I Corps at Fleurus, Gilly and Gosselies in southern Belgium, causing some 1,200 casualties for the loss of half that number of their own. Surprise was almost complete. The effective attack on Ziethen's I Corps on 15 June made French morale soar; this job was going to be a repeat of the 1806 walkover; the Prussians had learned nothing.

But Ziethen should not be portrayed as a fool; he had reported enemy activity on his immediate front to headquarters the day before, but had been left in his extended posture. The I Prussian corps was not destroyed; it fell back to Ligny where it joined the II Corps; there were now eighty thousand Prussians concentrated under Marshal Prince Blücher. In Brussels, Wellington received news of this attack from the Prussians at about 1330 hours on the afternoon of the 15th. By 1400 hours orders had been dispatched to his troops to concentrate at the agreed positions. To maintain calm in Brussels, the news was kept secret and Wellington and his officers attended the Duchess of Richmond's ball as previously arranged.

The next step in Napoleon's master plan was the rapid twin assault on the allied and Prussian armies in their separated locations. Speed and determination were of the essence if it were to succeed. The Emperor decided – correctly – to strike his main blow at the Prussians to exploit his initial success and their confusion. He would take charge of this thrust, with the Guard, the III and IV Corps, part of the I and VI Corps and the bulk of the four cavalry corps. With him he had seventy battalions, seventy-four squadrons and 248 guns.

Marshal Ney had rejoined Napoleon on 15 June and was given command of the secondary force designed to seize the strategically vital crossroads of Quatre-Bras, on the road connecting the allies. His aim was to take the crossing and to ward off any interference from Wellington in the struggle at Ligny. For this purpose he commanded d'Erlon's I Corps, Reille's II Corps and part of the Guard Cavalry (later replaced by part of the III Cavalry Corps); thirty-two battalions, fifty-eight squadrons, fifty-eight guns, some forty thousand men. Napoleon retained eighty thousand men and 248 guns for the assault on Ligny.

But herein lie two imperial errors. Napoleon underestimated the combat value of the Prussian army – perhaps lingering lovingly on the fields of Jena and Auerstädt. This underestimation led him to give Ney too many of the available assets, leaving himself with too few for his own task on 16 June. Napoleon's second error was to send no orders to Mouton's VI Corps of nine thousand men and thirty-eight guns to move on Ligny, and so even fewer forces were available than planned.

Was this overconfidence? He had said: 'My presence on the battlefield is worth ten thousand men.' Wellington put it at forty thousand. Maybe in June 1815 Napoleon's presence was overvalued.

Ney's thrust on Quatre-Bras on 15 June failed to take the vital crossroads, as General Perponcher, with Prince von Weimar's brigade of the 2nd Dutch-Belgian Division – some four thousand men – just happened to be there at midday and hung on grimly in the face of all French assaults, ignoring orders to fall back to the north-west on Enghien. This was because Wellington assumed that the French would strike at his western flank – a completely wrong assumption. Perponcher's disobedience probably saved the entire 1815 campaign.

On 16 June, the small allied defence force, hastily cobbled together under the Prince of Orange, managed to hold off Ney's late and poorly co-ordinated attacks – they began only at two o'clock – and reinforcements began to pour down the road from Brussels as Wellington finally realised his error.

The action at Ligny on 16 June was also late, beginning only at half past two in the afternoon. The men of the new Prussian army proved their worth there (even if their commanders had fallen short of the expected standard) and gave Napoleon and his men a nasty shock. Their resistance was so fierce that he was forced to send orders to Ney that day to send him d'Erlon's I Corps. Obediently, the corps set off south-east towards Ligny.

Ney, fired up by the Emperor to redeem himself with a convincing victory, felt that he had to call d'Erlon back from his trek to Ligny to help him break the allies, who were now reinforced to some thirty thousand men. With d'Erlon's corps in limbo, Ney was now outnumbered on the field. All his assaults failed. He called d'Erlon back.

The legendary wanderings of Count d'Erlon's I Corps between these two battlefields, a hapless football kicked one way and then another by the orders of the Emperor and Marshal Ney, meant that it played very little part in either battle. Indeed, at one point in the day, the appearance of its advanced guard to the north-west of Ligny caused a halt in Napoleon's assaults as it was feared that the unidentified troops might be hostile. So near yet so far.

Ney, then, made no headway at Quatre-Bras; the allies lost about 5,600 men there, and the French about 4,400. Wellington pulled his forces back north to the Mont St-Jean position.

The battle of Ligny on 16 June saw the Prussians badly mauled, but still unbowed, having lost between twelve and twenty thousand men (there is much confusion as to exact numbers) and some twenty-one guns. Blücher had been rolled on by his horse and was incapable of action for some hours. His Chief of Staff, von Gneisenau, openly assumed the command that he usually exercised behind the scenes. The Prussian retreat was well ordered. The French had lost about twelve to fifteen thousand men.

Ney, however, seemed to be in an operational coma; he mounted no pursuit of Wellington's men on 17 July, and it was not until the Emperor himself rode over and found, to his rage, Ney's men lounging about at the side of the road, that they were rudely galvanised into action. It was two o'clock in the afternoon when they finally marched off. The whole day had been lost.

The courageous decision of the Prussian command on 16 June, after their defeat at Ligny, to abandon their lines of communication and march north through Tilly to join Wellington, leaving only one corps to keep contact with the French at Wavre, was to encompass Napoleon's doom.

Despite these setbacks, the Emperor's plan seemed to be working quite well. Having dealt the Prussians – as he hoped – a crushing blow, his aim was now to drive them away to the east (along their lines of communication) and to deal with Wellington himself.

Marshal Grouchy commanded the French left wing. He was a cavalryman with little experience of using infantry. He was now sent after Blücher with over twenty-eight thousand men. The Prussians were able to mount such a clever cavalry screen to cover their movements that Grouchy's men lost them for some vital hours. When the French cavalry scouts picked up traces of the Prussians, they had in fact found only General Baron von Thielmann's III Corps (twenty-seven thousand men) in the direction of Wavre, some twenty kilometres east of Waterloo. Once again, Napoleon had left himself short of assets by allocating too many to Grouchy, whose task was only to hold off any Prussians and then return to join Napoleon's right wing.

The main body of Napoleon's army now hurried across to the main road to Brussels, to join Ney, crash through Wellington's army and take Brussels.

~ Waterloo ~

During 17 June, Wellington's allied army concentrated on his pre-selected position along the ridge across the main road to Brussels from Quatre-Bras, south of the forest of Soignies and near the village of Waterloo. That day and night it rained heavily, soaking the heavy clay of the battlefield.

On 18 June 1815 Wellington had about sixty-eight thousand men, some twenty-four thousand of whom were British. He had 288 guns and was opposed by the Emperor with seventy-two thousand men and 246 guns. Blücher's fifty-two thousand Prussians would be sorely needed.

Wellington is justly famed for husbanding his assets – he never had enough to be able to squander them as liberally as Napoleon so often did – and for making best use of the ground in all his battles. All his skills would be tested to the limit here today; they were not found to be wanting.

Apologists for Napoleon find many excuses for his defeat: the weather; his piles or stomach ulcers; his bladder infection, his acromegaly, his incompetent or treacherous subordinates, his premature ageing. No one has ever thought to find excuses for any of his opponents for their defeats at his hands on the grounds of their health or age. Melas, defeated by Desaix at Marengo in 1800, was seventy-one years old at the time of that battle, and he had defeated Napoleon (then thirty-one) prior to Desaix's appearance on the field. Kutusov was sixty-eight years of age when he chased Napoleon out of Russia, and the state of his health was so poor that he died on 28 April 1813.

In 1815 Napoleon was forty-six years old, as was Wellington.

What of Wellington's state of health on this fateful day? Were all his staff and commanders paragons of military virtue whose performances were faultless? Was incompetence the monopoly of the Emperor's subordinates? Hardly.

At dawn on the 18 June 1815 the opposing armies were already drawn up, not more than 1,500 metres apart in some places. At about half past eight, some of the senior members of Napoleon's entourage remarked that the fight would be hard and that Wellington was a good general; the Emperor's response was typical: 'There are ninety chances in our favour and not ten against us. I tell you Wellington is a bad general, the English are bad soldiers; we will settle the matter by lunchtime!'

To which Marshal Soult (remembering the repeated drubbings Wellington had inflicted on him in 1813 and 1814) replied: 'I sincerely hope so!'

It was to be a very late lunch.

THE DUKE OF WELLINGTON

Why the delay? Napoleon was always acutely aware of the value of time in military affairs, so why did he waste precious hours? Did he waste them? Or was a delay in launching the assault dictated by factors outside even his control?

According to Napoleon's own subsequent account of events, the saturated state of the ground on the French side of the field made off-road movement of artillery and cavalry impracticable in the early morning. As this account was written well after the battle, and as it is the nature of the writers of memoirs to remember to advantage, a pinch of salt may well be added here.

In any event, much time was lost while the Emperor, accompanied by his numerous, glittering staff, rode along the front of his army, bathing in the frenzies of adulation which such appearances inevitably provoked. Was this the big ego again? His track record suggests it.

But was his ego of such dimensions that it would cause him to ignore all his well-proven awareness of the importance of time and speed? After all, among his many famous words we find:

'Ask of me anything but time!'

'Ground I may recover, time never!'

'I may lose ground, but I will never lose a minute.'

Was it overconfidence? As far as he knew at that point, Marshal Grouchy was pushing the Prussians away from the battlefield, but would soon turn to join him. Why not indulge in another display of hero worship?

Whatever the real reason for the late start to the battle of Waterloo, this same mud did not prevent the weary Prussians from marching throughout the day to break in on Napoleon's right flank and to bring about the most famous defeat in western military history.

Soult's order for the battle (dictated by Napoleon at about eleven o'clock) is of interest: 'As soon as the army is in position, about one o'clock, when the Emperor gives the order to Marshal Ney, the attack will commence for capturing the village of Mont St-Jean, where the crossroads are. Count d'Erlon will open the attack.' So, from early in the day, the start of the assault was set for one o'clock. It is also remarkable that Marshal Ney, despite his mistakes of the last three days, had not been removed from command.

Prior to the commencement of the French bombardment just before midday, a cavalry patrol from General Count von Bülow's IV Prussian Corps reached the village of Smohain, on the eastern edge of the battlefield, and passed on the information that Blücher's battered army was marching to join the allies. The message was taken by Lieutenant Lindsey of the 10th Hussars to Wellington's command post.

When firing commenced at Waterloo, Marshal Grouchy was about to take breakfast with his staff at Walhain, convinced that the Prussian main body was at Wavre. They heard the gunfire. It was suggested that they should at once return to the west, but Grouchy insisted on adhering to his orders – and has been condemned for it ever since.

At about 1130 hours, troops from Prince Jerome's division advanced to attack Hougoumont, the fortified chateau on the western end on the battlefield which Wellington had ordered to be occupied. They were engaged by Wellington's artillery; by midday, the artillery engagement was general from both sides. Battle had commenced.

The struggle for Hougoumont – intended by Napoleon to be merely a feint – was to absorb the bulk of Reille's II Corps for most of the day. It was not Napoleon's intention that this feint should become the meat-grinder that it did. The fault for this misinterpretation of intentions must lie with the Emperor; his orders should have been more specific. He also should have ordered the action to be broken off if he saw it going astray.

Shortly after one o'clock some troops were noticed approaching from the east; hoping that they were Grouchy's men, Napoleon sent an orderly officer and some men to confirm their identity. They returned with a captured Prussian officer courier, who informed them that thirty thousand Prussians of von Bülow's IV Corps were close behind him.

Instead of calling off the battle and withdrawing, the Emperor said to Soult: 'This morning we had ninety chances in our favour. Even now we have sixty chances, and only forty against us.' The inveterate gambler had reassessed the odds; the fateful day dragged on, as the allied vice closed ever more tightly about its wilfully immobile prey.

At about half past one, d'Erlon's great infantry assault on La Haye Sainte began, which was shattered by Lord Uxbridge with the cavalry brigades of Ponsonby and Somerset. In typical British cavalry fashion, these horsemen 'galloped at everything', and were destroyed in their turn by a French cavalry counter-attack. Later in the day, at four o'clock, the famous, tragically wasteful charges of the French Imperial Guard cavalry against the British squares took place.

A quotation from a letter written in 1835 by ex-captain Fortune Brack, of the 2nd Chevaux-Légers-Lanciers of the Guard, a participant in the battle of the 18 June, reveals a new aspect of this futile exercise.

Impassioned by our recent success against Ponsonby, and by the forward movement that I had noticed being executed by the Cuirassiers to our right, I exclaimed, 'The English are lost! The position on which they have been thrown back makes it clear. They can only retreat by one narrow road confined between impassable woods. One broken stone on this road and their entire army will be ours! Either their general is the most ignorant of officers, or he has lost his head! The English will realise their situation – there – look – they have uncoupled their guns.' I was ignorant of the fact that the English batteries usually fought uncoupled.

I spoke loudly, and my words were overheard. From the front of our regiment a few officers pushed forward to join our group. The right-hand file of our regimental line followed them; the movement was copied in the squadrons to the left to restore the alignment; and then by the Chasseurs à Cheval of the Guard. This movement, of only a few paces at the right, became more marked [as it passed] to the left. The brigade of the Dragoons and Grenadiers à Cheval, who were awaiting the order to charge at any moment, believed this had been given.

They set off – and we followed!

That is how the charge of the Imperial Guard cavalry took place, over the reason for which so many writers have argued so variously.

So there we have it; the charge of five thousand cavalrymen was a pure accident, which accounts for the fact that it was not supported by infantry or artillery. The French army was out of control.

This imposing mass of horse crested the ridge, filtered through the guns ranged along the crest and were then among the allied infantry squares, each well formed and ready to receive them. The crews of the allied guns, in accordance with Wellington's orders, abandoned them as the French cavalry surged over the crest and took refuge in the nearest of the squares.

The horsemen swirled impotently about the squares, taking well-aimed fire from all sides as they did so. Finally, they turned and rode for their own lines. But, as they cleared the allied gun lines, the crews ran back to their pieces and bade them farewell with another salvo.

But worse was to come; after the first charge was defeated, the cavalry fell back to their start position.

Captain Brack continued:

It was then that Marshal Ney, alone and without a single member of his staff accompanying him, rode along our front and harangued us, calling out to the officers he knew by their names. His face was distracted, and he cried out again and again: 'Frenchmen, let us stand firm! It is here that the keys to our freedom are lying!' I quote him word for word.

Napoleon saw this second movement begin. 'This is a premature movement which may well lead to fatal results! He [Ney] is compromising us as he did at Jena!' he snapped; but it was too late for him to stop this charge. The Emperor was later even to throw Kellermann's III Cavalry Corps into the disaster to try to extract Ney. This was just to present the allies with bigger and better targets.

Siborne, in his *History of the Waterloo Campaign*, describes the scene as follows:

> When the tremendous cavalry force which Ney had thus assembled, moved forward to the attack, the whole space between La Haye Sainte and Hougoumont appeared one moving glittering mass; and as it approached the Anglo-allied position, undulating with the conformation of the ground, it resembled a sea in agitation.
>
> Disorder and confusion, produced by the commingling of corps, and by the scattering fire from the faces of the chequered squares, gradually led to the retreat of parties of horsemen across the ridge: these were followed by broken squadrons, and, at length, the retrograde movement became general. Then the allied dragoons, who had been judiciously kept in readiness to act at the favourable moment, darted forward to complete the disorganisation and overthrow of the now receding waves of the French cavalry.

Captain Brack's account of this amazing phase of this critical battle continues:

> Five times we repeated the charge; but since the conditions remained unchanged, we returned to our position at the rear five times.
>
> There, at 150 paces from the enemy infantry, we were exposed to the most murderous fire. Our men began to lose heart: they were being hit at the same time by bullets from the front and by cannonballs from the flank, and by new projectiles (small shells) which exploded over their heads and fell. These were Shrapnel shells and we had not come against them before.
>
> At last a battery of the Guard was sent over to support us; but

instead of the light artillery, it belonged to the Foot Artillery of the Reserve of 12-pounders. It had the utmost difficulty in moving forward through the mud and only took up position behind us after endless delay. Its first shots were so badly aimed that they blew away a complete troop of our own regiment.

As was said of the British cavalry riding into the jaws of death at Balaclava, 'It is magnificent, but it is not war!'

This extraordinary odyssey continued, as Ney squandered the Emperor's precious heavy cavalry to no avail at all. For some three hours the French cavalry threw themselves at the allied lines; it would have taken Napoleon ten minutes to send an orderly officer to Ney to tell him to stop the slaughter; he did nothing. By five o'clock he no longer had a cavalry reserve left.

Shortly after six o'clock, Marshal Ney finally regained his senses and launched a co-ordinated assault of cavalry, infantry and artillery from Donzelot's 3rd Division, I Corps at La Haye Sainte, whose gallant German garrison had run out of ammunition, and took it.

But it was too late. The Prussians were thrusting deep into Napoleon's right flank. He threw in the Guard; they were initially successful but were then pushed back.

Meanwhile, some common sense seems to have prevailed in the shattered remains of the Guard cavalry, as Captain Brack tells us:

> So a movement to the rear was ordered. We carried this out at ordinary pace and formed up again behind the battery. The Chasseurs à Cheval, Dragoons and Grenadiers à Cheval extended their movement further and took position in echelon a short distance behind and to the left of us.
>
> The English cavalry advanced on and off to follow us, but as soon as they came up with our line they stopped, respecting our Lancers above all – the long lances intimidated them. They were limited to firing their pistols at us before retiring behind their infantry line, which made no move.
>
> Then a voluntary truce was reached between the combatants due to the complete exhaustion of the troops. Half our squadrons dismounted within musket range.
>
> This suspension of arms lasted about three-quarters of an hour, during which we were hoping that the Emperor's genius would change the face of the battle, forming a general, supported and decisive attack – But nothing! Absolutely nothing!
>
> It was then that we changed from participants to spectators of

an incomprehensible drama of which the terrible absurdity was soon recognised, and roundly condemned, by even the least of our simple troopers.

The small plain which we bordered on one side, was as it were, a great circus whose boxes were occupied by the English. Into this bloody arena descended, one after another, poor men destined for death, whose sacrifice was all the easier and quicker since the English, without danger to themselves, were waiting for them at point-blank range.

At first, a few battalions came past our left and presented themselves in column to the English right and its fearless Scots under cover in a wood. When these had been stretched on the ground it was the turn of our Carabinier brigade. This emerged on our right at a gentle trot, crossed the arena alone in column of troops, and rode along all the enemy batteries to attack the English right.

Then Wellington's musketry and batteries awoke together, aiming at the same point, and despite the thunder of their fire, we heard three butcher's cheers. Within a few seconds the Carabiniers had vanished, in death or flight.

Incredible folly! Incredible waste!

To make our grief complete, rumours were running through our ranks: Our right was routed; Grouchy had sold himself to the enemy; Bourmont, Clouet, du Barail and many other officers had deserted. A senior officer of the column that had just attacked the Scots had fallen, hit by a case shot, and two hundred white cockades had spilled from his shako.

When the English retired from their first position they had left proclamations on the field signed by Louis XVIII which promised pardon, amnesty, retention of rank and post.

When there were no more victims to offer for the great sacrifice, when the circus games had come to an end, our attention was drawn to a new spectacle which worthily crowned that day. On the plateau to our right appeared black lines; they came forward, preceded by their guns. They were the Prussians, which had escaped Grouchy!

So the great game was finally over; the Imperial Guard infantry had by this time advanced on Wellington's right and been shattered, thrown back. Plancenoit had been taken by the Prussians. It was the final straw for the French army; they broke and fled the field.

Captain Brack's moving account of that rout continues:

Ah! How can I describe to you the consternation among the Guard cavalry? They cried out for the Emperor, whom they had not seen since their commitment to battle – and they would not see him yet!

The order to retreat was given. How ominous was that retreat – a funeral procession.

Our light cavalry brigade was reduced to two-and-a-half squadrons and commanded by Generals Lefebvre-Desnouettes, Lallemand and Colbert (wounded), retreated slowly and extended its line in order to form a curtain which somewhat concealed our routed army from English observation.

So we marched until we met again on our left what remained of the Old Guard infantry which, with us, formed the extreme rearguard. They were facing to the rear; we halted level with them and turned about too. We numbered at that time one hundred to 150 officers and troopers of the Lancers and Chasseurs à Cheval,

CHARLES LEFEBVRE-DESNOUETTES

exhausted and wretched.

The sun had almost disappeared, and it was nearly dark.

Our three generals came together in front of our line and some officers joined them – I was a member of this group. A powerful assault column of the enemy was marching on the road and was heading for the Foot Guards' square.

Its head had barely appeared on the crest behind which the Foot Guards were standing, when the latter opened fire. This shooting was well enough co-ordinated, but was perhaps premature; and it seemed to me that it would have produced more effect if it had been delivered from closer to the crest and thus as plunging fire. This fire was answered by a rather poor salvo from the enemy, this was followed by a mêlée which was concealed from me by the night and the distance.

General Lefebvre-Desnouettes cried out in the greatest excitement that, 'It is here that we must all die; that no Frenchman could outlive such a horrible day, that we must look for death among this mass of English facing us.'

We tried to calm him down. A discussion began in which we all took part and, strangely enough, the man who maintained his sangfroid – who still thought that we had a tomorrow to look forward to, who talked about making a useful retreat all the way to Paris – was the one man who would instantly lose his life if the Bourbons laid hands on him: General Lallemand.[*] He ignored his own interests in order to consider the general situation, discussing matters coolly and with authority.

Captain Brack has also left us a telling account of the Emperor's state of mind on the night of his last defeat:

After several hours we began to make out a muffled noise to our left. This grew louder, and soon we broke out onto the road at Quatre-Bras. Here we came upon the most crowded, breathless and disordered retreat that I ever saw.

We lined up in battle formation, facing to the rear, our right being close to the Charleroi road. This movement was barely completed, when one of our officers said: 'There is the Emperor!' At once all eyes turned in the direction of the road and there, among a mass of infantry, vehicles, cavalry and wounded, we saw the

---

[*] Lallemand was condemned to death in the 'White Terror', but reprieved, released and went to the United States where he set up a colony of French refugees in Louisiana. He later returned to Paris, where he died on 4 March 1859.

Emperor riding, accompanied by two officers wearing greatcoats just like him and followed by four or five Gendarmes d'élite. This was, I believe, at one o'clock in the morning.

Recognising troops still under discipline, the Emperor came towards us. Never has such a bright moon lit a more horrible night. The moonlight fell full on the face of the Emperor as he stood in front of our ranks.

Never, even during the retreat from Moscow, had I seen a more confused and unhappy expression on that majestic face.

'Who are you?' asked his majesty.

'The Lancers of the Guard.'

'Ah, yes! The Lancers of the Guard! And where is Pire?'

'Sire, we know nothing of him.'

'What, and the 6th Lancers?'

'Sire, we do not know, he was not with us.'

'That's right . . . but Pire?'

'We have no idea,' replied General Colbert.

'But who are you?'

'Sire, I am Colbert, and here are the Lancers of your Guard.'

'Ah, yes . . . and the 6th Lancers? . . . and Pire? Pire?'

One of the generals with him dragged him away, and he disappeared into the night. Our grief knew no bounds.

The French army scattered. So, after such a brilliant beginning, which appeared to offer the Emperor so much, the great adventure crumbled into the defeat of Waterloo.

In popular mythology, peace descended across Europe on 19 June 1815. In fact, fighting went on until 24 September of that year, when the fortresses of Charlemont and Givet finally surrendered to the Prussians.

In Paris, on 19 June cannon fired salutes for the victories of Charleroi, Ligny and Quatre-Bras. On the morning of the 21st, it became known in the capital that Napoleon had returned alone to the Elysée palace; his army was no more.

He was quickly in urgent conference with his senior ministers, anxious to cobble something together from the wreckage of 18 June, when they were told that both Chambers were in permanent session, signifying defiance to the wishes of the Emperor.

Lucien, his brother, urged continued resistance; Napoleon was in a state of vacillation for the entire day. Later that night he called a conference to which the presidents and vice-presidents of both Chambers were admitted.

Maret, Secretary of State, called for severe measures against all royalists. 'Had such been resorted to earlier,' he said, 'one who hears me would not be smiling at the misfortunes of France and Wellington would not be marching on Paris!' This was a reference to Fouché, once again Napoleon's Minister of Police, but deeply involved in treacherous negotiations with the royalists and with Metternich, to such an extent that it was almost public knowledge. But Maret's suggestion was unrealistic; there was no longer any spirit for yet another return to the Glory Years.

The veteran democrat, Marie-Joseph de Lafayette, rose to speak in the Chamber: 'I can see only one man between us and peace; if we rid ourselves of him, peace will be ours for the asking!'

Carnot, Minister of the Interior and veteran defender of the democratic republic, almost wept when Napoleon's abdication was mentioned.

The meeting closed without any decision having been taken.

At the next session, the Chambers voted to demand that Napoleon appear before them to answer their questions; he refused to go – a decision he subsequently regretted.

'I ought to have gone, he later said, 'but I was tired out. I could have dissolved them, but I lacked courage; I am only a man after all. My memories of the Nineteenth Brumaire terrified me.' So, with all the arrogance, pomp and bombast finally stripped away, the Emperor was 'only a man after all'.

The Chambers now summoned the ministers; Napoleon forbade them to go. The Chambers' response was that they would depose him if they did not appear; Napoleon gave way, and sent Lucien with them, to say that he would negotiate with the enemy powers. The response was that he had been declared an outlaw by these powers; they would not negotiate with him. Voices were raised in the Emperor's defence; a call was made to rally round him to drive the barbarians from French soil.

Carnot tried to whip up enthusiasm for continuing the war with Grouchy's men, whom he guesstimated at sixty thousand. Marshal Ney entered the debate in the Chamber:

> Grouchy cannot have more than twenty thousand – at most twenty-five thousand men; and as to Soult – I myself commanded the Guard in the last assault – I did not leave the field until they were exterminated.
>
> Be assured there is but one course – negotiate and recall the Bourbons.
>
> In their return I see nothing but the certainty of being shot as a deserter.
>
> I shall seek all I have henceforth to hope for in America.
> Take you the only course that remains for France.

Lafayette rose again to address the Chamber: 'Have you forgotten where the bones of our sons and our brothers whiten? In Africa, on the Tagus, on the Vistula, amid the snows of Russia. Two million have been the victims of this one man who wanted to fight all Europe! Enough!'

A deputation from the Chambers went to Napoleon and presented to him the only viable course – his second abdication.

Next day, the two Chambers were in session and the topic of Napoleon's abdication was about to be put to the vote, when Fouché entered and read out the following proclamation:

> TO THE FRENCH PEOPLE.
>
> Frenchmen! In commencing war for the maintenance of the national independence, I relied on the union of all wills and all authorities. I had reason to hope for success, and I braved all the declarations of the powers against me. Circumstances appear to be changed. I offer myself as a sacrifice to the hatred of the enemies of France. May they prove sincere in their declarations, and to have aimed only at me!
>
> My political life is ended; and I proclaim my son, Napoleon II, Emperor of the French. Unite for the public safety, if you would remain an independent nation.
>
> Done at the Palace of the Elysée.
> 22 June 1815 – NAPOLEON.

On 8 October 1815 Napoleon was to write: 'The men of 1815 were not the men of 1792. The generals were afraid of everything. I needed someone to lead the Guard; had Bessières or Lannes been there I should not have been defeated. Soult did not have a good staff.'

Epilogue

Napoleon hoped to go to the United States to spend the rest of his life as a private citizen; fate – in the shape of HMS *Bellerophon*, which blocked the entrance to Rochefort harbour – decided otherwise.

To the Prince Regent of Great Britain he addressed this note:

> *14 July, Ile d'Aix.*
>
> Your Royal Highness,
> Exposed to the factions which distract my country and to the enmity of the greatest powers of Europe, I have closed my political career, and I come, like Themistocles, to throw myself upon the hospitality of the British people. I put myself under the protection of their laws, and beg Your Royal Highness, as the most powerful, the most persistent, and the most generous of my enemies, to grant me this protection.
> Napoleon.

He boarded the British warship on 15 July, having decided to throw himself on the mercy of the British government; his most implacable foes. The considered response of the British government was to exile him to the remotest spot that they could think of – St Helena, in the south Atlantic.

Napoleon and his small party were transferred to HMS *Northumberland* for the trip to St Helena. There he spent six miserable years, writing his memoirs and fighting with the governor of the island, General Sir Hudson Lowe.

Napoleon died on St Helena on 5 May 1821. Controversy rages still as to the exact manner of his death, the validity of the investigations into it and the real identity of the body that was returned to France in 1840 and reinterred, in great pomp, in Les Invalides, in Paris.

Appendix A
French Exports 1805-1815 (Millions of Francs)

	1805–6	1807	1808	1809
Confederation of the Rhine	126,132	99,465	115,618	115,618
Spain	65,311	65,614	33,202	33,907
NL	56,546	45,123	80,217	66,667
Kingdom of Italy	40,059	40,607	44,310	43,840
USA	45,923	43,159	1,825	1,384
Swiss Confederation	26,673	23,577	23,331	18,815
Denmark	30,806	35,556	2,652	28,435
Italy **	20,172	17,121	11,648	14,721
Hanseatic Cities	24,119	3,376	5,797	3,717
Turkey ***	5,826	2,445	3,954	6,633
Prussia	10,718	1,207	1,122	2,005
Portugal	9,280	6,946	91	–
Russia	1,588	382	802	4,030
Austria	1,436	505	591	785
Britain	–	–	–	–
Totals	464,589	385,083	325,160	340,557

* included in the Hanseatic Cities' figures.
** The rest of the Italian peninsula: Etruria (until 1809), Naples, Rome, Sardinia and other minor states.
*** Ottoman Empire and Barbary.

The states are arranged in diminishing volumes of trade, except for Britain, which is purposely placed at the base of the chart.

This very informative chart shows that the bulk of France's exports through this period went into the Confederation of the Rhine; how much of this was re-exported to other states is not recorded.

The volume of licensed trade exports to Britain from 1810 to 1815 shows that she had the potential to be one of France's major customers. The volumes of smuggled goods – in both directions – can only be guessed at. The loss of such a major export market in the years 1805–10 surely hurt the French and British economies.

Source: Geoffrey Ellis, *Napoleon's Continental Blockade: The Case of Alsace.*

1810	1811	1812	1813	1814	1815
143,391	110,544	111,034	72,514	65,303	81,178
38,343	40,427	38,183	22,168	61,774	54,337
44,574	16,432	*	*	53,549	64,664
51,646	52,563	56,906	47,944	30,622	20,427
4,411	14,655	24,799	31,622	4,498	56,113
21,217	20,706	16,877	22,829	27,122	26,871
799	9,401	30,145	9,349	1,466	3,380
20,505	20,388	31,263	16,262	16,001	35,280
1,967	3,128	24,534	9,564	4,972	3,195
5,367	6,055	3,928	5,624	3,132	4,488
728	1,130	2,125	859	2,028	10,565
–	–	–	–	10,541	10,805
817	207	145	–	4,674	4,152
3,441	1,894	1,146	281	1,805	677
38,918	29,987	76,973	114,632	53,369	38,624
376,124	327,517	418,058	353,648	340,847	414,756

Appendix B: The Berlin Decree

FROM OUR IMPERIAL CAMP AT BERLIN,

21 November 1806.

Napoleon, Emperor of the French and of Italy, considering:

1. That England does not admit the rights of nations as universally acknowledged by civilised people;

2. That she declares as an enemy every individual belonging to an enemy State and, in consequence, makes prisoners of war, not only of the crews of *armed* vessels, but also of *merchant* vessels, and even of the supercargoes of the same;

3. That she attends or applies to mere vessels, to articles of commerce, and to the property of individuals, the right of conquest, which can only be applied or extended to what belongs to an enemy state;

4. That she extends to ports not fortified, to harbours and mouths of rivers, the right of blockade, which according to reason and the usage of civilised nations, is applicable only to strong or fortified ports;

5. That she declares blockaded, places before which she has not a single vessel of war, although a place ought not to be considered blockaded but when it is so invested as that no approach to it can be made without imminent hazard; that she declares even places blockaded which her united forces would be incapable of doing, such as entire coasts, and a whole empire;

6. That this unequalled abuse of the right of blockade has no other object than to interrupt the communications of different nations, and to extend the commerce and industry of England upon the ruin of those of the continent;

7. That this being the evident design of England, whoever deals on the continent in English merchandise favours that design and

becomes an accomplice;

8. That this conduct of England (worthy of the first ages of barbarism) has benefitted her, to the detriment of other nations;

9. That it being right to oppose to an enemy the same arms she makes use of to combat as she does, when all ideas of justice and every liberal sentiment (the result of civilisation among men) are discarded;

We have resolved to enforce against England the usages which she has consecrated in her maritime code.

The present decree shall be considered the fundamental law of the empire, until England has acknowledged that the *rights of war* are the same on land as at sea; that it cannot be extended to any private property whatever, nor to persons who are not military, and until the right of blockade be restrained to fortified places, actually invested by competent forces.

~ Imperial Decree of 21 November 1806 ~

Art. 1. The British islands are declared in a state of blockade.

Art. 2. All commerce and correspondence with the British Isles are forbidden. In consequence, letters and packages addressed either to England or to an Englishman in the English language, shall not pass through the post office and shall be seized.

Art. 3. Every subject of England, of what rank or condition so-ever, who shall be found in the countries occupied by our troops, or by those of our allies, shall be made a prisoner of war.

Art. 4. All magazines, merchandise or property whatsoever belonging to a subject of England, shall be declared lawful prize.

Art. 5. The trade in English merchandise is forbidden. All merchandise belonging to England, or coming from its manufactories and colonies, is declared lawful prize.

Art. 6. One-half of the proceeds of the confiscation of the merchandise and property declared good prize by the preceding articles, shall be applied to indemnify the merchants for the losses which they have suffered by the capture of merchant vessels by English cruisers.

Art. 7. No vessel coming directly from England, or from the English colonies, or having been there since the publication of the present decree, shall be received in any port.

Art. 8. Every vessel contravening the above clause, by means of a false declaration, shall be seized, and the vessel and cargo confiscated as if they were English property.

Art. 9. Our tribunal of prizes at Paris is charged with the definitive adjudication of all controversies, which may arise within our empire, or in countries occupied by the French army, relative to the execution of the present decree. Our tribunal of prizes at Milan shall be charged with the definitive adjudication of the said controversies, which may arise within the extent of our kingdom of Italy.

Art. 10. The present decree shall be communicated by our Minister of External Relations to the Kings of Spain, of Etruria, and to our allies whose subjects, like ours are the victims of the injustice and barbarism of the English maritime laws.

Our Ministers of External Relations. Of War, of Finances, of Police and our Postmasters General, are charged each in what concerns him with the execution of the presaid decree.

NAPOLEON.

Appendix C: The Milan Decree

At our Royal Palace at Milan, 17 December 1807. Napoleon, Emperor of the French, King of Italy, and Protector of the Rhenish Confederation:

Observing the measures adopted by the British Government on 11 November last, by which vessels belonging to neutral, friendly, or even Powers the allies of England, are made liable, not only to be searched by British cruisers, but to be compulsorily detained in England, and to have a tax laid on them of so much per cent of the cargo, to be regulated by the English Legislature:

Observing that, by these acts, the British Government denationalise ships of every nation of Europe; that it is not competent of a Government to detract from its own independence and rights, all the sovereigns of Europe having in trust the sovereign independence of the flag; that if, by an unpardonable weakness, and which in the eyes of posterity would be an indelible sin, if such a tyranny was allowed to be established into principles, and consecrated by usage, the English would avail themselves of it to assert it as a right, as they have availed themselves of the tolerance of Government to establish the infamous principle that the flag of a nation does not cover goods, and to have their right of blockade an arbitrary extension, and whch infringes on the sovereignty of every State; we have decreed and do decree as follows:

Art. 1. Every ship, to whatever nation it may belong, that shall have submitted to be searched by an English ship, or to a voyage to England, or shall have paid any tax whatsoever to the English Government, is thereby and for that alone declared to be denationalised, to have forfieted the protection of its King, and have become English property.

Art. 2. Whether the ships thus denationalised by the arbitrary measures of the English Government enter into our ports, or those of our allies, or whether they fall into the hands of our ships of war, or of our privateers, they are declared to be good and lawful prize.

Art. 3. The British Isles are declared to be in a state of blockade, both by land and by sea. Every ship, of whatever nation, or whatsoever the nature of its cargo so may be, that sails from the ports of England, or those of the English colonies, or of countries occupied by English troops, and proceeding to England, or to the English colonies, or to countries occupied by English troops, is good and lawful prize, as contrary to the present decree, and may be captured by our ships of war, or our privateers, and adjudged to the captor.

Art. 4. These measures, which are resorted to only in just retaliation of the barbarous system adopted by England, which assimilates its legislation to that of Algiers, shall cease to have any effect with respect to all nations who shall have the firmness to compel the English to respect their flag. They shall continue to be rigorously in force as long as that Government does not return to the principle of the law of nations, which regulates the relations of civilised States in a state of war. The provisions of the present decree shall be abrogated and null, in fact, as soon as the English abide again by the principles of the law of nations, which are also the principles of justice and honour.

Our ministers are charged with the execution of the present decree, which shall be inserted in the bulletin of the laws.

NAPOLEON.

H-B. MARET, Secretary of State.

Appendix D: The Chappe Telegraph System

This system was installed in France starting in 1793. It was based on pure semaphore signals, thus successful operation was limited to conditions of good visibility between the relay stations. These stations were built on prominent features within eyesight of one another. Poor visibility, rain, cloud, mist, snow and darkness limited the operation of the relay chain. Messages were sent in the 196 recorded combinations of the two arms. Using pre-arranged code reduced transmission times.

The telegraph relay station chains linked Paris with the following cities; the best transmission times for each link (if known) are shown in brackets after the station concerned.

Amsterdam, Angouleme, Antwerp, Bayonne, Behobia (in north-eastern Spain), Blaye, Boulogne, Brest (eight minutes), Brussels, Calais (three minutes), Cherburg, Dijon, Dunkirk, Flushing, Hueningen, Lille (two minutes), Lyons (nine minutes), Mainz, Mantua, Metz, Milan, Montpellier, Nantes, Nîmes, Poitiers, Strasbourg (six minutes thirty seconds), Toulon (twelve minutes), Tours, Turin, Venice (six hours).

At its height in 1810, this amazingly effective communications network included 556 stations covering over five thousand kilometres. Claude Chappe committed suicide in 1805.

Napoleon was not a great user of this system; it was too liable to be interrupted by poor light and it was too liable to misinterpretation of the intended signal.

Appendix E: Population and Armies of States in 1800

Population	(millions)	Army (thousands)
France	26.9	620
Russia	37.5	507
Austria	23.3	352
Prussia	9.7	220
England	10.9	184
Spain	11.5	80
Naples	4.6	32
Holland	4	31
Bavaria	3.4	28
Saxony	2	20
Portugal	2.9	15
Württemberg	1.3	15
Baden	0.95	11
Switzerland	1.4	?
Hessen-Darmstadt	0.6M	4
Hessen-Kassel	0.4	4
USA	5.3M	4
Nassau	0.25	2
Würzburg	0.28	2
Brunswick	0.2	2

Appendix F: The Navies in 1790

Population	SOL*	Frigates	Sloops	SHIPS	GUNS	CREW	TOTALS (millions)
England	10.9	195	210	256	661	12,000	100,000
France	26.9	81	69	141	291	14,000	78,000
Spain	11.5	72	41	109	222	10,000	50,000
Russia	37.5	67	36	700	803	9,000	21,000
Italy	6.5 includes Genoa, Rome, Tuscany, Modena, Parma; totals unknown.						
USA in 1812**	5.3	-	7	2	9	246	5,500
Holland	4	44	43	100	187	2,300	15,000
Denmark	?	38	20	60	118	3,000	12,000
Turkey	?	30	50	100	180	3,000	50,000
Sweden	?	27	12	40	79	3,000	13,000
Venice	?	20	10	58	88	1,000	14,000
Portugal	2.9	10	14	29	53	1,500	10,000
Naples	4.6	10	10	12	32	1,000	5,000

* Ship of the line.

** The frigate *Constitution* carried forty-four 24-pounder guns and twenty carronades in her battle in 1812 with various British frigates and weighed 1,600 tons with a crew of 460 men. The British *Guerriere*, with thirty-eight 9-pounders, was completely outclassed.

The population of the United States excludes the native Americans.

Appendix G: Naval Supplies

Most ships were built of oak and vast amounts were consumed in the naval dockyards to build them. Britain's main supplies of naval stores came from the Baltic region; Sweden and Russia being the main suppliers. The commodities included oak for the hull, elm for the keel, pine for the masts, flax and hemp for the sails, rigging and cables, iron ore, copper, tar and pitch. This same region was also a major supplier of grain to the UK and elsewhere. The amount of wood needed to build a ship was calculated in 'loads'; one load equalled 50 ft^3, or one large tree. A one-hundred-gun First Rater would require about 5,750 loads; a seventy-four-gunner about 3,500; a fifty-gunner about 2,450. After 1800 Indian teak became popular for ship-building.

Due to the blockade of the French fleet in their ports by the Royal Navy, French ships might be idle for months on end. The ships deteriorated, as did the skills of their crews. If at last they managed to leave port, the results were often disastrous even without an encounter with the enemy, as collisions, rigging failures and ships running aground were often the immediate consequences.

Appendix H: Napoleon's Finances

Reference has been made to certain aspects of some of Napoleon's financial dealings – and those of his marshals. This is a complex subject of which I know but little and understand less. I am much indebted to Dominique Contant for the following information.

King Louis XVI received a salary governed by the equivalent of our Civil List. On 26 May 1791 this amounted to twenty-six million francs for the king and his household; the queen received another four million francs. The king was given the use of the palaces, furniture, carpets, paintings, statues and other objets d'art of the Louvre and the Tuileries, the great and small parks of Fontainebleau, Marly, Meudon, Pau, Rambouillet, Saint-Germain-en-Laye, Saint-Cloud, Versailles, including all buildings and facilities upon them. He also had the porcelain factory at Sèvres and the tapestry works at Les Gobelins.

During his reign, he had use of the crown jewels and other regalia.

As First Consul, Napoleon's salary was five hundred thousand francs a year; when he was elected 'Emperor of the French', this rose to twenty-five million francs; he reputedly saved twelve million per year.

He also had use of the *domaine de la couronne* and the *domaine d'extension*, but did not own them. Apart from these assets, he had his *domaine privée*, or private funds, valued at two hundred million francs, all of which seems to have been acquired since 1796, as we know he was poor up to that point.

These private funds were administered by the Baron de la Bouillerie. Napoleon also had between two hundred and three hundred thousand francs with the Italian banker, Torlonia.

At the time of leaving Paris in 1814, Marie-Louise seems to have taken some two million francs in gold. Also at this point, the Emperor gave two million francs to Prince Eugène.

In 1815 he gave six million francs to the banker Lafitte.

All the *domaines* were taken over by Louis XVIII on his accession to the throne.

On St Helena he is known to have had some three hundred thousand francs in gold and silver.

Bibliography

Robert Asprey, *The Rise and Fall of Napoleon Bonaparte*, London, 2001.

Louis Bergeron, *France under Napoleon*, Princeton NJ, 1990.

Owen Connelly, *Napoleon's Satellite Kingdoms*, London and New York, 1965.

Vincent Cronin, *Napoleon*, London, 1971.

Geoffrey Ellis, *Napoleon's Continental Blockade: The Case of Alsace*, Oxford, 1981.

Baron Fain, *Memoires du Baron Fain, Premier Secretaire du Cabinet de L'Empereur*, Paris, 1908.

J. C. Herold, *The Age of Napoleon*, London, 1963.

R. M. Johnston (ed.), *In the Words of Napoleon*, London, 2001.

Emmanuel-Auguste Dieudonné, Count de Las Cases, *Memoirs of the Life, Exile and Conversations of the Emperor Napoleon*, London, 1836.

John Gibson Lockhart, *The History of Napoleon Buonaparte*, London, 1866.

Lady Mary Loyd, *New Letters of Napoleon I Omitted from the Edition Published under the Auspices of Napoleon III, from the French*, New York, 1897, and London, 1898.

Emil Ludwig, *Napoleon*, London, 1927.

F. Markham, *Napoleon*, New York, 1963.

Freiherr Otto von Odeleben, *Napoleons Feldzug in Sachsen im Jahr 1813*, Dresden, 1816.

Sir Charles Oman, *History of the Peninsular War*, 7 volumes, Oxford, 1902–30, reprinted London, 1995–7.

Alan Palmer, *Napoleon and Marie Louise, 'The Second Empress'*, London, 2001.

Alan Schom, *One Hundred Days: Napoleon's Road to Waterloo*, Atheneum, 1992.

—— *Napoleon Bonaparte*, New York, 1997.

Desmond Seward, *Napoleon's Family*, London, 1986.

Captain W. Siborne, *History of the War in France and Belgium in 1815*, London, 1844, reprinted as *History of the Waterloo Campaign*, London, 1990.

W. Sloane, *The Life of Napoleon Bonaparte*, New York, 1906.

Digby Smith, *Greenhill Napoleonic Wars Data Book*, London, 1998.

—— *1813: Leipzig, Napoleon and the Battle of the Nations*, London, 2001.

—— *Armies of 1812*, Staplehurst, 2002.

—— *Napoleon's Regiments: Battle Histories of the Regiments of the French Army, 1792–1815*, London, 2002.

J. M. Thompson, *Napoleon Bonaparte*, Oxford, 1952.

J. Tulard, *Napoleon, the Myth of the Saviour*, London, 1984.

Colonel Jean-Baptiste-Modeste-Eugène Vachée, *Napoleon at Work*, London, 1914.

Gerhart Werner, *Wuppertal in Napoleonischer Zeit*, Wuppertal, 1967.

Index